EXCHANGE RATE DETERMINATION AND ADJUSTMENT

Jagdeep S. Bhandari

Praeger Studies in
International Monetary Economics and Finance

General Editors:
J. Richard Zecher, D. Sykes Wilford

PRAEGER

PRAEGER SPECIAL STUDIES • PRAEGER SCIENTIFIC

Library of Congress Cataloging in Publication Data

Bhandari, Jagdeep S.
    Exchange rate determination and adjustment.

    (Praeger studies in international monetary economics
and finance)
    Includes bibliographical references
    1. Foreign exchange—Mathematical models. I. Title.
II. Series.
HG3823.B47   332.4'56'0724   81-11933
ISBN 0-03-059008-6   AACR2

Published in 1982 by Praeger Publishers
CBS Educational and Professional Publishing
A Division of CBS, Inc.
521 Fifth Avenue, New York, New York 10175 U.S.A.

© 1982 by Praeger Publishers

23456789   145   987654321

Printed in the United States of America

FOREWORD

D. Sykes Wilford and J. Richard Zecher

Over the past decade the world of international trade in goods, services, and money has changed dramatically. From the glory days of Bretton-Woods to the dark periods of 1977/78 the dollar has seen its ups and downs. The financial system of the world, once undergirded by the almighty dollar, has found itself going through one vicious or virtuous cycle after another. The 1970s brought us devaluations; revaluations; managed (sometimes not too managed) floating, freely fluctuating exchange rates; "snakes" and "super-snakes"; the European Monetary Community; monetary neglect and reform; monetarism and supply-side economics; and even interest rate wars. The rhetoric changes as fast as the journalists or central bankers can think up new plans for saving the system. What is amazing—or at least what seems amazing after reading the deluge of rhetoric written about one crisis or another—is that the system has somehow survived. Not only has it survived, but in many ways it is even stronger.

Exchange markets have become more efficient at providing this crucial form of financial intermediation as it is daily tested by new and changing international conditions. The structure of the market has evolved over the decade as it has been faced with different challenges and as its participants have become more skilled. One of the critical elements in its adaptability has been how quickly its participants have learned to deal with new information. Indeed, the OPEC shocks, monetary shocks, political shocks, and so on, have all been tests that the market has dealt with very well—in spite of predictions of doom and gloom.

As the market has adapted, so has the economics profession. Not many years ago a book such as Jagdeep Bhandari's *Exchange Rate Determination and Adjustment* would have been ridiculed as being based upon unproven monetary tenents. The existence of this type of intellectual exercise is a testament to the profession's ability to change from its old structured habits as new information about the reality of exchange rate determination is realized. It was just a decade ago that the monetary approach to exchange rate determination—and the balance of payments—first came to the forefront of the literature. Or, more aptly stated, it was just a decade ago that the literature began to fully appreciate the work of Hume and others in previous centuries who understood the basic mechanics of international transactions. From these beginnings a set of literature has developed in and around this school of thought; and it has transformed the whole thrust of exchange rate and balance of payments analysis.

Building upon work in the 1960s of Robert Mundell and Harry Johnson, this literature has come of age. Today several aspects of this literature are being examined and understood as greater refinements take place. To help clarify and extend the knowledge of exchange rate determination in a changing and dynamic world has been one of the major tasks undertaken by Bhandari in this volume. He has lived up to that task admirably. His presentation carries the reader through the logic of exchange rate determination built upon earlier work in this area by Rudiger Dornbusch, as well as others, as he attempts to flesh out the various modern monetary theories of exchange rate determination. He does not attempt to have the final say on what the "truth" is but attempts to move the literature toward that ultimate goal, even if unobtainable in a dynamic world.

Bhandari's efforts, no doubt, will be rewarded, as this volume will certainly add to the efforts now under way in the profession to understand and solve many of the unanswered questions that plague market participants and academics daily. More important, users of this volume will be rewarded with new and fresh looks at a problem that is as old as money itself— exchange rate determination.

ACKNOWLEDGMENTS

It is difficult to write a work of this kind without incurring intellectual debt. I have run up large deficits with several people. In some cases the help and encouragement I have received is direct—Michael Mussa wrote Chapter 12, and Stephen Turnovsky, Robert Driskill, and David Burton contributed fruitful ideas conceived in earlier joint work with them.

I have also benefited from the comments and suggestions of several friends and colleagues. I am particularly grateful to Willard Witte, Jay Levin, Don Hanson, Matt Canzoneri, John Bilson, Sven Arndt, Don Mathieson, and especially Jeffrey Frankel. Others have been extremely generous in allowing me access to their recent unpublished work and offering advice. I also wish to thank Jeff Sachs, Paul Krugman, William Branson, Robert Stern, Maurice Obstfeld, André Burgstaller, Jacob Frenkel, Dale Henderson, Masanao Aoki, David Laidler, and Doug Purvis. None of these people are in any way responsible for the opinions I have expressed or for the errors and inconsistencies that remain.

The editorial staff at Praeger has been particularly patient. The manuscript was typed with speed and accuracy by Heather Ryan. Finally, I am grateful to my wife Karen for having provided a home environment conducive to the writing of this book.

CONTENTS

1

AN AGENDA

This book is not and was not intended to be a textbook on international monetary economics. Rather, it is a collection of studies on exchange rate determination and adjustment. A common unifying theme to the chapters in this volume is that the models that are constructed and analyzed are of a general equilibrium nature. The takeoff point for the investigations is Dornbusch's seminal contribution, and some of the essays are in the spirit of this kind of "sticky-price monetary model,"[1] although the scope of the book is by no means limited to this framework.

Chapter 2 begins by reviewing the well-known model of exchange rate dynamics proposed by Dornbusch. In the second half of this chapter two alternative expectations hypotheses are introduced and their implications for exchange rate volatility and dynamics examined. One of these hypotheses is the adaptive expectations hypothesis; the other recognizes that for certain types of exogenous disturbances the prediction of the long-run equilibrium exchange rate may be a matter as complex as the prediction of the adjustment path itself. Accordingly, a two-stage expectations hypothesis is proposed to address this issue.

In Chapter 3 the assumption of perfect capital mobility and instantaneous money market equilibrium is relaxed. Thus, the model now permits transitory disequilibrium in both commodity and money markets as well as a role for the balance of payments in exchange rate determination. It is shown that the well-known exchange rate overshooting property is conditioned upon certain specific parameter magnitudes. It also becomes apparent that the spot exchange rate is not determined exclusively in asset markets.

Chapter 4 returns to the continuous money market equilibrium and perfect capital mobility assumption of Chapter 2 but distinguishes between short- and long-run elasticities of aggregate demand. Thus, the fact that the adjustment of aggregate demand to a change in the terms of trade or interest rates is essentially a dynamic process is explicitly recognized here. A further notable feature of this model is that the sticky-price assumption of the previous chapters is dropped, and continuous price flexibility ensures full and continual equilibrium in all markets. Price flexibility notwithstanding, the model does involve dynamic adjustment as aggregate demand adjusts over time to its fully adjusted value. The short-run results of this model are quite antithetical to those emerging from Chapter 2. Specifically, it is real expenditure disturbances rather than monetary shocks that are now associated with exchange rate overadjustment, in contrast to the Dornbusch framework.

Chapter 5 considers two competing scenarios to endogenize income. Both assume that real income is demand determined (that is, a perfectly elastic supply schedule). The first approach is a simple extension of the basic model discussed in Chapter 2, while the second utilizes the distributed lag specification of aggregate demand introduced in Chapter 4 but reintroduces the sticky-price assumption. Thus, the latter model involves both elasticity and price dynamics and is capable of explaining a variety of dynamic adjustment patterns. The short-run results from this model continue to retain the property that expenditure disturbances lead to an exaggerated extent of exchange rate volatility in comparison with monetary disturbances.

Chapter 6 extends the analysis of Chapter 2 to consider anticipated disturbances. The analysis incorporates concepts introduced by Wilson (1979) and Gray and Turnovsky (1979).

Chapter 7 provides a framework to incorporate steady-state or ongoing inflation and exchange depreciation. In some ways this model can be interpreted as being the moving equilibrium analogue to the basic model of Chapter 2. A notable feature of the analysis is that a range of alternative monetary rules are considered, one of which is close to the "optica" intervention rule. Thus, this chapter considers a simple (passive) X% monetary growth rule as well as activist intervention rules that stabilize the rate of domestic inflation, exchange depreciation, and so on. It is seen that there is a correspondence between the behavior of the exchange rate under a passive X% monetary growth rule and that of the money supply under an activist intervention rule that pegs the rate of depreciation.

Chapter 8 constructs and analyzes a two-country macrodynamic model. Previous chapters have utilized the small-country assumption—a scenario that is clearly inapplicable to many situations of bilateral trade. The framework of analysis here is basically the two-country analogue to the simple model in the second chapter. One of the results in this chapter is that despite floating exchange rates both monetary and real disturbances tend to get transmitted internationally and that insulation may require a costly policy of continual adjustments in the domestic economy. Another related point of interest is that the inflation that is "imported" by the domestic economy (as a response to foreign monetary expansion) is only imported during the first part of the dynamic adjustment process. Thus, movements in the two price levels are positively correlated in the initial period, after which they are negatively correlated.

Chapter 9 is similar in spirit to Chapter 8 but considers a three-country trading world. The advantage of this approach is that it does not enforce the symmetry between countries necessitated in a two-country model. However, the cost of this added bit of descriptive realism is that the dynamics of the model are now of the third-order variety. The model focuses on the instantaneous effects of monetary disturbances originating in one country on the two bilateral exchange rates.

Chapter 10 introduces the supply side to the small open economy model, and equilibrium income is now determined by both supply and demand considerations. The focus of the analysis is on the effects of both unanticipated and anticipated increases in the price of an imported input (such as oil), although the effects of monetary disturbances are also investigated. Both the short-run and long-run effects of these disturbances are examined as well as the dynamic adjustment path. The model embodies instantaneous equilibrium in both commodity and asset markets, the source of dynamic movement being the adjustment over time of (sticky) nominal wages. One of the central results of this chapter is that neither spot nor steady-state depreciation is the inevitable consequence of such an input price increase. Rather, this outcome is contingent upon specific (although perhaps plausible) parameter magnitudes. Thus, the conventional belief associating the weakness of certain currencies with increases in imported input prices needs to be viewed with caution.

Chapter 11 also focuses on the effects of an input price disturbance, although the framework of analysis is quite different. Specifically, this chapter utilizes a portfolio balance-type approach to model imperfect asset substitutability while a fairly standard real sector representation is employed. Unlike the previous chapter this model assumes continuous full employment, and the economy's movement over time is governed by asset accumulation and the evolution of exchange rate expectations.

Chapter 12, written by Michael Mussa, analyzes exchange rate and price dynamics in a simple monetary model that assumes purchasing power parity. A distinguishing feature of his framework is that the analysis of exchange rate and price dynamics is not primarily an analysis of the process of convergence of the exchange rate and price level toward fixed long-run levels or growth paths. Rather, the analysis of equilibrium dynamics incorporates both (1) a determination of expected changes in the equilibrium exchange rate and price level due to expected changes in money supplies and the exogenous factors influencing money demands and (2) a determination of unexpected changes in the equilibrium exchange rate and price level due to new information that alters expectations about the future course of the exogenous factors governing the exchange rate and price level.

Finally, Chapter 13 constructs a rational expectations stochastic general equilibrium model and analyzes the nature of optimal exchange rate management in response to various structural, foreign, and domestic disturbances. The approach is not based upon the usual small-country model in that the rational expectations solution to the foreign price level and interest rate (in terms of their fundamental determinants) is first computed and then fed into the domestic economy model. An innovative feature of the model is the rehabilitation of the balance of payments in exchange rate determination. The model has implications for the debate on the international transmission of shocks under floating exchange rates, and one of the counterintuitive results in this respect is that external monetary disturbances may tend to get negatively transmitted to the domestic economy, in the form of a falling price level in the latter. In contrast, a small-country analysis—ignoring the correlation between foreign price and interest rate movements concomitant with the foreign monetary expansion—would have produced the opposite result. The chapter also examines various types of optimal intervention policies when the optimality criterion is defined in terms of output stabilization or, alternatively, as trade balance stabilization.

For all practical purposes these chapters are self-contained and include their own references. I have tried to be selective in citing other works— mainly because so many excellent surveys on exchange rate determination already exist, and complete bibliographical references can be found in these sources. Among them are Isard (1978), Schadler (1977), Frankel (forthcoming), Frenkel (forthcoming), and Dornbusch (forthcoming).

NOTE

1. Frankel (forthcoming) in a recent survey has provided a taxonomical structure to analyze recent work on exchange rate determination.

REFERENCES

Dornbusch, R. Forthcoming. "Exchange Rate Economics: Where Do We Stand?" In *Economic Interdependence and Flexible Exchange Rates*, edited by J. Bhandari and B. Putnam. Cambridge: MIT Press.

Gray, M., and S. Turnovsky. 1979 "The Stability of Exchange Rate Dynamics under Perfect Myopic Foresight." *International Economic Review* 20 (October): 643–66.

Frankel, J. Forthcoming. "Monetary and Portfolio Balance Models of Exchange Rate Determination." In J. Bhandari and B. Putnam, op. cit.

Frenkel, J. Forthcoming, "Flexible Exchange Rates, Prices and the Role of "News' Lessons from the 1970s." In J. Bhandari and B. Putnam, op. cit.

Isard, P. 1978. "Exchange Rate Determination: A Survey of Popular Views and Recent Models." *Princeton Studies in International Finance*, no. 42 (May).

Schadler, S. 1977. "Sources of Exchange Rate Variability: Theory and Empirical Evidence." *IMF Staff Papers* 24 (July): 253–96.

Wilson, C. 1979 "Anticipated Shocks and Exchange Rate Dynamics." *Journal of Political Economy* 87 (June): 639–47.

2

SIMPLE MODELS OF
EXCHANGE RATE DYNAMICS

This chapter first reviews the simple but elegant framework proposed in the pioneering work of Dornbusch (1976). Subsequently, other authors such as Mathieson (1977), Bilson (1979), and Witte (1979) have added various innovations to the basic Dornbusch model.

The organization of this chapter involves the detail of the basic framework, its steady-state characteristics, and the nature of adjustment paths. First, the perfect foresight path is obtained directly, and then the expectations scheme consistent with perfect foresight is discussed. This is followed by the usual comparative dynamic exercises (for fixed income). These matters occupy the first three sections. In the fourth section we introduce two alternative expectational schemes as opposed to the regressive scheme popularized by Dornbusch. One of these is the adaptive expectations model, while the other is a two-stage scheme that permits errors not only along the adjustment path but also in the prediction of the steady-state level of the exchange rate. Finally, the fifth section briefly considers the nature of activist monetary policy in terms of the Dornbusch framework and the implications for the associated exchange rate behavior. Later chapters progressively widen the scope of the analysis by relaxing some of the assumptions of this chapter.

THE DORNBUSCH MODEL

Security Markets

Assume that the country under consideration is small in world markets in that it faces a given world interest rate (that is, the yield on foreign

7

currency-denominated bonds) and a given foreign currency price of foreign goods. Domestic residents may hold three assets—domestic and foreign currency-denominated securities and domestically issued money. They do not hold foreign currency—there is no advantage in doing so, since foreign bonds yield the certain rate $i*$ and transactions costs in security markets are not considered. These bonds can be assumed to be riskless short-term government bonds. Further, bonds denominated in terms of domestic or foreign currency are assumed to be perfect substitutes, given a proper premium or discount to offset anticipated appreciation or depreciation of domestic currency.[1] Accordingly, if domestic currency is expected to depreciate, interest rates on assets denominated in terms of domestic currency will exceed those abroad by the expected rate of depreciation. This relationship is expressed as

$$i = i* + z, \tag{2.1}$$

where i is the yield on domestic securities, $i*$ is the yield on foreign securities and, z is the expected rate of depreciation of domestic currency vis-à-vis foreign currency. Equation (2.1) is the uncovered interest arbitrage condition or the net interest parity condition and holds continuously except at the instant that an unanticipated disturbance occurs, at which time it is suspended.[2] The implication of (2.1) is that portfolio compositions of domestic residents are indeterminate. Further, the small-country assumption along with (2.1) implies that the domestic security market is always in equilibrium in the sense that any domestic bond issue can be traded on the world market at the uncovered world rate.

The Money Market

The money market in the home country is always in stock equilibrium.[3] Foreigners do not hold domestic currency nor domestic residents any foreign currency—that is, there is no currency substitution[4]—and all domestic money enters the system via a series of random nondistorting governmental transfers—that is, "helicopter drops." Thus, the government's financing constraint is ignored at this point.[5] All money is to be interpreted as high-powered money: there is no distinction between base money and domestic credit. Domestic monetary equilibrium is described by

$$m - q = -\lambda i + \phi \bar{y}, \tag{2.2}$$

where m is the log of domestic monetary stock, q is the log of domestic price level (to be discussed below), and $\bar{y}$ is the log of full employment or natural output.[6] λ is the semilog interest elasticity of money demand, and ϕ is the income elasticity of money demand. The notation is the same as in Dornbusch (1976).

The Goods Market

Domestic output is assumed to be imperfectly substitutable for foreign output on the demand side; the aggregate demand function for domestic output is given by

$$d = u + \delta(e + p^* - p) + \gamma\bar{y} - \sigma r, \qquad \gamma < 1, \qquad (2.3)$$

where d is the log of real aggregate demand for domestic output, p^* is the log of the foreign currency price of the imported good, e is the log of the spot exchange rate (defined as the domestic currency price of foreign exchange), and r is the real interest rate.[7] The domestic currency price p is endogenously determined, while p^* is exogenous in view of the small-country assumption. It can be seen, therefore, that smallness extends over import markets but not export markets. Specifically, the domestic economy faces an infinitely elastic supply of imports at the going world currency price; on the other hand, it faces the usual downward-sloped demand curve for its exports to world markets since both domestic residents and foreigners regard the two goods as being imperfectly substitutable. The term u is intended to capture the effects of governmental action and structural shifts (for example, a structural change in autonomous exports). Postulate the linearized relation

$$u = u_0 + u_1 g, \qquad (2.4)$$

where u_0 is the structural term and g is the real government expenditure (in log terms). u_1 depends upon the fraction of real government expenditure that falls on home output.

From (2.3) it can be seen that a decrease in the relative price of domestic goods (that is, an increase in $e + p^* - p$) switches demand toward home goods. An increase in the real interest rate reduces aggregate demand via an adverse effect on investment decisions. To the extent that consumption is determined by permanent income or wealth, the nominal interest rate may also be expected to exert an additional influence on aggregate demand.

The price level relevant for domestic agents, q, will depend upon prices of both domestic and foreign goods. If the underlying utility functions are of the Cobb-Douglas variety, then the log-additive price index defined in (2.5) can be shown to be the "true" cost-of-living index:

$$q = \alpha p + (1 - \alpha)(e + p^*). \qquad (2.5)$$

Equation (2.5) has been utilized, for example, by Mathieson (1977) and Bilson (1979). The real interest rate is defined via Fisher's equation

$$r = i - \dot{q}^E, \tag{2.6}$$

where $\dot{q}^E$ is the expected rate of inflation of the domestic price index and can be obtained from (2.5).

Adjustment Equations

Domestic prices are assumed to respond sluggishly to an excess demand measure, that is,

$$\dot{p} = \pi(d - \bar{y}), \tag{2.7}$$

where π is a finite nonnegative constant. Since π is finite, the goods market is characterized by transient disequilibrium in contrast to the money market, which is always in stock equilibrium. Further, no instantaneous jumps are permitted in the domestic price level. No such constraint is placed on any other variable of the system.

Expectation Formation

Clearly the mechanism of expectations formation needs to be specified in order to complete the specification of the model. Dornbusch (1976) discusses an arbitrary regressive expectations hypothesis that can be consistent with a convergent perfect foresight path, while Mathieson (1977) also examines the continuous time analogue of adaptive expectations.

In what follows we focus on the class of perfect foresight paths that the model implies without any reference to a specific expectational scheme. The perfect foresight steady state of the model will be seen to involve a saddle point. We then discuss the expectational scheme that forces the system onto the stable arm of the saddle (the expectational scheme employed by Dornbusch does precisely this). The continuous time analogue of adaptive expectations as well as more complicated two-stage expectational schemes are discussed in this chapter.

SOLUTION OF THE MODEL

At the outset make the simplifying assumption that the general price level q is adequately represented by the domestic price level p, that is, we do away with the price index. Also assume that the nominal rate i rather than r is the relevant argument in the aggregate demand function (2.3). This eliminates the need to specify price expectations and makes little difference to the qualitative nature of the results under perfect foresight.

The Class of Perfect Foresight Paths

Let the stationary equilibrium of the model be described by the price and exchange levels $\bar{p}$ and $\bar{e}$, respectively. These levels correspond to

$$\dot{e}^E = \dot{e} = \dot{p} = 0$$

and

$$i = i^*.$$

By implication

$$(m - \bar{p}) = -\lambda i^* + \phi\bar{y} \tag{2.8}$$

and

$$u + \delta(\bar{e} + p^* - \bar{p}) + (\gamma - 1)\bar{y} - \sigma i^* = 0. \tag{2.9}$$

Equations (2.8) and (2.9) determine the equilibrium values of the price level and the exchange rate in terms of exogenous variables and parameters as

$$\bar{p} = m + \lambda i^* - \phi\bar{y} \tag{2.10}$$

and

$$\bar{e} = (m - p^*) + \left(\frac{1 - \gamma}{\delta} - \phi\right)\bar{y} - \frac{u}{\delta} + \left(\lambda + \frac{\sigma}{\delta}\right)i^*, \tag{2.11}$$

where we note the long-run neutrality of money, that is, $d\bar{p} = d\bar{e} = dm$.[8] Now, from the money market equation (2.2)

$$i = \frac{p - m}{\lambda} + \frac{\phi}{\lambda}\bar{y} \tag{2.12}$$

This is the interest rate that, given real income, clears the money market. Further,

$$\bar{i} = i^* = \frac{\bar{p} - m}{\lambda} + \frac{\phi}{\lambda} \bar{y}.$$

Hence,

$$(i - i^*) = \dot{e}^E = \dot{e} = \frac{p - \bar{p}}{\lambda}, \tag{2.13}$$

where we have imposed the perfect foresight requirement $\dot{e}^E = \dot{e}$. Next,

$$\dot{p} = \pi[u + \gamma\bar{y} + \delta(e + p^* - p) - \sigma i - \bar{y}]. \tag{2.14}$$

Using (2.9) and substituting for $(i - i^*)$ from (2.13), we obtain

$$\dot{p} = \pi\delta(e - \bar{e}) - \pi\left(\delta + \frac{\sigma}{\lambda}\right)(p - \bar{p}). \tag{2.15}$$

Equations (2.13) and (2.15) form a system of simultaneous differential equations that yield adjustment paths for p and e. With no new shocks they describe the time profile of the price level and the spot rate. In general, there is no reason why these adjustment paths should necessarily converge to the stationary equilibrium. In fact, in the current context, unless restricted, these adjustment paths are indeed explosive.

The system (2.13) and (2.15) can be represented by the homogeneous matrix equation

$$\begin{bmatrix} \dot{e} \\ \dot{p} \end{bmatrix} = \begin{bmatrix} 0 & \frac{1}{\lambda} \\ \pi\delta & -\pi\left(\delta + \frac{\sigma}{\lambda}\right) \end{bmatrix} \begin{bmatrix} (e - \bar{e}) \\ (p - \bar{p}) \end{bmatrix} \tag{2.16}$$

whence the characteristic equation is

$$\lambda s^2 + \pi(\sigma + \delta\lambda)s - \pi\delta = 0,$$

the roots of which are real and opposite in sign. That is,

$$s_1, s_2 = \frac{-\pi(\sigma + \delta\lambda) \pm \sqrt{\pi^2(\sigma + \delta\lambda)^2 + 4\pi\delta}}{2\lambda}, \quad s_1 < 0, \ s_2 > 0.$$

Hence, the stationary equilibrium is characterized by a saddle point. The exchange rate solution is given by

$$(e_t - \bar{e}) = A \exp^{s_1 t} + B \exp^{s_2 t}.$$

Since $s_2 > 0$, e_t is unbounded unless $B \equiv 0$. The stable arm of the saddle point is thus described by the locus $B \equiv 0$, along which the exchange rate path is

$$(e_t - \bar{e}) = A \exp^{s_1 t}$$

Hence, $\dot{e}$ along the stable arm is given by

$$\dot{e} = s_1 A \exp^{s_1 t}. \tag{2.17}$$

Now from (2.15)

$$\dot{e} = \frac{p_t - \bar{p}}{\lambda}, \tag{2.17'}$$

so that

$$s_1 A \exp^{s_1 t} = \frac{p_t - \bar{p}}{\lambda},$$

whence

$$A = \frac{p_t - \bar{p}}{\lambda s_1 \exp^{s_1 t}}. \tag{2.18}$$

Hence,

$$e_t = \frac{p_t - \bar{p}}{\lambda s_1 \exp^{s_1 t}} \exp^{s_1 t} + \bar{e} = \frac{p_t - \bar{p}}{\lambda s_1} + \bar{e}$$

is the solution along the stable arm or, equivalently,

$$(e_t - \bar{e}) = \frac{p_t - \bar{p}}{\lambda s_1}. \tag{2.19}$$

Finally, dynamics along the stable arm can be described from (2.19) as

$$\dot{e} = s_1(e - \bar{e}), \qquad s_1 < 0, \tag{2.20}$$

implying a first-order exponential decay adjustment process. Equation (2.19) is a key equation of the model. For given values of $\bar{p}$ and $\bar{e}$ it determines e_t in terms of p_t. It also shows that prices and exchange rates converge (along the stable arm) to their steady states from opposite directions.

To ensure dynamic stability it is essential that (2.19) and, more specifically,

$$(e_0 - \bar{e}) = \frac{p_0 - \bar{p}}{\lambda s_1} \tag{2.19'}$$

hold. Since change in m will change $(\bar{e}, \bar{p})$ such that $dm = d\bar{e} = d\bar{p}$, the only way that (2.19') can hold (except by accident) is by allowing e_0 to adjust appropriately. The appropriate extent is given by (2.19'). In other words, whatever the fixed money supply happens to be, the initial value of the exchange rate must adjust so as to place the system on the stable arm of the saddle passing through the corresponding equilibrium.

The economic mechanism of this is essentially the same as that in the well-known perfect foresight models of Brock (1974) and Sargent and Wallace (1973). That is to say, the economy's agents compute the final equilibrium first; then, given this, the initial condition e_0 is determined via a solution to (2.20), which describes dynamics along the stable arm of the saddle.

Consequently, the exchange rate path described by the solution to (2.20) originates at e_0^+, that is,

$$e_t = \bar{e} + (e_0^+ - \bar{e}) \exp^{s_1 t},$$

where e_0^+ refers to the exchange rate level following the jump.

Gray and Turnovsky (1979) point out that the flexibility of e_0 is not by itself sufficient to guarantee stability and that other terminal conditions may be required as well. The terminal condition they invoke is that real balances remain finite.

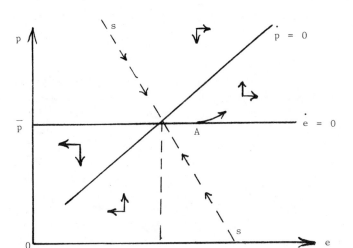

Figure 2.1

Diagrammatically the system (2.16) can be represented as shown in Figure 2.1. The $\dot{e} = 0$ curve [9] generates a stable exchange rate, which occurs for $p = \bar{p}$. The $\dot{p} = 0$ curve is upward sloped with slope $\delta\lambda/(\delta\lambda + \sigma) < 1$. All points to the right (left) of $\dot{p} = 0$ imply rising (falling) prices. Points above the $\dot{e} = 0$ line imply depreciation and those below appreciation. Hence, the arrows show the movement of the system. The stable arm of the saddle point path is depicted as ss above. The presence of this path, as discussed earlier, implies a knife-edge problem. Any point not on this path implies portfolio and price adjustments that lead continuously away from the steady state. For example, A is on the unstable arm of the saddle. The problem that most ad hoc perfect foresight models face is to provide a rationale in terms of economic behavior for the assumption that a path such as ss is the actual adjustment path that is followed. The technical conditions that ensure the selection of the stable saddle point trajectory were noted earlier.

Quasi-Rational and Rational Expectational Schemes

In this section we discuss a stable expectation scheme that is consistent with perfect foresight. As pointed out earlier, Dornbusch (1976) uses this route to compute the perfect foresight trajectory.

It is clear from the foregoing discussion that an expectational scheme that leads to equation (2.19) will be consistent with a stable perfect foresight adjustment path. Specifically, Dornbusch uses the extrapolative scheme

$$z = -\theta(e - \bar{e}), \qquad \theta > 0. \tag{2.21}$$

Equation (2.21) states that the expected rate of depreciation is proportional to the discrepancy between the spot and steady state exchange rates, where the long-run rate, $\bar{e}$, is known to be given by (2.12). It will be demonstrated below that the perfect foresight value of the expectational parameter θ is $\hat{\theta} = -s_1$. But, in general, any positive value of θ is in the class of quasi-rational schemes. Quasi-rational expectations imply that the relevant agents "know" the steady state but have knowledge only about the qualitative characteristic of the adjustment path, such as the direction of movement. Subsequently we frequently refer to quasi-rational expectations as directionally consistent expectations. Perfect foresight, of course, implies that the exact path is known.

A negative value of θ can be ruled out in the present context, since it implies that speculators expect depreciation when the current spot rate is above $\bar{e}$ (that is, already too high). Since

$$i = \frac{p - m}{\lambda} + \frac{\phi}{\lambda}\bar{y}$$

and

$$i^* = \frac{\bar{p} - m}{\lambda} + \frac{\phi}{\lambda}\bar{y},$$

using $i = i^* + \theta(\bar{e} - e)$,

$$\frac{p - m}{\lambda} + \frac{\phi}{\lambda}\bar{y} = \frac{\bar{p} - m}{\lambda} + \frac{\phi}{\lambda}\bar{y} - \theta(e - \bar{e})$$

or

$$\frac{p - \bar{p}}{\lambda} = -\theta(e - \bar{e})$$

or

$$(e - \bar{e}) = -\frac{(p - \bar{p})}{\lambda\theta}. \tag{2.22}$$

The similarity between (2.19) and (2.22) is obvious now. For a specific value $\hat{\theta} = -s_1$, the expectational scheme (2.21) will yield perfect foresight. Equation (2.15) in view of (2.22) is

$$\dot{p} = -\pi\left(\frac{\delta + \sigma\theta}{\lambda\theta} + \delta\right)(p - \bar{p}) \tag{2.23}$$

or

$$\dot{p} = -v(p - \bar{p}),$$

whence the actual solutions

$$p_t = \bar{p} + (p_0 - \bar{p})\exp^{-vt}$$

and

$$e_t = \bar{e} + (e_0 - \bar{e})\exp^{-vt}$$

immediately follow. Since the expected exchange rate follows the path

$$e^E(t) = \bar{e} + (e_0 - \bar{e})\exp^{-\theta t},$$

the solution to the quadratic equation $\theta = v$ yields the perfect foresight value of θ as $\hat{\theta}$, which is equal to $-s_1$. The positive (and therefore stable) root of the solution to $\theta = v$ is

$$\hat{\theta}(\lambda, \delta, \sigma, \pi) = \frac{\pi\left(\frac{\sigma}{\lambda} + \delta\right)}{2} + \left[\frac{\pi^2\left(\frac{\sigma}{\lambda} + \delta\right)^2}{4} + \frac{\pi\delta}{\lambda}\right]^{1/2}. \tag{2.24}$$

In effect, then, when Dornbusch introduces perfect foresight by setting $\theta = -s_1$, he also imposes stability by rejecting the negative value of θ. Finally, (2.21) is the only expectation scheme that is consistent with perfect foresight in this framework.

The line AA in Figure 2.2 represents equation (2.22), that is, asset equilibrium. This line is downward sloped with slope $= -\lambda\theta$. The arrows indicate that assets markets clear instantaneously as assumed—that is, the

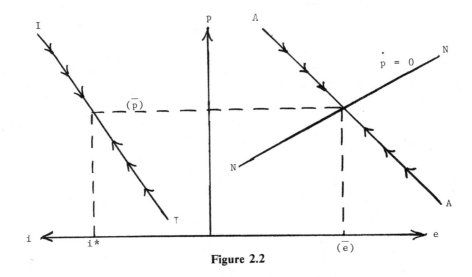

Figure 2.2

economy is always on the AA locus. The NN curve represents combinations of p and e for which the commodity markets clear, that is $\dot{p} = 0$. This line is positively sloped and flatter than a 45° line for the following reason. An increase in the exchange rate creates excess demand for commodities by lowering their relative price. To restore equilibrium prices must increase, though proportionately less, since rising prices reduce aggregate demand via higher interest rates as well. The slope of this schedule is

$$\frac{dp}{de}\bigg|_{NN} = \frac{\delta}{\delta + \dfrac{\phi}{\lambda}} < 1 \ .$$

The II curve represents

$$i = \frac{p - m}{\lambda} + \frac{\phi}{\lambda}\bar{y}$$

that is, it depicts combinations of i and p that clear the money market given $\bar{y}$ and m. And

$$\frac{di}{dp} = \frac{1}{\lambda} > 0,$$

for example this line is positively sloped. Combined asset and commodity market equilibrium occurs when $i = i^*$, $p = \bar{p}$, and $e = \bar{e}$.

COMPARATIVE DYNAMICS FROM THE STEADY STATE

An Increase in Nominal Money

Consider first the effects (under perfect foresight) of a one-time unanticipated increase in nominal money, m.

Recalling the long-run homogeneity properties of the model (see equations [2.11] and [2.12]), it is clear that the new state is such that $d\bar{p} = d\bar{e} = dm$, that is, changes in prices and exchange rates are exactly proportional to the monetary expansion. Long-run homogeneity is not surprising since there are no underlying sources of money illusion in the model.

There is no impact effect upon the price level while the impact effect upon the spot exchange rate is given from

$$\frac{de_0^+}{dm} = 1 + \frac{1}{\hat{\theta}\lambda}.^{10}$$

Using (2.22) where $\hat{\theta}$ is the "correct" perfect foresight value $-s_1$, which is also given explicitly in (2.24), we have

$$\frac{de_0^+}{dm} = \frac{d\bar{e}}{dm} + \left[\frac{1}{\left(\dfrac{\pi(\sigma + \delta\lambda)}{2} + \dfrac{\pi^2(\sigma + \lambda\delta)^2}{4} + \pi\delta\lambda \right)^{1/2}} \right].$$

$$(2.25)$$

Equation (2.25) clearly indicates that the spot exchange rate overshoots its long-run value $\bar{e}$, the extent of overshooting depending in a precise way upon all the structural parameters of the model.

Consider now the adjustment process. At the initial level of prices the monetary expansion creates an excess supply of money and hence induces an instantaneous reduction in the nominal interest rate. At the same time the monetary expansion causes the public to expect depreciation of the steady-state exchange rate (since there is perfect foresight). Domestic assets therefore become less attractive, causing incipient capital outflows, which causes actual spot depreciation. The actual spot depreciation must be so large that there is now expected appreciation at a rate just sufficient to maintain the uncovered interest arbitrage condition

$$i = i* + z .$$
$$\downarrow \qquad \downarrow$$

The reduction in the interest rates plus the spot depreciation implies excess demand in the commodity market at the initial price level—that is, the adjustment process is characterized by appreciating exchange rates and rising prices, so that purchasing power parity does not hold during the adjustment. The effects of monetary expansion on the balance of trade and the capital account are as follows. Since $i < i*$ implies incipient capital outflows, the adjustment process is characterized by an improving capital account and a deteriorating trade account. Changes in the trade and capital accounts may be obtained via reference to the following equation:

$$\text{trade surplus} = g[(p* + e - p), \bar{y}] .$$
$$\phantom{\text{trade surplus} = g[} (+) \qquad (-)$$

At any instant t the values p_t^*, e_t, p_t, and $\bar{y}_t$ are known by the solution to the model. These values are then plugged into the above equation (with the appropriate functional form) to obtain the nominal trade surplus. The nominal capital account is clearly the mirror image of this.

Actually, the fact that $de_0 > d\bar{e}$ can be verified without reference to the functional form of the model. Two assumptions are necessary: that expectations be at least approximately correct on average and that the underlying model be such that price adjustment is monotonic. Consider a monetary shock, given by an increase in m. From the condition of monetary equilibrium and the fact that $p_0^- = p_0^+$, the implication is $i_0^+ < i*$ where $y = \bar{y}$ is also assumed. Since $i = i* + \dot{e}^E$ always holds, $\dot{e}^E$ must now be less than zero. Directional consistency in expectations now requires expected appreciation on average. Given a monotonically upward path of p, the path of i will be similar. Hence e_0^+ will decline monotonically to $\bar{e}(m_1)$, that is, $e_0^+ > \bar{e}(m_1)$.

It is obvious from the preceding explanation that the impact effects of monetary expansion are dominated entirely by asset market considerations—specifically by the assumption of differential speeds of adjustment in the two markets. Had prices been completely flexible, no dynamics would have been implied, that is, the system would jump from one steady state to another. Consider now the extent to which the parameters of the system contribute to the amount of overshooting (which is $de_0^+/dm - d\bar{e}/dm$). The contribution of π, δ, λ and, σ to the amount of overshooting can be obtained from equation (2.25).

The extent of overshooting is given by

$$A \equiv \frac{1}{\left[\dfrac{\pi(\sigma + \delta\lambda)}{2} + \dfrac{\pi^2(\sigma + \delta\lambda)^2}{4} + \pi\delta\lambda\right]^{1/2}} \tag{2.26}$$

from which it is immediately seen that A is decreasing in each of the parameters π, δ, σ and λ. Evaluating the limits

$$\lim_{\pi \to \infty} A = 0 \quad,$$

$$\lim_{\pi \to 0} A = \infty \quad,$$

$$\lim_{\lambda \to 0} A = \frac{1}{\left(\dfrac{\pi\sigma}{2} + \dfrac{\pi^2\sigma^2}{4}\right)^{1/2}} \tag{2.27}$$

$$\lim_{\delta \to 0} A = \lim_{\lambda \to 0} A$$

$$\lim_{\sigma \to 0} A = \frac{1}{\left[\dfrac{\pi\delta\lambda}{2} + \dfrac{\pi^2\delta^2\lambda^2}{4} + \pi\delta\lambda\right]^{1/2}} \quad,$$

it follows that a nonzero interest semielasticity of money demand is not necessary for a finite extent of overshooting, contrary to what may have been implied for other exogenous values of the expectations parameter θ. Also, with either zero terms of trade or interest elasticities of aggregate demand, the extent of overshooting remains finite.

Diagrammatically, all the effects can be illustrated as shown in Figure 2.3. Initial equilibrium occurs at $(i^*, \bar{p}_1, \bar{e}_1)$. The increase in nominal money disturbs all three curves. Specifically, the AA curve shifts to the right—that is, for the initial price level a higher exchange rate is required to maintain combined monetary plus asset equilibrium.

Since the increase in nominal money causes excess demand in the commodity market at the initial price level, the NN curve shifts to the left. The vertical shift in the AA curve is $1 + \lambda\hat{\theta}$, while that in the NN curve is less, that is, $\sigma/(\delta\lambda + \sigma)$. At the same time the II curve shifts to the right, since

$$\left.\frac{di}{dm}\right|_{dp=0} = -\frac{1}{\lambda}.$$

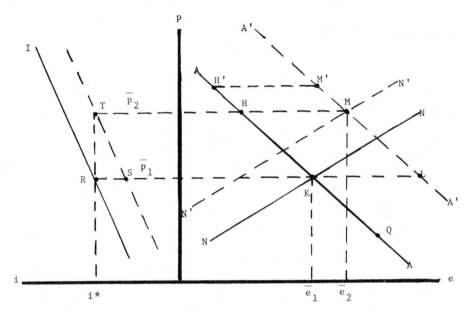

Figure 2.3

The adjustment path is shown as *KLM* in the right-hand panel and *RST* on the left. Final equilibrium is attained at $(i^*, \bar{p}_2, \bar{e}_2)$. The horizontal segment *KL* indicates that on impact prices do not change. The extent of overshooting is $(KL - \bar{e}_1\bar{e}_2)$.

It will be convenient for later purposes to refer to (RS, KL) as the impact effect and (ST, LM) as the trend component.

Alternatively, the diagrams in Figure 2.4 depict the behavior of the system. Using the phase-diagram associated with the class of perfect foresight paths (see Figure 2.5), we can also illustrate the effects of an increase in nominal money on the stable path.

The effect of the increase in *m* is to cause the instantaneous jump to L'. L' is a point on the new saddle point path. After that, the system proceeds on the saddle point path to M'. Were the system to jump to any other point such as L'' or L''', prices and exchange rates would explode.

Foreign Disturbances: A Change in *i**

Consider now an increase in *i** that results from either contractionary monetary policy in the "world" or bond issue abroad. [11] The steady effects of a change in *i** are readily obtained from (2.10) and (2.11) as

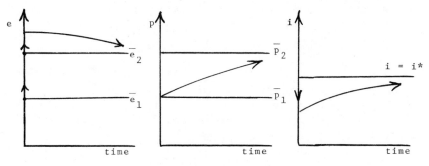

Figure 2.4

$$\frac{d\bar{p}}{di*} = \lambda > 0$$

and

$$\frac{d\bar{e}}{di*} = \left(\lambda + \frac{\sigma}{\delta} \right) ,$$

that is, the system is not homogeneous with respect to *i** or long-run

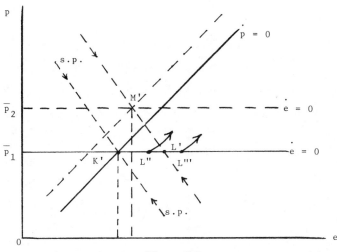

Figure 2.5

exchange rates are affected more than long-run prices compared with the case of monetary shocks. The effect on spot exchange rates is

$$\left. \frac{de}{di^*} \right|_{p=p_0} = \frac{1}{\hat{\theta}} + \lambda + \frac{\sigma}{\delta} ,$$

whence the extent of overshooting is $1/\hat{\theta}$.

The results are diagrammatically shown in Figure 2.6. The AA curve shifts rightward as does the NN curve, while the II curve is unaffected. There is no impact effect upon i as can be seen from

$$i = \frac{p - m}{\lambda} + \frac{\phi}{\lambda} \bar{y} .$$

Hence, the foreign disturbance is transmitted to the home country in the form of domestic inflation of home prices and interest rates (see Figure 2.7).

Foreign Disturbances: Foreign Price Level Changes

Inspection of equations (2.10) and (2.11) indicates that

$$\frac{d\bar{p}}{dp^*} = 0$$

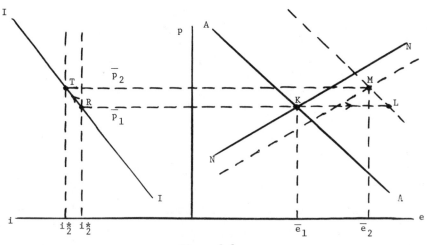

Figure 2.6

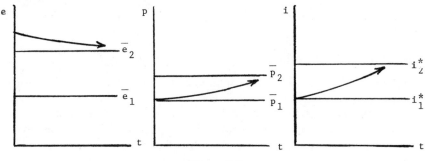

Figure 2.7

and

$$\frac{d\bar{e}}{dp^*} = -1$$

from which it immediately follows that this model is too simple to allow for any dynamics resulting from foreign inflation—that is, the system jumps instantaneously to the new equilibrium

$$\frac{dp}{dp^*} = \frac{d\bar{p}}{dp^*} = 0$$

and

$$\frac{de}{dp^*} = \frac{d\bar{e}}{dp^*} = -1 \ .$$

Hence there is full insulation from foreign inflation. In later chapters more complicated dynamics will preclude this simple possibility. As a matter of fact, any shock that does not affect $\bar{p}$, the long-run price level, will not set up any dynamics (see equation [2.10]).

Changes in g, u_0, or u_1 fall in the above category and imply only instantaneous jumps to the new equilibrium.

OTHER EXPECTATIONAL SCHEMES

This section considers two alternative expectational hypotheses: the continuous-time adaptive expectations scheme and a two-state predictor that is a combination of adaptive and regressive expectations. The two-stage scheme that is discussed below bears some resemblance to that used in Frenkel (1975).

The Adaptive Expectations Model

This section examines the continuous-time analogue to Dornbusch's model provided by Mathieson (1977) and concludes that the interpretation of adaptive expectations provided by the latter results in the requirement that not only do agents make systematic errors (which is, in fact, inherent to adaptive expectations) but that expectations are also directionally perverse—agents continually expect depreciation while there is actual appreciation and vice versa. It is also shown that a proper reformulation of continuous-time adaptive expectations eliminates this paradoxical property, and the conclusion regarding exchange rate volatility under rational versus adaptive expectations is reversed—exchange rate volatility under rational expectations is relatively greater than under adaptive expectations.

Mathieson refines the basic model by defining a price index, which is used in the money market equation, and in the definition of the *real interest rate*, which is used in the aggregate demand function instead of the nominal interest rate. To keep the analysis as close as possible to the original Dornbusch framework, we shall ignore these complications introduced by Mathieson and focus instead on the use of the alternative expectational assumption, that is, adaptive expectations. Thus, the model is described by the following set of equations:

$$i = i^* + \dot{e}^E,$$
$$\dot{e}^E = \beta(e - e^E),$$
$$m = p = -\lambda i + \phi\bar{y},$$
$$d = u + \delta(e + p^* - p) - \sigma i + \gamma\bar{y},$$
$$\dot{p} = \pi(d - \bar{y}),$$

all parameters being defined positively. The only difference between the model represented by the above equations and Dornbusch (1976) lies in the second equation, which specifies that exchange rate expectations are formulated adaptively. Two further assumptions are made to close the model. First, the domestic price level may not jump; second, the expected exchange rate is also similarly constrained.

Consider now a one-time unanticipated permanent increase in domestic nominal money supply m. Mathieson now (erroneously) assumes that the fixity of e^E (the level of the expected exchange rate) implies the fixity of $\dot{e}^E$ (the rate of expected depreciation). Mathieson contends that "as long as the expected exchange rate remains fixed, asset market arbitrage will tie the domestic interest to the world interest rate" (p. 547). The consequence of all these assumptions is that continuous monetary equilibrium cannot be maintained, contrary to the third equation above. Mathieson's route out of this dilemma is to postulate a deflator q(equal to $\alpha p + [1 - \alpha][p^* + e]$) rather than p in the money market condition. Once this is done, the actual exchange rate can depreciate on impact to maintain continuous monetary equilibrium. this is the basis for the claim that adaptive expectations imply large extents of overshooting (of the exchange rate).

All is not well even now. For if one interprets $\dot{e}^E$ as the rate of expected depreciation, then the initial fixity of e^E and the second equation must imply that the rate of expected depreciation is positive (at least initially), while if there is overshooting of the actual exchange rate and if the exchange rate converges from above to its new equilibrium, there must be actual appreciation (that is, $\dot{e} < 0$). Thus expectations are directionally perverse.[12] These facts can be represented in a simple diagram such as Figure 2.8. It remains unclear how speculators can continue to operate despite perpetual losses, as implied, for example, in figure 2.8.

A Suggested Reinterpretation

This section demonstrates that a proper reformulation of the framework discussed above eliminates the paradoxical conclusion noted. To facilitate easier comparison with the rational expectations (or perfect foresight) case,

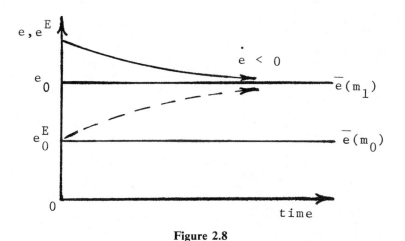

Figure 2.8

we make one more simplifying assumption: $\sigma = 0$. No qualitative difference is made by this assumption.

The first element in the reformulation lies in recognizing that the initial level of the expected spot exchange rate cannot be fixed. If it were in fact fixed, and assuming that monetary expansion results in actual spot depreciation, then from the expectational scheme it is immediately clear that there must be expected depreciation, while actual overshooting, if it occurs, requires that there be actual appreciation along the trend path. Thus, in order for directional consistency to obtain it is necessary that both e and e^E be allowed to vary. The initial jump in the actual and expected spot rates immediately following the shock can be calculated by reference to the dynamic properties of the model.

Since the steady state of the model implies that $\dot{e} = \dot{e}^E = \dot{p} = 0$, the price adjustment equation is

$$\dot{p} = \pi\delta(e - \bar{e}) - \pi\delta(p - \bar{p}). \tag{2.28}$$

Next, we obtain

$$\dot{e}^E = \frac{p - \bar{p}}{\lambda}. \tag{2.29}$$

Further, the expectational equation can be rewritten as

$$\dot{e}^E = \beta(e - \bar{e}) - \beta(e^E - \bar{e}), \tag{2.30}$$

so that (2.29) and (2.30) yield

$$(e - \bar{e}) = \frac{p - \bar{p}}{\lambda\beta} + (e^E - \bar{e}). \tag{2.31}$$

Substitute (2.31) into (2.28) to obtain the final form of the price adjustment equation:

$$\dot{p} = \pi\delta(\frac{1}{\lambda\beta} - 1)(p - \bar{p}) + \pi\delta(e^E - \bar{e}). \tag{2.32}$$

Equations (2.29) and (2.32) describe the dynamics of the system and are conveniently represented as

$$
\begin{bmatrix} \dot{p} \\ \dot{e}^E \end{bmatrix} = \begin{bmatrix} \pi\delta(\dfrac{1}{\lambda\beta} - 1) & \pi\delta \\ \dfrac{1}{\lambda} & 0 \end{bmatrix} \begin{bmatrix} p - \bar{p} \\ e^E - \bar{e} \end{bmatrix}. \quad (2.33)
$$

The characteristic equation to (2.33) is

$$
\lambda s^2 - \lambda\pi\delta\left(\frac{1}{\lambda\beta} - 1\right) s - \pi\delta = 0,
$$

where s is the eigenvector. The solution is

$$
s_1, s_2 = \frac{\lambda\pi\delta\left(\dfrac{1}{\lambda\beta} - 1\right) \pm \left(\lambda^2\pi^2\delta^2\left(\dfrac{1}{\lambda\beta} - 1\right)^2 + 4\pi\delta\right)^{1/2}}{2}.
$$

$$(2.34)$$

It is seen that regardless of $(1/\lambda\beta - 1) \lessgtr 0, s_1 < 0$, while $s_2 > 0$—that is, the system is saddle point stable. The general solution to the expected spot rate is described by

$$
(e^E - \bar{e}) = A \exp^{s_1 t} + B \exp^{s_2 t}. \quad (2.35)
$$

To ensure stability we restrict the system to the stable arm of the saddle, which is described by $B = 0$.[13] The initial constant A can thus be calculated as

$$
A = \frac{p_t - \bar{p}}{s_1\lambda \exp^{s_1 t}}
$$

Consequently, the expected exchange rate and price level must be related along the stable arm via

$$
(e^E - \bar{e}) = \frac{p_t - \bar{p}}{\lambda s_1}. \quad (2.36)
$$

Evaluating (2.36) at $t = 0$ yields the initial jump in e^E that is required to stabilize the system, which is

$$\frac{de_0^E}{dm} = \left(1 - \frac{1}{\lambda s_1} \right) > 1. \tag{2.37}$$

The jump in the actual exchange rate must, as was seen earlier, be less than that in (2.37). From (2.29) and the specification of expectations

$$\frac{1}{\lambda}(p_t - \bar{p}) = \beta(e_t - e_t^E). \tag{2.38}$$

Evaluating (2.38) at $t = 0$, we obtain

$$\frac{de_0}{dm} = \left(1 - \frac{1}{\lambda s_1} - \frac{1}{\lambda \beta} \right). \tag{2.39}$$

Equation (2.39) indicates that the initial jump in the actual spot rate falls short of that in the expected spot rate by a factor that depends inversely upon the speed of adjustment of expectations and the semi-interest elasticity of money demand.

Is there actual overshooting? This depends upon whether the expression in (2.39) exceeds unity. The condition that ensures this is

$$2\lambda^2 \beta^2 + \pi \delta[\lambda(1 - \lambda\beta) - 2] > 0. \tag{2.40}$$

An obvious interpretation of (2.40) is hard to find, but it is easy to verify that (2.40) is clearly satisfied for large β or small values of π.[14] Thus, for relatively quick adjustment in expectations the actual exchange rate overshoots, and there is both actual and expected appreciation along the trend path. But if expectational adjustment is very sluggish, there may again be the problem of directional inconsistency in expectations.

Consider next the perfect foresight case. This is given by setting $\dot{e}^E = \dot{e}$ and ignoring the expectational scheme. This procedure yields the adjustment system[15]

$$\begin{bmatrix} \dot{p} \\ \dot{e} \end{bmatrix} = \begin{bmatrix} \pi\delta & \pi\delta \\ \dfrac{1}{\lambda} & 0 \end{bmatrix} \begin{bmatrix} p - \bar{p} \\ e - \bar{e} \end{bmatrix}. \tag{2.41}$$

Exchange rate overshooting is inevitable in the perfect foresight case. By a procedure identical to the above it can be shown that the initial jump in the spot exchange rate is (see Gray and Turnovsky 1979).

$$\frac{de_0^*}{dm} = \left(1 - \frac{1}{\lambda s_1^*} \right) > 1, \tag{2.42}$$

where the asterisk refers to the perfect foresight case. Since $s_1^* = \lim_{\beta \to \infty} s_1$, it can be shown that $s_1^* < s_1$ for finite β. It is then unambiguously true that

$$\frac{de_0^*}{dm} > \frac{de_0}{dm},$$

that is, exchange rate volatility under perfect foresight is relatively greater than under adaptive expectations. In either case the domestic interest rate must decline below the world rate in view of the expected appreciation.

The Two-Stage Structural Expectations Model

This section considers an expectations structure that is based on errors in both the path of exchange rates as well as the equilibrium exchange rate itself. Until now it has been assumed that the equilibrium exchange rate corresponding to every level of all the exogenous variables of the economy is always correctly known. While this assumption may be quite defensible for nominal monetary shocks (the kind of the disturbance considered by Dornbusch), it will be seen below that the prediction of the equilibrium exchange rate following a real shift (which alters the equilibrium terms of trade) is by no means a trivial matter and may require almost as much information as the prediction of the perfect foresight path itself.

Consider now the problem of predicting the equilibrium exchange rate, which is given by equation (2.11) repeated here for convenience:

$$\bar{e} = (m - p^*) + \left(\frac{1 - \gamma}{\delta} - \phi \right) \bar{y} - \frac{u}{\delta} + \left(\lambda + \frac{\sigma}{\delta} \right) i^*. \tag{2.11}$$

It is clear from (2.11) that the equilibrium exchange rate is proportional to the stock of nominal money, m. Thus, given a change in the latter of the amount Δm, the new equilibrium exchange rate can be directly inferred as

$$\bar{e}_1 = (\bar{e}_0 + \Delta \bar{e}) = m_0 + \Delta m,$$

where $\bar{e}_0$ and m_0 are the predisturbance levels of the equilibrium exchange rate and money supply, respectively. Provided that these are correctly observed, the new equilibrium exchange rate can be predicted without reference to any of the structural parameters of the economy. The only piece of information required is knowing that nominal money is ultimately neutral.

Consider next a disturbance that alters the equilibrium terms of trade $(\bar{e} + p^* - \bar{p})$. Such a disturbance can be parameterized within this framework by considering a change in the world interest rate i^*.[16] As shown in an earlier section, such a shift alters the equilibrium exchange rate and price level in the proportions

$$\frac{d\bar{e}}{di^*} = \lambda + \frac{\sigma}{\delta} \; ; \; \frac{d\bar{p}}{di^*} = \lambda. \tag{2.43}$$

Consequently, the equilibrium terms of trade are seen to unambiguously depreciate. Meanwhile, the spot exchange rate overshoots the equilibrium exchange rate and adjusts in the proportion $(\lambda + \sigma/\delta + 1/\theta)$, as can be seen by using the asset curve (2.22).

A moment's reflection indicates, however, that this overshooting result crucially depends upon the assumption that the new equilibrium exchange rate and price levels following the unanticipated interest rate disturbance be exactly known to market participants (that is, the formulas in [2.43] are known with certainty).[17] Specifically, it is necessary that speculators (and other agents) know that an increase in i^* will raise the equilibrium domestic level by a factor of λ and the equilibrium exchange rate in the proportion of exactly $(\lambda + \sigma/\delta)$.

Consider next the value of θ that is consistent with perfect foresight along the adjustment path. As shown by Dornbusch (1976), it is

$$\theta^* = \frac{\pi\left(\dfrac{\sigma}{\lambda} + \delta\right)}{2} + \left[\frac{\pi^2\left(\dfrac{\sigma}{\lambda} + \delta\right)^2}{4} + \frac{\pi\delta}{\lambda}\right]^{1/2}, \tag{2.44}$$

that is, a complex quadratic function involving the parameters of the economy $\lambda, \sigma, \delta,$ and π. Thus if one admits the possibility of lack of perfect foresight along the adjustment path (that is, $\theta \neq \theta^*$), then the conclusion follows that this must result from lack of knowledge on the part of domestic speculators concerning either the parameters involved ($\sigma, \lambda, \delta,$ and π) or the form of (2.44). Now consider equation (2.11), which indicates that the true equilibrium exchange rate following the interest rate shift is obtained by adding to the predisturbance exchange rate the amount $(\lambda + \sigma/\delta)di^*$. Thus, three of the four parameters involved in the correct computation of $\theta*$ are also involved in the correct calculation of the new equilibrium exchange rate. Consequently, unless one assumes that domestic speculators can solve linear equations such as (2.11) but not quadratic equations such as (2.44), or that it is only the parameter π (speed of price adjustment) that is not correctly known, it follows that lack of perfect foresight along the adjustment path implies that the equilibrium exchange rate is also misestimated.

It has been argued above that the estimation of the equilibrium exchange rate (following interest rate shifts) may not be an easy matter and that the same reasons that permit errors in forecasting the rate of depreciation at each future point in time also apply in predicting the level of the long-run equilibrium. We now propose a simple theory of expectational errors for both the rate of short-run depreciation and the level of equilibrium depreciation. The implication of this is to modify both the response of the instantaneous exchange rate and its evolution over time.

An Alternative Specification

Rather than assuming that the correct equilibrium exchange rate is perfectly forecast, it is supposed that market participants have an estimate of the equilibrium exchange rate corresponding to every level of the autonomous variables (in particular, $i*$) of the system. Implicit in the knowledge of the expected equilibrium exchange rate and the currently observed spot rate is an estimate of the rate of depreciation/appreciation. Moreover, market agents believe in the inherent stability of the system in the sense that equilibrium is eventually expected to be attained. The simplest hypothesis that expresses these assumptions is

$$\dot{e}_t^E = -\theta(e_t - \tilde{e}_t), \ \theta > 0, \tag{2.45}$$

where $\tilde{e}_t$ *is the estimate of the equilibrium exchange rate at time t.* Equation (2.45) is seen to be very similar to (2.21), except for the fact that the correct equilibrium exchange rate $\bar{e}$ in (2.21) has been replaced in (2.45) by its available forecast $\tilde{e}_t$. A more complex setting would attempt to make the speed parameter θ endogenous, depending possibly on the other known parameters of the economy as well as on time, but we shall ignore this possibility.

The next step is to describe the determination of the expected long-run exchange rate $\tilde{e}$. For expositional purposes suppose that the economy starts at a long-run equilibrium point characterized by the level of world interest rate i_0^*. Further, any long-run equilibrium is such that long-run expectations are fulfilled—that is, $\tilde{e}(i_0^*) = \bar{e}(i_0^*)$ where $\bar{e}(i_0^*)$ is the actual long-run exchange rate corresponding to i_0^*. An analytical expression for $\bar{e}(i_0^*)$ was derived in

(2.11). Assume now, that at $t = 0$ an unanticipated increase in i^* occurs. The new level is i_1^*, corresponding to which is the new actual long-run (or equilibrium) exchange rate $\bar{e}(i_1^*)$. If market participants were endowed with equilibrium perfect foresight, the new expected equilibrium exchange rate $\tilde{e}(i_1^*)$ would equal $\bar{e}(i_1^*)$. This being not the case, however, at the instant the actual equilibrium shifts the new expected equilibrium exchange rate is misestimated. As time goes by, market participants acquire more information and experience, so that the error associated with the initial forecast of the long-run equilibrium diminishes, and eventually expectations about the location of the long-run equilibrium are fulfilled. These ideas can be expressed formally as

$$\bar{e}(i_1) = \bar{e}(i_0) + \left(\lambda + \frac{\sigma}{\delta} \right) di^*, \qquad (2.46)$$

where $di^* = i_1^* - i_0^*$. Further, the initial forecast of the long-run equilibrium is

$$\tilde{e}_0(i_1^*) = \bar{e}(i_0) + \alpha_0 \left(\lambda + \frac{\sigma}{\delta} \right) di^*, \qquad \alpha_0 > 0, \qquad (2.47)$$

that is, the initial error in the long-run forecast is

$$\tilde{e}_0(i_1^*) - \bar{e}(i_1^*) = (\alpha_0 - 1) \, di^*.$$

Over time, the error associated with an estimate of $\bar{e}(i_1^*)$ diminishes

$$\alpha_t = 1 + (\alpha_0 - 1) \exp^{-\beta t}. \qquad (2.48)$$

Later estimates of $\bar{e}(i_1^*)$ are given by (2.49) analogously to (2.47):

$$\tilde{e}_t(i_1^*) = \bar{e}(i_0^*) + \alpha_t \left(\lambda + \frac{\sigma}{\delta} \right) di^*. \qquad (2.49)$$

Equations (2.48) and (2.49) yield

$$\tilde{e}_t(i_1^*) = \bar{e}(i_1^*) + \left(\lambda + \frac{\sigma}{\delta} \right) di^* (\alpha_0 - 1) \exp^{-\beta t},$$

whence the expected rate of depreciation of the long-run exchange rate is

$$\dot{\tilde{e}}_t = -\beta(\alpha_0 - 1) \left(\lambda + \frac{\sigma}{\delta} \right) di^*$$

or

$$\dot{\tilde{e}}_t = -\beta[\tilde{e}_t(i^*_1) - \bar{e}(i^*_1)].$$ (2.50)

The theory of expectations, put forward above, thus consists of two parts and shares some common elements with Frenkel (1975). First, market participants possess an estimate of the rate of depreciation between equilibriums, and this is hypothesized in (2.46). Second, their perception of the equilibrium is itself an estimate that is subject to revision over time, with subsequent implications for intraequilibrium expectations. At best this theory is extremely crude, for nothing has been said about α_0, which determines the extent of the initial miscalculation. Nor is it likely in an actual situation that information is acquired smoothly and continually and that the amount of the initial error diminishes at a constant rate β. Despite these drawbacks, it would appear that these assumptions allow for more realism than the commonly made assumption that the long-run exchange rate corresponding to every level of all exogenous variables is inevitably correctly known.

The rest of the model is given by (2.2), (2.3), and (2.7).[18] Consider now an unanticipated increase in the world interest rate, i^*. Given the level of prices and other exogenous variables, real money demand declines by a factor of λ, so that the maintenance of monetary equilibrium requires expected appreciation to offset this effect.[19]

It is clear, therefore, that the spot rate overshoots the initially expected long-run exchange rate $\tilde{e}_0$. Whether it overshoots the actual long-run exchange rate depends upon the sign of

$$\frac{de_0}{di^*} - \frac{d\bar{e}}{di^*} = (\alpha_0 - 1)\left(\lambda + \frac{\sigma}{\delta}\right) + \frac{1}{\theta}.$$ (2.51)

If the initial forecast of the long-run exchange rate were a serious underestimate, then (2.51) might conceivably be negative. On the other hand, if $\tilde{e}_0$ is an overestimate of $\bar{e}$, the extent of the initial overshooting is even more serious than that implied by the Dornbusch model. There is thus a certain ambiguity about the effects of interest rate shifts on the instantaneous exchange rate—an ambiguity that hinges on the magnitude of the parameter α_0. While a more complete theory of expectational errors might attempt to endogenize this (and it is hoped that future research will be directed at this issue), a few remarks are in order. First, α_0 must almost certainly be positive, but there is no reason to suspect that it should necessarily be a constant. It may, for example, be related to the size of the disturbance, implying a systematic relationship between the error of prediction and the magnitude of the prediction problem. Or, it may be related to previous experience that speculators have had in estimating the equilibrium exchange rate. The latter consideration would make α_0 depend upon the variance of previous shifts in exogenous variables. Thus, the exchange rate response to exogenous disturbances may depend not only upon expectations about the future but also upon past history.

The dynamic behavior of the model is governed by equations (2.11), (2.45), (2.7), and (2.50). First, the revised asset curve is now

$$(e - \check{e}) = -\frac{1}{\lambda\theta}(p - \bar{p}), \tag{2.52}$$

while (2.7) can be rewritten

$$\dot{p} = \pi\delta(e - \bar{e}) - \pi\delta(p - \bar{p}) + \pi\sigma\theta(e - \check{e}). \tag{2.53}$$

Next,

$$(e - \bar{e}) = (e - \check{e}) + (\check{e} - \bar{e}).$$

Using this along with (2.52), (2.53) can be reduced to

$$\dot{p} = -\left[\pi\delta + \frac{\pi}{\lambda\theta}(\delta + \sigma\theta)\right](p - \bar{p}) + \pi\delta(\check{e} - \bar{e}). \tag{2.54}$$

Equation (2.54) along with (2.50) form a second-order dynamic system and adjustment is characterized by the distinct real roots $-\beta$ and $-A$ where

$$A \equiv \frac{\pi\delta(1 + \lambda\theta) - \pi\sigma\theta}{\lambda\theta}, \quad \text{(assuming } A > 0\text{)}.$$

Since the interest is on the path of the actual spot rate, the latter is to be obtained as follows. First, the price solution can be hypothesized to be

$$(p_t - \bar{p}) = c_1 \exp^{-At} + c_2 \exp^{Bt}, \tag{2.55}$$

where c_1 and c_2 are determined from initial conditions and are

$$c_1 = \frac{-\pi\delta}{A - B}(\check{e}_0 - \bar{e}) + (p_0 - \bar{p})$$

and

$$c_2 = \frac{\pi\delta}{A - B}(\check{e}_0 - \bar{e}).$$

The actual exchange rate path can now be obtained by substituting these results in (2.52), after recalling that the solution to (2.50) is

$$(\check{e}_t - \bar{e}) = (\check{e}_0 - \bar{e})\exp^{-\beta t}.$$

The result is

$$(e_t - \bar{e}) = (\check{e}_0 - \bar{e})\exp^{-\beta t}\left[1 - \frac{\pi\delta}{\lambda\theta(A - \beta)}\right.$$
$$\left. + \frac{\pi\delta}{\lambda\theta(A - \beta)}\exp^{(\beta - A)t}\right] - \frac{p_0 - \bar{p}}{\lambda\theta}\exp^{-At}. \qquad (2.56)$$

The reader may verify that (2.56) will lead to (2.51) when evaluated at $t = 0$ and differentiated with respect to i^*. Next, differentiating (2.56) with respect to time,

$$\dot{e} = -\beta(\check{e}_0 - \bar{e})\exp^{-\beta t} + \frac{\beta\pi\delta}{\lambda\theta(A - \beta)}(\check{e}_0 - \bar{e})\exp^{-\beta t}$$
$$- \frac{A\pi\delta}{\lambda\theta(A - \beta)}(\check{e}_0 - \bar{e})\exp^{-At} + \frac{A}{\lambda\theta}(p_0 - \bar{p})\exp^{-At};$$

evaluating at $t = 0$ yields

$$\dot{e}_0 = -\left(\beta + \frac{\pi\delta}{\lambda\theta}\right)(\check{e}_0 - \bar{e}) + \frac{A}{\lambda\theta}(p_0 - \bar{p}). \qquad (2.57)$$

Equation (2.57) cannot be unambiguously signed, since $\check{e}_0 \lessgtr \bar{e}$ depending upon whether the initial forecast of $\bar{e}$ is an over- or underestimate. Recalling that $(p_0 - \bar{p}) = -\lambda di^*$ while $(\check{e}_0 - \bar{e}) = (\alpha_0 - 1)(\lambda + \sigma/\delta)di^*$ and the definition of A, (2.57) can be used to place an upper bound on the value of α_0 that will result in an initially rising spot rate. This is

$$\hat{\alpha}_0 < 1 - \frac{\pi\delta[\delta(1 + \lambda\theta) + \theta\sigma]}{(\pi\delta + \beta\lambda\theta)(\delta\lambda + \sigma)} \cdot {}^{20} \qquad (2.58)$$

On the other hand, the condition that implies undershooting of the instantaneous exchange rate is (from [2.51])

$$\alpha_0^* < 1 - \frac{\delta}{\theta(\delta\lambda + \sigma)} \cdot \qquad (2.59)$$

There is no conflict between (2.58) and (2.59), since in this framework the exchange rate may overshoot its long-run equilibrium and then proceed to deviate even further away from the latter. From (2.59) it can be seen that the likelihood of instantaneous undershooting is positively related to θ, λ, and σ and inversely to δ.

Even if the instantaneous exchange rate falls short of its equilibrium value, there may be delayed overshooting. The latter situation is seen to occur if (2.58) is satisfied for $\alpha_0 > 0$ and if $t' > 0$ can be found such that $(e_t' - \bar{e}) = 0$. From (2.56) this involves a positive value of t' that satisfies

$$\exp^{(\beta - A)t'} = \frac{(\alpha_0 - 1)\left(\lambda + \dfrac{\sigma}{\delta}\right)\left[\dfrac{\pi\delta}{\lambda\theta(A - \beta)} - 1\right]\lambda\theta}{\dfrac{\pi\delta}{A - \beta}\left[\alpha_0\lambda + \dfrac{\sigma}{\delta}(\alpha_0 - 1)\right]} .$$

Other characteristics of the exchange rate path may similarly be explored and will be seen to be dependent upon the precise parameter magnitudes involved. In any case exchange rate adjustment can assume a variety of dynamic patterns in contrast with the simple first-order exponential process implied in Dornbusch.

OPTIMAL POLICIES

So far we have noted the descriptive aspects of monetary and other policies. A natural question to ask is, What money supply rule (or government expenditure rule) should be pursued in the face of exogenous shocks? Turnovsky (1979) provides a partial answer.

The model

$$i = i^* + z,$$

$$z = -\theta(e - \bar{e}),$$

$$m - p = -\lambda i + \phi\bar{y},$$

and

$$\dot{p} = \pi(d - \bar{y}) = \pi[u + (\gamma - 1)\bar{y} - \sigma i + \delta(e - p)]$$

can be rewritten as

$$m - p = \phi\bar{y} - \lambda[i* + \theta(\bar{e} - e)]$$

and

$$\dot{p} = \pi[u + (\gamma - 1)\bar{y} - \sigma(i* + \theta(\bar{e} - e)) + \delta(e - p)],$$

which in the steady state are

$$\bar{m} - \bar{p} = \phi\bar{y} - \lambda i*$$

and

$$u + (\gamma - 1)\bar{y} - \sigma i* + \delta(\bar{e} - \bar{p}) = 0.$$

Denote

$$m_d = m - \bar{m},$$

$$p_d = p - \bar{p},$$

and

$$s = e - \bar{e},$$

so that

$$\dot{p} = \pi\left[\left(\frac{\delta + \sigma\theta + \delta\lambda\theta}{-\lambda\theta}\right) p_d + \left(\frac{\delta + \sigma\theta}{\lambda\theta}\right) m_d\right] \qquad (2.60)$$

expresses the dynamics of the system.

The optimal monetary rule requires the solution to the following optimum control problem:

$$\min_{[m_d(t)]} \int_0^t \tfrac{1}{2}(c_1 s^2 + c_2 p^2)\exp^{-bt}dt,$$

subject to (2.28) and

$$(p_d - m_d) = -\lambda\theta s. \tag{2.61}$$

The solution is a liner feedback rule:

$$m*d = -\mu*s,$$

where the sign of the feedback coefficient $\mu*$ is not determinate without a knowledge of the regret coefficients c_1 and c_2. Hence, "leaning with the wind" may be more desirable than "leaning against the wind."

This implies the existence of a procyclical rather than countercyclical optimum monetary policy. Actually, these terms are somewhat misleading in view of the fact that in this model the state variables s and p_d are always of opposite sign at any instant t. What is procyclical with respect to one state variable is countercyclical with respect to the other. For example, if prices are too low and the exchange rate too high, the optimum monetary policy may not involve expansion of nominal money if c_1 is much greater than c_2.

One may compare the extent of overshooting under optimal and passive ($m_d = 0$) monetary policies. Not surprisingly, the answer depends on the feedback coefficient $\mu*$. Finally, adjustment speeds and the amounts of overshooting may be compared under arbitrary X% rules and the optimal rule and again turn out to depend on c_1 and c_2.

NOTES

1. Hence, the analysis deals with perfect international capital mobility. This assumption as well as that of instantaneous money market adjustment will be relaxed in the next chapter.

2. The similarity between (2.1) and the Fisher equation linking nominal and real interest rates is quite notable.

3. By implication the speed of adjustment of the money market to equilibrium is infinitely great. The next chapter allows for noninstantaneous clearing of the money market.

4. Currency substitution models are analyzed in Canto and Miles (forthcoming).

5. The government budget constraint implies an additional source of dynamics (see Turnovsky [1977]) and, if incorporated, would lead to fruitless complexities at this stage.

6. Income is assumed to be fixed at its full-employment level at this stage. This assumption will be relaxed in a later chapter.

7. Equation (2.3) can also be rationalized by appealing to the fact that aggregate demand is composed of domestic absorption plus the net trade surplus. The latter can be assumed to be determined by the real exchange rate and the former by the interest rate and income. Chapter 3 employs this rationalization.

8. Since the model is log linear, $d\bar{e}/dm = 1$ implies that the elasticity of $\bar{e}$ with respect to m is 1.

9. This curve is negatively sloped if q instead of p is used.

10. For the effects under quasi-rational expectations the reader should substitute the general unknown value θ for $\hat{\theta}$.

11. This experiment is also considered later in a different context. But see note 16 at this point.

12. This conclusion must clearly be modified if adjustment is cyclical rather than monotonic. Formally, the problem occurs because of the lack of "weak consistency" in the sense of Turnovsky and Burmeister (1977).

13. See Gray and Turnovsky (1979) for similar use of this procedure in a perfect foresight context. We have also followed this method earlier.

14. This can be seen by writing (2.40) as

$$2\lambda^2 + \pi\delta\left(\frac{\lambda}{\beta^2} - \frac{\lambda^2}{\beta} - \frac{2}{\beta^2} \right) > 0.$$

15. Equation (2.41) can be derived from (2.33) by setting $\beta \to \infty$. This ensures $e_t = e_t^E$ for all t—that is, there is perfect foresight. Note that this procedure need not always work.

16. This experiment—that is, a shift in i^* without a concomitant change in p^*—strains the usefulness of a one-country model. For expository purposes it may be supposed that the change in i^* is brought about by an appropriate mix of foreign monetary and fiscal policies such that p^* is not altered. It should be noted, however, that were p^* allowed to change simultaneously with i^*, this would render the prediction of $\bar{e}$ even more difficult (see [2.11]). Specifically, domestic agents would now need information on world economic parameters—that is, the reduced-form elasticity of p^* with respect to i^*.

17. If these formulas are not correctly known, (2.22) cannot hold in a relevant way.

18. Again, we do not consider the price index or the real interest rate and follow instead the original Dornbusch specification.

19. This can be seen by writing the monetary equilibrium condition as

$$m - p = -\lambda i^* - \lambda \dot{e}^E + \phi\bar{y}.$$

20. Equation (2.58) is derived from the assumption that $\dot{e}_0 > 0$.

REFERENCES

Bilson, J. 1979 "The Vicious Circle Hypothesis." *IMF Staff Papers* 26 (March): 1–37.

Brock, W. 1974 "Money and Growth: The Case of Long-Run Perfect Foresight." *International Economic Review* 15 (June): 750–77.

Canto, V., and M. Miles. Forthcoming. "Exchange Rates and Inflation in a Global Monetarist Model with Currency-Substitution." In *Economic Interdependence and Flexible Exchange Rates,* edited by J. Bhandari and B. Putnam. Cambridge: MIT Press.

Dornbusch, R. 1976 "Expectations and Exchange Rate Dynamics" *Journal of Political Economy* 84 (December): 1161–76.

Gray, M., and S. Turnovsky. 1979 'The Stability of Exchange Rate Dynamics under Perfect

Myopic Foresight." *International Economic Review* 20 (October): 643–60.

Frenkel, J. 1975 "Inflation and the Formation of Expectations." *Journal of Monetary Economics* (October): 403–21.

Mathieson, D. 1977 "The Impact of Monetary and Fiscal Policy under Flexible Exchange Rates and Alternative Expectations Structures." *IMF Staff Papers* 24 (November): 535–68.

Sargent, T., and N. Wallace. 1973 "The Stability of Models of Money and Growth with Perfect Foresight." *Econometrica* 41: (November) 1043–48.

Turnovsky, S. 1979 "Optimal Monetary Policies under Flexible Exchange Rates." *Journal of Economic Dynamics and Control Theory* (February): 85–100.

_____. 1977 *Macroeconomic Analysis and Stabilization Policy.* Cambridge, England: Cambridge University Press.

Turnovsky, S., and E. Burmeister. 1977 "Perfect Foresight, Expectational Consistency and Macroeconomic Equilibrium." *Journal of Political Economy* 85 (April): 379–94.

Witte, W. 1979 "Dynamic Adjustment in an Open Economy with Flexible Exchange Rates." *Southern Economic Journal* 45 (April): 1072–90.

3

EXCHANGE RATE
OVERSHOOTING REVISITED

This chapter is concerned with investigating in further detail the exchange rate overshooting hypothesis popularized by Dornbusch (1976). Although the principal statement of this view is expressed by Dornbusch (1976, 1979), similar results are also stressed in subsequent work by Mathieson (1977), Bilson (1979), and Witte (1979). The opposite view, however, is expressed by Niehans (1977) who argues that the main drawback of Dornbusch (1976) (and of subsequent work within that framework) is the neglect of the interaction between trade flows and asset stocks. Thus Niehans finds that monetary expansion is inevitably associated not with overshooting but with undershooting of instantaneous exchange rates. Niehans's analysis, while interesting, is, however, marred by limitations of its own. For example, the real sector is completely excluded and all considerations of expectations and of the capital account (which appears to be an important source of exchange rate volatility) are ignored.

This chapter may be viewed as an extension of the Dornbusch and Niehans lines of inquiry and is an attempt to integrate them. Specifically, it extends Niehans's analysis by incorporating interest-bearing assets and expectations as well as by providing a role for the trade and capital accounts. It also generalizes Dornbusch's work by allowing for noninstantaneous adjustment in money and security markets. The resulting framework involves considerable interplay between the real and asset sectors of the economy. An implication of the analysis is that unlike the Dornbusch model (1976) the short-run exchange rate is not determined exclusively in asset markets but instead by the full general equilibrium interaction of commodity and asset markets, and only in special cases (of which Dornbusch's work is one example) does a valid dichotomy exist. The central result of this chapter is that neither overshooting nor undershooting is the inevitable consequence of monetary disturbances. Rather, the short-run exchange rate response is governed by a variety of factors such as the relative speeds of adjustment in real and asset markets, by the responsiveness of trade and capital flows, and by other structural parameters of the economy.

THE FRAMEWORK

The model applies to a small open economy with floating exchange rates. Domestic consumption is divided up between two goods—an exportable (which is locally produced) and an importable (of which there is no domestic production). These goods are regarded by domestic agents as being imperfectly substitutable on the demand side. The domestic economy is small enough to regard the world supply of importables as well as the world supply of foreign currency-denominated securities to be perfectly elastic at the going world currency price and yield, respectively. The domestic currency price of the exportable is determined endogenously. All goods are perishable, so that domestic wealth owners allocate their wealth to the available financial assets. These are domestic money and domestic and foreign currency-denominated securities. There is no currency substitution, and domestic output is fixed at its full-employment level.

The Commodity Market

Aggregate demand for the exportable is given by the sum of domestic absorption and the net trade balance. Domestic absorption is assumed to depend upon domestic income (output) and the domestic interest rate, while the trade balance is determined by the real exchange rate. The dependence of domestic absorption upon the nominal interest rate can be rationalized either through the induced wealth–effect or via its influence on permanent income, which in turn determines consumption. Although the real interest rate can also be regarded as affecting the investment component of domestic absorption, this effect is ignored in the interest of computational simplicity. It is assumed that domestic absorption is linear in the interest rate and the income, while the net trade balance is linear in the log of the real exchange rate.[1] By an appropriate choice of units it can be ensured that the trade balance corresponding to the equilibrium real exchange rate (to be defined below) is zero. Thus, aggregate demand for domestic output can be characterized as

$$D = u + \gamma \bar{Y} - \sigma i + \delta(e + p^* - p), \tag{3.1}$$

where $A = u + \gamma \bar{Y} - \sigma i$ is domestic absorption and $T = \delta(e + p^* - p)$ is the trade balance. u is the autonomous component of aggregate demand, $\bar{Y}$ is full-employment output, i is the domestic interest rate, and $(e + p^* - p)$ is the (log) real exchange rate. The parameter δ measures the sensitivity of trade flows to the real exchange rate. The percentage change in the domestic price level $\dot{p}$ is assumed to be proportional to excess demand in the domestic output market—that is,

$$\dot{p} = \pi(D - \bar{Y}), \tag{3.2}$$

where π measures the speed of adjustment in the goods market.

The Money Market

It is assumed that the logarithm of real money demand, $(m^* - p)$, is linear in the interest rate and the logarithm of real income. Thus,

$$m^* - p = -\lambda i + \phi \bar{y}. \tag{3.3}$$

The adjustment of real money demand to real money supply is not instantaneous. Specifically, actual real balances are adjusted according to a measure of stock excess demand in the money market,

$$\dot{m} - \dot{p} = \mu[m^* - p - (m - p)] = \mu(m^* - m), \tag{3.4'}$$

where m is the logarithm of the actual money supply and μ the speed of adjustment. Since domestic money supply is assumed to be exogenously fixed, (3.4′) can be rewritten as

$$\dot{p} = \mu(m - m^*). \tag{3.4}$$

The symmetry between (3.2) and (3.4) is notable. These equations state that excess demand in the commodity market is reflected by excess supply in the money market. No disequilibrium is observed in the bond market because the domestic interest rate is allowed to adjust instantaneously. The commodity market disequilibrium causes domestic prices to rise; this reduces aggregate demand, thus alleviating the excess demand here. At the same time the increase in the price level is also the mechanism whereby the money market adjusts toward equilibrium. The spillover from excess money supply directly onto the commodity market is not made explicit here, since this effect operates via real wealth.

The Capital Account and Expectations

Unlike the Dornbusch model (1976), it is assumed here that financial capital is only imperfectly internationally mobile. More specifically, capital flows occur at a finite rate in proportion to the uncovered differential between yields on domestic currency- and foreign currency-denominated securities. Thus,

$$C = \beta(i - i^* - x), \tag{3.5}$$

where C is the net capital inflow, and x is the expected rate of depreciation of domestic currency vis-à-vis foreign currency. β is a measure of the degree of capital mobility and as $\beta \rightarrow \infty$ (3.5) reduces to the uncovered interest arbitrage condition. Expected depreciation is described by the simple regressive scheme

$$x = -\theta(e - \bar{e}), \tag{3.6}$$

where $\bar{e}$ is the logarithm of the equilibrium exchange rate. The lags in the money market and security market notwithstanding, it will be clear presently that (3.6) is the only scheme consistent with perfect foresight for properly chosen θ.

The final equation of the model is the condition of equilibrium in the total balance of payments under a floating exchange rate—that is,

$$\delta(e + p^* - p) + \beta(i - i^* - x) = 0. \tag{3.7}$$

Equation (3.7) states that the sum of the trade balance and the capital account surplus must equal zero. This completes the specification of the model.

MONETARY EXPANSION: THE ANATOMY OF OVERSHOOTING

Consider now the impact effects of an unanticipated permanent monetary expansion. Defining the steady state of the model by $i = i^*$, $x = 0$, $\dot{p} = 0$, and $m^* = m$ as well as by $p = \bar{p}$ and $e = \bar{e}$, it is easily verified that both the equilibrium exchange rate and the price level increase proportionately with the money stock. Thus, the model retains the standard property of long-run neutrality of money. In the short run, however, owing to the assumption that domestic prices are initially sticky and may not jump, the increase in nominal money is in fact an increase in real money supply, and, consequently, real effects emerge. First, equation (3.1) can be written in deviation form as

$$(D - \bar{Y}) = \delta(e - \bar{e}) - \delta(p - \bar{p}) - \sigma(i - i^*). \tag{3.8}$$

Recalling (3.2) and (3.4), (3.8) can alternatively be expressed as

$$\mu(m - m^*) = \pi\delta(e - \bar{e}) - \pi\delta(p - \bar{p}) - \pi\sigma(i - i^*). \tag{3.9}$$

Differentiating (3.9) with respect to m and using (3.3) to eliminate m^*, we obtain

$$\pi\delta\frac{de}{dm} - (\mu\lambda + \pi\sigma)\frac{di}{dm} = \mu. \tag{3.10}$$

Next, write the balance of payments condition (3.7) in deviation form and substitute for x from (3.6):

$$(\delta + \beta\theta)(e - \bar{e}) - \delta(p - \bar{p}) + \beta(i - i^*) = 0. \tag{3.11}$$

Differentiating (3.11) with respect to m yields the following expression for di/dm:

$$\frac{di}{dm} = \theta - \left(\frac{\delta + \beta\theta}{\beta}\right)\frac{de}{dm}. \tag{3.12}$$

Substitute from (3.12) into (3.10) to obtain the final expression for the effect on the spot exchange rate:

$$\frac{de}{dm} = \frac{\beta[\mu + \theta(\mu\lambda + \pi\sigma)]}{\beta\pi\delta + (\mu\lambda + \pi\sigma)(\delta + \beta\theta)} > 0. \tag{3.13}$$

What is at once clear from (3.13) is that the spot exchange rate response depends upon the money market and the capital market as well as the goods market parameters. Thus, in no sense can one speak of a valid dichotomy between the real and asset sectors in the short-run determination of exchange rates. Such a dichotomy is present, of course, in Dornbusch (1976) and is imposed perforce in other so-called asset market theories of the exchange rate. The conditions under which a valid dichotomy may exist can be seen from a proper understanding of (3.13). To gain further insight into the short-run exchange rate response rewrite (3.13) in terms of deviations from the equilibrium exchange rate response—that is,

$$\left(\frac{de}{dm} - 1\right) = \frac{\beta(\mu - \pi\sigma) - \delta(\mu\lambda + \pi\sigma)}{\beta\pi\delta + (\delta + \beta\theta)(\mu\lambda + \pi\sigma)} \lessgtr 0. \qquad (3.14)$$

It is immediately clear from (3.14) that as long as $\mu < \pi\sigma$, there will always be exchange rate undershooting for all finite values of β (the degree of capital mobility). Nor is this conclusion altered for the case of perfectly mobile capital ($\beta \to \infty$), for in this case (3.14) becomes

$$\lim_{\beta \to \infty} \left(\frac{de}{dm} - 1\right) = \frac{\mu - \pi\delta}{\pi\delta + \theta(\mu\lambda + \pi\sigma)}. \qquad (3.15)$$

Therefore, in one sense undershooting can be related to the relation between the speeds of adjustment in the money and commodity markets and the responsiveness of trade flows to the real exchange rate, as long as money market adjustment is not instantaneous. It is tempting to argue that if money markets adjust instantaneously, undershooting will be eliminated. But this is entirely incorrect as may be seen by taking the limit of (3.14) for $\mu \to \infty$:

$$\lim_{\mu \to \infty} \left(\frac{de}{dm} - 1\right) = \frac{\beta - \delta\lambda}{\lambda\delta + \beta\lambda\theta}. \qquad (3.16)$$

Equation (3.16) makes it clear that even if money markets are continuously in equilibrium, the exchange rate will undershoot its equilibrium response provided that the responsiveness of capital flows does not exceed a certain critical magnitude, which is determined by the semiinterest elasticity of money demand and the responsiveness of trade flows. It can also be seen from (3.15) and (3.16) that in neither case is there a valid dichotomy, for goods market parameters enter into each.

If, however, two conditions are satisfied—that the money market adjusts instantaneously and that capital flows are infinitely sensitive to uncovered interest differentials—(3.14) degenerates into the precise result obtained by Dornbusch (1976). For

$$\lim_{\substack{\beta \to \infty \\ \mu \to \infty}} \left(\frac{de}{dm} - 1\right) = \frac{1}{\lambda\theta} > 0. \qquad (3.17)$$

Equation (3.17) exhibits the special case considered by Dornbusch and demonstrates the basis of the overshooting claim as well as of the view that the short-run exchange rate is determined exclusively in asset markets (no commodity market parameters are present in equation [3.17]). The lack of generality of these two claims can, however, be seen even more sharply by the fact that (3.14) can be consistent with one view (that is, overshooting) but not with the other (the asset market view). From (3.14) the formal condition for exchange rate overshooting is (for finite β and μ)

$$\beta\mu > \beta\pi\delta + \delta(\mu\lambda + \pi\sigma). \tag{3.18}$$

The absence of θ—the expectations parameter—in (3.18) is quite notable. Equation (3.18) depends only upon the structural parameters of the model.

Having examined certain special cases—(3.15), (3.16), and (3.17)—it is worthwhile to investigate the properties of the general expression (3.14). Straightforward differentiation establishes that (3.14) is increasing in β (the degree of capital flow responsiveness) and increasing in μ (the speed of money market adjustment), so that (3.15) and (3.16) denote the maximum exchange rate response for the associated degrees of capital mobility and money market speeds. It can also be verified that (3.14) is decreasing in δ (the responsiveness of trade flows). Next, it can be demonstrated that the effect of λ (the interest rate semielasticity) upon the exchange rate response is, unlike the Dornbusch model, ambiguous. Specifically, it depends upon the three parameters μ, π, and δ. If the money market clears relatively fast (that is, $\mu > \pi\delta$), (3.14) is unambiguously decreasing in λ, although it is possible to observe such a response for the opposite case. Further, (3.14) is unambiguously decreasing in π (the speed of goods market adjustment), as may be expected, and an interesting special case arises for $\pi \to \infty$. Specifically,

$$\lim_{\pi \to \infty} \frac{de}{dm} = \frac{\sigma\beta\theta}{\beta\delta + \delta\sigma + \sigma\beta\theta} < 1. \tag{3.19}$$

The interest of (3.19) lies in the fact that even with instantaneous goods market adjustment the exchange rate does not immediately jump to its new equilibrium (unless $\delta = 0$). More interestingly, this case inevitably results in undershooting and is independent of the speed of money market adjustment μ. Finally, unlike what may be suggested by the Dornbusch expression in (3.17), (3.14) demonstrates that the exchange rate response remains finite for static expectations ($\theta = 0$) and also for $\lambda = 0$. In fact, provided that speeds in the capital and money markets are sufficiently high, the possibility of overshooting is enhanced in either case.

This analysis has been carried out for a fixed arbitrary value of the expectation parameter θ. The next section discusses the perfect foresight value of this parameter and the nature of dynamic adjustment. It will quickly become apparent that, the lags in the money and capital markets notwith-standing, (3.6) is the only expectational scheme that is consistent with perfect foresight.

DYNAMICS AND PERFECT FORESIGHT

The key to dynamic adjustment and to the perfect foresight solution of the model lies in recognizing that adjustment occurs according to a single first-order differential equation.

Writing (3.3) in deviation form and using (3.4), we have

$$-\frac{\dot{p}}{\mu} - (p - \bar{p}) = -\lambda(i - i^*). \tag{3.20}$$

Next, eliminate the interest-differential term by using the balance of payments condition, whence

$$(i - i^*) = \frac{\delta}{\beta}(p - \bar{p}) - \frac{\delta + \beta\theta}{\beta}(e - \bar{e}). \tag{3.21}$$

Substitute (3.21) into (3.20) to solve for the exchange rate deviation as

$$(e - \bar{e}) = \frac{\lambda\delta - \beta}{\lambda(\delta + \beta\theta)}(p - \bar{p}) - \frac{\beta}{\mu\lambda(\delta + \beta\theta)}\dot{p}. \tag{3.22}$$

Next, writing (3.2) in deviation form and using (3.1) and (3.21), we obtain

$$\dot{p} = \pi\left[\delta + \frac{\sigma(\delta + \beta\theta)}{\beta}\right](e - \bar{e}) - \pi\left(\delta + \frac{\sigma\delta}{\beta}\right)(p - \bar{p}). \tag{3.23}$$

Finally, substitute (3.22) into (3.23), yielding

$$\dot{p} = -\left[\frac{\beta\pi\mu\delta(\beta + \sigma) + \beta^2\theta\mu\pi(\sigma + \lambda\delta)}{\beta^2\pi\delta + (\delta + \beta\theta)(\beta\mu\lambda + \pi\beta\sigma)}\right](p - \bar{p}). \tag{3.24}$$

Given $\dot{p} = -w(p_t - \bar{p})$, where w is the bracketed expression contained in (3.24), the price path is

$$p_t = \bar{p} + (p_0 - \bar{p}) \exp^{-wt},$$

while the exchange rate solution is of the identical form

$$e_t = \bar{e} + (e_0 - \bar{e}) \exp^{-wt}. ^2 \qquad (3.25)$$

Given (3.6) and (3.25), perfect foresight requires the solution to the quadratic equation

$$\theta = w \qquad (3.26)$$

where

$$w = \frac{\beta \pi \mu \delta (\beta + \sigma) + \beta^2 \theta \pi \mu (\sigma + \delta \lambda)}{\beta (\delta + \beta \theta)(\mu \lambda + \pi \sigma) + \pi \beta^2 \delta}.$$

One root of the solution is clearly negative and thus inadmissible, while the positive (and hence stable) solution is

$$\theta^* = -[\pi \beta \sigma + \delta(\mu \lambda + \delta \pi) - \beta \pi \mu(\delta + \delta \lambda)]$$

$$+ \frac{\sqrt{[\pi \beta \sigma + \delta(\mu \lambda + \sigma \pi) - \beta \pi \mu(\sigma + \delta \lambda)]^2 + 4\beta(\mu \lambda + \pi \sigma)(\sigma + \beta)\pi \mu \delta}}{2\beta(\mu \lambda + \pi \delta)}.^3$$

Thus, the rational expectations solution involves all the parameters of the economy including the speed of adjustment in money and capital markets. It is possible to assess the contribution of each of these parameters to θ^* and then recompute the solutions (3.14) through (3.19) corresponding to the endogenously chosen value of the expectations parameter. While these recomputed solutions are of course of interest, they do represent a single special case—that of perfect foresight—and will be left to the interested reader.

CONCLUSION

This chapter has attempted to integrate within a single unified frame-work the analysis of exchange rate dynamics pioneered by Dornbusch and

Niehans. It was shown that the results obtained in either of the latter works can be obtained as special cases of the more general framework proposed in this chapter. This framework also has implications for the debate on the dichotomy between the real and asset sectors of the economy in relation to the short-run determination of the exchange rate. Specifically, the dichotomy is valid only if the money market adjusts instantaneously and if capital flows are infinitely sensitive to uncovered interest differentials. The likelihood of occurrence of either exchange rate overshooting or undershooting in the general case can be related to the association between certain key parameters of the economy and the contribution of each of these parameters to the short-run exchange rate response was investigated.

NOTES

1. Little qualitative change would result if absorption is assumed to be autonomous.
2. This can be seen by noting that

$$(e_t - \bar{e}) = \frac{\mu(\lambda\delta - \beta) + \beta w}{\mu\lambda(\delta + \beta\theta)}[p_0 - \bar{p}]\exp^{-wt}$$

and the fact that

$$(e_0 - \bar{e}) = \frac{\mu(\lambda\delta - \beta) + \beta w}{\mu\lambda(\delta + \beta\theta)}(p_0 - \bar{p}).$$

3. Recall that w is defined to be positive.

REFERENCES

Bilson, J. F. O. 1979. "The Vicious Cycle Hypothesis." *IMF Staff Papers*, 26 (March): 1–37.

Dornbusch, R. 1979 "Monetary Stabilization, Intervention and Real Appreciation." Mimeographed. Rio de Janeiro, Brazil. October.

_____. 1976 "Expectations and Exchange Rate Dynamics." *Journal of Political Economy* 84 (December): 1161–76.

Mathieson, D. 1977 "The Impact of Monetary and Fiscal Policy under Flexible Exchange Rates and Alternative Expectations Structures." *IMF Staff Papers* (November): 535–68.

Niehans, J. 1977 "Exchange Rate Dynamics with Stock/Flow Interaction." *Journal of Political Economy* 85 (December): 1245–57.

Witte, W. 1979 "Dynamic Adjustment in an Open Economy with Flexible Exchange Rates." *Southern Economic Journal* 45 (April): 1072–90.

4

AN ALTERNATIVE THEORY OF EXCHANGE RATE DYNAMICS

Recent empirical work on international price elasticities indicates statistically significant differences between long-run and short-run export and import price elasticities in virtually all industrial countries. Econometric evidence from recent studies (Beenstock and Minford 1976; Deppler and Riley 1978; Goldstein and Khan 1978; Hooper 1978; Stern, Francis, and Schumacher 1976) indicates that the long-run (two to three years) price elasticity demand for total imports is about −0.75 to −1.25, while that for total exports is −1.25 to −2.50. On the other hand, short-run (up to one year) price elasticities are generally about half as large, implying that only about 50 percent of total adjustment occurs within one year. The difference in magnitude between short- and long-run elasticities appears reasonably robust with respect to several alternative specifications—as, for example, if the analysis is conducted on a disaggregated level, simultaneous equation techniques are employed, or if alternative price deflators are employed, and so on.

Despite this wealth of evidence indicating that adjustment of aggregate demand to a change in terms of trade is essentially a dynamic process, there appears to be little theoretical modeling of this fact. This chapter constructs and analyzes a simple macrodynamic model of the open economy. The central aspect of this analysis is the attention given to the lags involved in complete adjustment of aggregate demand to a given change in terms of trade (and interest rates). The framework is similar in spirit to that developed in Dornbusch (1976) with one very significant difference. While the latter analyzes a model based on sticky prices and consequent goods market disequilibrium, the present framework assumes freely flexible prices (as well as exchange rates) and is consequently more in line with monetary or portfolio balance-type models on this score. Despite this difference, the final adjustment equation of this model is seen to be deceptively similar to that proposed by Dornbusch (1976), Mathieson (1977), or Bilson (1979). An implication of the model (to be detailed below) is that domestic real expenditure shifts may induce greater short-run exchange rate volatility than domestic monetary shocks. In this sense this model provides results that are quite antithetical to those that emerge from models emphasizing sticky prices. Even though this is a flexible price model, it will become apparent that different speeds of adjustment in the real and asset sectors of the economy are implicit in the analysis. Asset markets clear instantaneously, while adjustment in the goods market is delayed owing to the distinction between short- and long-run elasticities.

The next three sections discuss, in turn, the analytical framework and the static and dynamic properties of the model.

THE MODEL

Consider a small open economy operating under floating exchange rates. The capital market of this economy is perfectly integrated with that of the rest of the world, and uncovered interest arbitrage ensures that security yields expressed in either domestic or foreign currency are equal, given a proper forward premium or discount to offset anticipated exchange depreciation or appreciation. On the other hand, the goods market is not completely integrated with the world market. Specifically, it is assumed that the economy under question is small enough for the supply of importables to be perfectly elastic at the going world currency price. On the export side, however, his economy faces a downward-sloping demand curve, because both domestic and world residents regard domestic and foreign goods as being imperfectly substitutable on the demand side. Domestic production is limited to the exportable commodity, and continuous price flexibility ensures that full employment prevails at all times. All goods are perishable, and there is no currency substitution so that domestic wealth owners must allocate their wealth between the available financial assets—domestic money and the internationally traded security. The distinction between base money and domestic credit and all considerations of physical growth, transactions costs, and uncertainty are ignored. The model is log-linear and all variables introduced below are to be understood to be in logarithmic terms, except interest rates, which are in natural form. The following notation is employed:

i: domestic interest rate,
i^*: world interest rate (assumed to be exogenous),
e: (log) domestic exchange rate (domestic currency price of foreign exchange),
m: (log) domestic nominal money supply,

p: (log) domestic currency price of exportables,

p^*: (log) foreign currency price of importables (assumed exogenous),

u: autonomous component of domestic real expenditure,

$\bar{y}$: (log) domestic full-employment output level,

d^s: (log) short-run level of real domestic aggregate demand,

d^L: (log) long-run level of real domestic aggregate demand, and $\alpha, \lambda, \theta, \phi, \sigma, \gamma$, and δ: parameters of the model, each defined positively.

Dots denote time derivatives, and overbars denote steady-state values; the superscripts s and L will stand for short- and long-run values, respectively.

The specification of the asset market includes a money market relation and a statement of uncovered interest arbitrage:

$$m - p = -\lambda i + \phi \bar{y} \qquad (4.1)$$

and

$$i = i^* - \theta(e - \bar{e}), \qquad (4.2)$$

where θ measures the rate of expected depreciation of domestic currency and will be constrained in accordance with perfect foresight presently.

In contrast to instantaneous adjustment in asset markets, it is assumed that aggregate demand is sluggish in the sense that it does not react instantaneously to the variables it depends upon. A given change in any of these endogenous variables, for example, the terms of trade, will cause a small partial effect on aggregate demand immediately; however, the full effect may not appear for a considerable length of time. Hence, the analysis distinguishes short-run and long-run aggregate demand elasticities. There are several theoretical reasons why, in fact, this distinction may arise. As indicated earlier, empirically the distinction is well founded.

1. Consumption depends upon permanent income, and permanent income is given by a distributed lag over past and current incomes.

2. There are lags between changes in short-term and long-term interest rates.

3. There are lags between changes in interest rates and planned changes in investment.

4. Changes in realized investment follow, often with long lags, changes in planned investment.

5. Because of lags in the transmittal of information on relative prices or because of currency contracts, a change in the terms of trade may not affect aggregate demand at once.

In view of these facts aggregate demand at any instant can be characterized by

$$d_t^s = u + \int_{-\infty}^{t} \gamma_{t-\tau} \bar{y}_\tau d\tau + \int_{-\infty}^{t} \delta_{t-\tau}(e_\tau + p^* - p_\tau)d\tau + \gamma_s \bar{y}_t$$

$$+ \delta_s(e_t + p^* - p_t) - \int_{-\infty}^{t} \sigma_{t-\tau} i_\tau d\tau - \sigma_s i_t, \tag{4.3}$$

where d_t^s refers to the short-run level of aggregate demand.[1] The form of (4.3) is quite similar to that in Dornbusch (1976), Bilson (1979), or Witte (1979) and posits that aggregate demand is determined by domestic interest rates, income, and the terms of trade. The distinction is that both current and previous levels of these variables affect current aggregate demand in (4.3), whereas in previous theoretical work the dependence of current demand on lagged endogenous variables is neglected—that is, no distinction between short- and long-run demand elasticities is made. A given change in current terms of trade will affect current aggregate demand to the extent given by the short-run elasticity δ_s. However, this is not its full effect—in particular, given sufficient time, the full effect will be given by the relevant long-run elasticity δ_L. The long-run or fully adjusted level of aggregate demand can thus be characterized as

$$d^L = u + \gamma_L \bar{y} + \delta_L(e + p^* - p) - \sigma_L i. \tag{4.4}$$

Equation (4.4) measures the level that aggregate demand would eventually attain if all the endogenous variables affecting aggregate demand remained at constant levels permanently—that is, when all adjustments are complete. If all adjustments could be made instantaneously, there would be no distinction between (4.3) and (4.4). At this point we invoke the assumption that the lag structure of weights (or elasticities) is of an extremely simple variety. Specifically,

$$\gamma_{t-\tau} = \gamma_0 \exp^{-\alpha(t-\tau)}, \qquad \alpha > 0,$$

$$\delta_{t-\tau} = \delta_0 \exp^{-\alpha(t-\tau)}, \tag{4.5}$$

$$\sigma_{t-\tau} = \sigma_0 \exp^{-\alpha(t-\tau)}.$$

That is, the weights on past variables decay exponentially at the common decay rate α. Utilizing (4.3) and (4.5), we obtain

$$\dot{d}_t^s = \gamma_0 \bar{y}_t - \alpha \int_{-\infty}^{t} \gamma_{t-\tau} \bar{y}_\tau d\tau + \gamma_s \dot{\bar{y}}_t + \delta_0 e_t - \alpha \int_{-\infty}^{t} \delta_{t-\tau} e_\tau d\tau$$

$$+ \delta_s \dot{e}_t - \delta_0 p_t + \alpha \int_{-\infty}^{t} \delta_{t-\tau} p_\tau d\tau - \delta_s \dot{p}_t - \sigma_s \dot{i}_t - \sigma_0 i_t$$

where it is assumed that p^* remains unchanged and that p, e, i, p^* and y are smoothly differentiable. Further, using (4.3), again,

$$
\dot{d}_t^s = \gamma_0 \bar{y}_t + \delta_0 e_t - \delta_0 p_t - \sigma_0 i_t
$$

$$
- \alpha(d_t^s - u - \gamma_s \bar{y}_t - \delta_s e_t + \delta_s p_t + \sigma_s i_t) + \gamma_s \dot{\bar{y}}_t + \delta_s \dot{e}_t
$$

$$
- \delta_s \dot{p}_t - \sigma_s \dot{i}_t, \tag{4.7}
$$

which yields

$$
\dot{d}_t^s = -\alpha \left\{ d_t^s - \left[u + \left(\gamma_s + \frac{\gamma_0}{\alpha} \right) \bar{y}_t + \left(\delta_s + \frac{\delta_0}{\alpha} \right) e_t \right. \right.
$$

$$
\left. \left. - \left(\sigma_s + \frac{\sigma_0}{\alpha} \right) i_t - \left(\delta_s + \frac{\delta_0}{\alpha} \right) p_t \right] \right\} + \gamma_s \dot{\bar{y}}_t
$$

$$
+ \delta_s \dot{e}_t - \delta_s \dot{p}_t - \sigma_s \dot{i}_t. \tag{4.8}
$$

Since d^L is the level of aggregate demand with all endogenous variables held constant

$$
d^L = u + \bar{y}_t \int_{-\infty}^{t} \gamma_{t-\tau} d\tau + e_t \int_{-\infty}^{t} \gamma_{t-\tau} d\tau + \gamma_s \bar{y}_t + \delta_s e_t
$$

$$
- i_t \int_{-\infty}^{t} \sigma_{t-\tau} d\tau - \sigma_s i_t - p_t \int_{-\infty}^{t} \delta_{t-\tau} d\tau - \delta_s p_t.
$$

Therefore,

$$
d^L = u + \bar{y}_t \left(\frac{\gamma_0}{\alpha} + \gamma_s \right) + e_t \left(\frac{\delta_0}{\alpha} + \delta_s \right) - p_t \left(\frac{\delta_0}{\alpha} + \delta_s \right)
$$

$$
- i_t \left(\frac{\sigma_0}{\alpha} + \sigma_s \right). \tag{4.9}
$$

Equation (4.1) gives a precise form to the relationship between short- and long-run demand elasticities, for example,

$$
\delta_L = \frac{\delta_0}{\alpha} + \delta_s,
$$

with similar relations for γ and σ. Thus, the long-run elasticities are each greater than corresponding short-run elasticities, the difference being inversely related to the speed of adjustment α. Next, from (4.8) and (4.9)

$$\dot{d}_t^s = - \alpha(d_t^s - d^L) + \gamma_s \dot{\bar{y}}_t + \delta_s \dot{e}_t - \delta_s \dot{p}_t - \sigma_s \dot{i}_t, \qquad (4.10)$$

which can be converted to final form by eliminating $\dot{e}_t$ and $\dot{i}_t$. First, note from (4.2) that $\dot{i} = -\theta\dot{e}$, while (4.1) and (4.2) also imply that $\dot{e} = -\dot{p}/\lambda\theta$. Using these substitutions in (4.10), along with the fact that actual aggregate demand is always equal to full-employment income Jevel (that is, $d_t^s = \bar{y}_t$) and that $\dot{\bar{y}} = 0$ (full-employment output is fixed) we obtain the price adjustment equation

$$\dot{p} = \frac{\alpha}{\dfrac{\delta_s}{\lambda\theta} + \delta_s + \dfrac{\sigma_s}{\lambda}} (d^L - \bar{y}). \qquad (4.11)$$

Equation (4.11) is superficially quite similar to the price adjustment equations employed by Dornbusch (1976), Mathieson (1977), or Bilson (1979). It is important to realize, however, that in the present context price dynamics are due entirely to the adjustment of aggregate demand, that is, to the shifting of the aggregate demand function owing to its dependence on lagged endogenous variables and not to any discrepancy between current aggregate demand and full-employment output resulting in commodity market excess demand/supply. Thus, there is no possibility of transitory commodity market disequilibrium in the present framework. Rather, aggregate demand is always equal to full-employment income, and the adjustment in aggregate demand due to the distinction between short- and long-run elasticities necessitates price movements to retain the equality.[2]

SOME COMPARATIVE STATISTICS

Changes in the Foreign Interest Rate i*

Consider an unanticipated increase in the world interest rate i^* due, say, to a world monetary disturbance.[3] The effects of this change on the steady state of the model are obtained via the steady-state solutions

$$\bar{p} = m + \lambda i^* - \phi\bar{y} \qquad (4.12)$$

and

$$\bar{e} = (m - p^*) + \left(\lambda + \frac{\sigma_L}{\delta_L}\right) i^* + \left(\frac{1 - \gamma_L}{\delta_L} - \phi\right)\bar{y} - \frac{u}{\delta_L},$$

(4.13)

whence

$$\frac{d\bar{p}}{di^*} = \lambda$$

and

$$\frac{d\bar{e}}{di^*} = \lambda + \frac{\sigma_L}{\delta_L}.$$

Next, using the asset market equation,

$$(e - \bar{e}) = -\frac{1}{\lambda\theta}(p - \bar{p})$$

and

$$\frac{de}{di^*} = \frac{1}{\theta} + \left(\lambda + \frac{\sigma_L}{\sigma_L}\right) - \frac{1}{\lambda\theta}\frac{dp}{di^*}.$$

(4.14)

Equation (4.14) clearly brings out the fact that the exchange rate response is damped to the extent that prices respond to i^* (it will be established below that $dp/di^* > 0$). Next, note that

$$\bar{y} = d^s = u + \gamma_s\bar{y} + \delta_s(e + p^* - p) - \sigma_s i + v,$$

where v is an omnibus term consisting of fixed-time integrals. Substituting for i above from the money market condition, we obtain

$$\frac{de}{di^*} = \frac{\delta_s + \frac{\sigma_s}{\lambda}}{\delta_s}\frac{dp}{di^*}.$$

(4.15)

Equations (4.14) and (4.15) can be solved simultaneously to yield

$$\frac{dp}{di^*} = \frac{\delta_s[\delta_L + \theta(\delta_L\lambda + \sigma_L)]\lambda}{\delta_L[\delta_s + \theta(\delta_s\lambda + \sigma_s)]} > 0. \tag{4.16}$$

Several aspects of these solutions should be noted. First, from (4.12), (4.13), and (4.15) it is clear that both the current and steady-state exchange rates are comparatively more sensitive to i^* than are current and steady-state prices on a semilog basis (that is, $d\bar{e}/di^* > d\bar{p}/di^*$ and $de/di^* > dp/di^*$), implying a spot and equilibrium deterioration of domestic terms of trade following the exogenous disturbance. Further, overshooting of prices in (4.16) cannot be ruled out. The price overshooting condition is

$$\frac{\delta_s}{\delta_L} > \frac{\sigma_s}{\sigma_L}. \tag{4.17}$$

Note, again, that with no difference between short- and long-run demand elasticities instantaneous jumps are implied, that is, no dynamics are involved. More interestingly, it can be verified that both the price level and the exchange rate cannot simultaneously overshoot their respective long-run values, but one must overshoot.

Changes in Domestic Real Expenditure

Stronger results than in the previous case are obtained for domestic real expenditure disturbances. Consider an autonomous increase in government real expenditure on exportables.[4] This can be analyzed by writing

$$u = u_0 + u_1 g,$$

where u_1 can be interpreted as the fraction of total government expenditure that falls on domestic exportables. From the steady-state solutions in (4.12) and (4.13) it follows that

$$\frac{d\bar{e}}{dg} = -\frac{u_1}{\delta_L}; \quad \frac{d\bar{p}}{dg} = 0.$$

Next, from the asset market equation the effect on the spot rate is

$$\frac{de}{dg} = -\frac{u_1}{\delta_L} - \left(\frac{dp}{dg}\right)\frac{1}{\lambda\theta}.$$

It will be demonstrated below that $dp/dg > 0$, so that

$$\left| \frac{de}{dg} \right| > \left| \frac{d\bar{e}}{dg} \right| ,$$

implying that the real expenditure disturbance leads inevitably to exchange rate overshooting. From the goods market side it is possible to derive

$$\frac{de}{dg} = \frac{\delta_s + \dfrac{\sigma_s}{\lambda}}{\delta_s} \left(\frac{dp}{dg} \right) - \frac{u_1}{\delta_s} . \qquad (4.18)$$

Equations (4.17) and (4.18) can be solved to yield

$$\frac{dp}{dg} = \frac{\lambda \theta u_1 (\delta_L - \delta_s)}{\delta_L [\delta_s + \theta(\lambda \delta_s + \sigma_s)]} > 0,$$

so that

$$\frac{di}{dg} = \frac{\theta u_1 (\delta_L - \delta_s)}{\delta_L [\delta_s + \theta(\lambda \delta_s + \sigma_s)]} > 0.$$

These results conform entirely to intuition. The adjustment process will be characterized by declining prices, a depreciating exchange rate, and declining interest rates. The next section will discuss the adjustment path in detail; meanwhile, the effects of the expenditure expansion on the domestic terms of trade are of some interest. Denoting by a subscript zero the level of a variable immediately following the shock, it has been shown that

$$e_0(g_1) < \bar{e}(g_1) < \bar{e}(g_0)$$

and

$$p_0(g_1) > \bar{p}(g_1) = \bar{p}(g_0),$$

where

$$g_1 > g_0,$$

implying

$$e_0(g_1) - p_0(g_1) < \bar{e}(g_0) - \bar{p}(g_0),$$

that is, the terms of trade initially improve. Over time e increases and p declines, implying that the initial improvement in the terms of trade is greater than the final improvement. Thus, the terms of trade are also seen to undergo overshooting. The trade balance implications of the fiscal expansion are readily obtainable. Assuming that the domestic real trade balance is an increasing function of the terms of trade $(e - p)$, the expenditure increase is seen to result in an initial worsening of the trade balance (following the improved terms of trade). Over time the improvement in the terms of trade is (partly) eroded, so that the initial trade deficit declines monotonically. Thus, the behavior of real trade balance is somewhat reminiscent of a J-curve response.

To conclude this section it may be pointed out that a monetary expansion in this framework will result in an immediate and equiproportionate increase in the price level and exchange rate, with no other effects. In particular there is no possibility of exchange rate overshooting or undershooting, the difference in short- and long-run elasticities notwithstanding. In this sense the results are quite antithetical to those of Dornbusch (1976), where it is monetary shocks that result in exchange rate overshooting, while real expenditure disturbances imply instantaneous jumps to the new steady state.[5]

DYNAMICS AND PERFECT FORESIGHT

The adjustment path of the economy is shown, in this section, to be characterized by a first-order differential equation. Using the definition of d^L from (4.4) and the fact that full-employment income must satisfy

$$\bar{y} = u + \delta_L(\bar{e} + p^* - \bar{p}) - \sigma_L i^* + \gamma_L \bar{y},$$

it is easy to show that

$$(d^L - \bar{y}) = - \left(\frac{\lambda \theta \delta_L + \delta_L + \sigma_L \theta}{\lambda \theta} \right) (p - \bar{p}). \qquad (4.19)$$

Using (4.19) in (4.11),

$$\dot{p} = - \alpha \left(\frac{\lambda \theta \delta_L + \delta_L + \sigma_L \theta}{\lambda \theta \delta_s + \delta_s + \sigma_s \theta} \right) (p - \bar{p}). \qquad (4.20)$$

Letting

$$W = \alpha \left(\frac{\lambda\theta\delta_L + \delta_L + \sigma_L\theta}{\lambda\theta\delta_s + \delta_s + \sigma_s\theta} \right),$$

(4.21)

the price path is

$$p(t) = \bar{p} + (p_0 - \bar{p}) \exp^{-Wt},$$

and the exchange rate path is

$$e(t) = \bar{e} + (e_0 - \bar{e}) \exp^{-Wt}.$$

From (4.21) it can be seen that the adjustment speed of the economy W exceeds (in an absolute sense) the elasticity decay rate α. Perfect foresight requires that $\hat{\theta}$ satisfy

$$\hat{\theta} = W(\hat{\theta}, \dots).$$

This involves the solution to

$$\hat{\theta}^2(\lambda\delta_s + \sigma_s) + \hat{\theta}(\delta_s - \alpha\lambda\delta_L - \alpha\sigma_L) - \alpha\delta_L = 0.$$

(4.22)

One of the roots of (4.22) is clearly negative (and thus inadmissible), while the other is

$$\hat{\theta} = \frac{(\alpha\lambda\delta_L + \alpha\sigma_L - \delta_s) + [(\alpha\sigma_L + \alpha\lambda\delta_L - \delta_s)^2 + 4\alpha\delta_L(\lambda\delta_s + \sigma_s)]^{1/2}}{2(\lambda\delta_s + \sigma_s)}.$$

(4.23)

The contribution of various parameters to the value of $\hat{\theta}$ on the extent of overshooting can easily be assessed, but this will be left as an exercise to the interested reader.

CONCLUSION

This chapter has considered the determination of exchange rates in a framework characterized by freely flexible prices. The latter consideration distinguishes this analysis from the sticky-price models introduced by Dornbusch and subsequently utilized by several other authors. Thus, as far as the specification of domestic prices is concerned, this model is more closely in line with portfolio balance models developed by Branson (1976) and Turnovsky (in press) or monetary models utilized by economists such as Frenkel (1976). The innovation in the present work is to introduce a new source of stickiness, that is, the distinction between short- and long-run demand elasticities. Such a distinction appears important empirically.

The results of this chapter are somewhat antithetical to those obtained from sticky-price Dornbusch-type models. Specifically, the latter framework predicts that the spot exchange rate is highly volatile with respect to monetary disturbances, while the spot and equilibrium response of the system is the same for a real expenditure shift. These conclusions are reversed in this chapter, and it is expenditure disturbances that are now inevitably associated with exchange rate overshooting. The policy implications of this analysis are also straightforward, and it can be seen that there is a role for fiscal policy in the short-run stabilization of nominal income, while in the Dornbusch model, as in the classic Mundell-Fleming models, fiscal policy is completely powerless.

NOTES

1. Strictly speaking, real rather than nominal interest rates should be used in (4.3). The choice of the latter over the former is dictated solely by considerations of computational simplicity in that the need to specify price expectations is eliminated. No qualitative change is made if this assumption is not retained; see, for example, Dornbusch (1976) and Frenkel (1979).

2. It is not our intention to suggest that a full-equilibrium model such as this is necessarily more realistic than one embodying transitory disequilibrium in commodity markets but merely that an important source of dynamics—the distinction between short- and long-run elasticities— is typically left out of recent macrodynamic models of the open economy. To bring this dynamic process to the fore, we have assumed instantaneous commodity market equilibrium, although one can easily construct models embodying both elasticity dynamics and disequilibrium dynamics (see Chapter 5).

3. It is assumed that p^* is not altered simultaneously with i^*. Such an assumption may be a weakness of this one-country approach.

4. Alternatively, the real expenditure shift could be interpreted as an autonomous increase in exports.

5. Dornbusch did not specifically analyze a real expenditure shift, although the result alluded to in the text follows directly from his framework and is discussed in Chapter 2.

REFERENCES

Beenstock, M., and P. Minford. 1976 "A Quarterly Econometric Model of Trade and Prices 1955–1972." *Inflation in Open Economies*, edited by M. Parkin and G. Zis. Manchester: Manchester University Press.

Bilson, J. 1979 "The Vicious Circle Hypothesis." *IMF Staff Papers* 26 (March): 1–37.

Branson, W. 1976 "Asset Markets and Relative Prices in Exchange Rate Determination." *Seminar Paper* no. 66. I.I.E.S., Sweden.

Deppler, M., and D. Riley. 1978 "The World Trade Model: Merchandise Trade." *IMF Staff Papers* 25 (March) 147–206.

Dornbusch, R. 1976 "Expectations and Exchange Rate Dynamics." *Journal of Political Economy* 84 (December): 1161–76.

Frankel, J. 1979 "On the Mark—A Theory of Floating Exchange Rates Based on Real Interest Differentials." *American Economic Review* 69 (September): 610–22.

Frenkel, J. A. 1976 "A Monetary Approach to the Exchange Rate: Doctrinal Aspects and Empirical Evidence." *Scandinavian Journal of Economics* 78 (May): 200–24.

Goldstein, M., and M. Khan 1978 "The Supply and Demand for Exports: A Simultaneous Approach." *Review of Economics and Statistics* 60 (May): 275–86.

Hooper, P. 1978 "The Stability of Income and Price Elasticities in U.S. Trade, 1957–77." *International Finance Discussion Paper* no. 119. Federal Reserve Board, Washington, D.C..

Mathieson, D. 1977 "The Impact of Monetary and Fiscal Policy under Flexible Exchange Rates and Alternative Expectations Structures." *IMF Staff Papers* 24 (November): 535–68.

Stern, R., J. Francis, and B. Schumacher. 1976 *Price Elasticities in International Trade—An Annotated Bibliography.* New York: Macmillan.

Turnovsky, S. In press. "The Asset Market Approach to Exchange Rate Determination." *Journal of Macroeconomics.*

Witte, W. 1979 "Dynamic Adjustment in an Open Economy with Flexible Exchange Rates." *Southern Economic Journal* 45 (April): 1072–90.

5

INCOME, PRICE, AND
EXCHANGE RATE ADJUSTMENT

This chapter endogenizes income, which has hitherto been held fixed at its full-employment level $y = \bar{y}$ in previous chapters. Dornbusch (1976) in an appendix has provided an extension wherein income is demand determined. In the first part of this chapter we review this framework. It will be seen that since income is representable as a linear combination of the price level and exchange rate, that the dynamic properties of the model are identical to those of the basic model discussed in the first part of Chapter 2, and adjustment still occurs according to a simple first-order exponential process. It will also be seen that monetary expansion temporarily stimulates income, and the income expansion in turn tends to increase money demand. Consequently, the interest decline necessary to maintain monetary equilibrium is moderated, which implies further that the extent of instantaneous exchange rate adjustment is reduced. In fact provided that the income response is sufficiently great, domestic nominal interest rates rise simultaneously with the monetary expansion, and the spot exchange rate response becomes one of undershooting.

The latter section of this chapter proposes an alternative theory of income, price, and exchange rate adjustment. Specifically, income is again demand determined, but we utilize the distributed lag specification of aggregate demand utilized in Chapter 4.[1] Meanwhile, price adjustment is hypothesized to occur sluggishly in response to a measure of excess demand (as in the first half of this chapter). Thus, the alternative framework involves both aggregate demand and price dynamics, and the model involves second-order adjustment and is capable of explaining a variety of dynamic adjustment patterns. To allow for expectational consistency it is necessary to extend the simple regressive scheme utilized earlier. While the perfect foresight values of the relevant expectational parameters can, in principle, be computed, in practice this turns out to be exceedingly tedious and requires the solution to a pair of highly nonlinear simultaneous quadratic equations.[2]

The impact results of the two alternative frameworks are also sharply distinguished from one another and are reminiscent of the differences in results between the Dornbusch fixed-income model reviewed in the first half of Chapter 2 and those in Chapter 4. In particular the Dornbusch variable-income model is, again, too simple to allow any dynamic adjustment in response to real expenditure disturbances, and adjustment occurs instantaneously from one steady state to the other. In this sense real disturbances imply neither overshooting nor undershooting in this framework. However, the alternative framework preserves the result noted in Chapter 4—that is, real disturbances always imply exchange rate overshooting or overadjustment. At the same time the richer detail of this model also allows for dynamic adjustment in response to monetary disturbances, although there is no clear presumption in favor of either overshooting or undershooting.[3]

THE DORNBUSCH VARIABLE-INCOME FRAMEWORK

Assume that income is demand determined, that is,

$$y = \mu[u + \delta(e + p^* - p) - \sigma i], \tag{5.1}$$

where

$$\mu = \frac{1}{1 - \gamma} > ,1$$

and assume further that the steady-state income level $\bar{y}$ is fixed at its full-employment level. Domestic price adjustment occurs according to

$$\dot{p} = \pi(y - \bar{y}), \qquad \pi > 0, \tag{5.2}$$

and all other aspects of the model are identical to the basic model discussed in the first part of Chapter 2. The interest parity plus monetary equilibrium conditions now yields

$$\phi(y - \bar{y}) + (p - \bar{p}) = -\lambda\theta(e - \bar{e}), \tag{5.3}$$

while from (5.1) above we obtain

$$(y - \bar{y}) + \mu\delta(p - \bar{p}) = \mu(\delta + \sigma\theta)(e - \bar{e}). \tag{5.4}$$

The solutions to (5.3) and (5.4) are

$$(y - \bar{y}) = -w(p - \bar{p}) \tag{5.5}$$

and

$$(e - \bar{e}) = -\frac{1 - \phi\mu\delta}{\Delta}(p - \bar{p}), \tag{5.6}$$

where

$$w \equiv \frac{\mu(\delta + \sigma\theta) + \mu\delta\theta\lambda}{\Delta} > 0$$

and

$$\Delta \equiv \phi\mu(\delta + \sigma\theta) + \theta\lambda > 0.$$

Hence,

$$\dot{p} = -w\pi(p - \bar{p})$$

and

$$\dot{e} = -w\pi(e - \bar{e}),$$

so that the perfect foresight value of θ, the expectational parameter, is

$$\hat{\theta} = w\pi, \tag{5.7}$$

which is given explicitly by

$$\hat{\theta} = \frac{(\pi\mu\sigma + \mu\delta\lambda\pi - \phi\mu\delta) + [(\phi\mu\delta - \pi\mu\sigma - \mu\delta\lambda\pi)^2 + 4\pi\mu\delta]^{1/2}}{2(\sigma + \lambda)} > 0.$$

Thus, dynamic adjustment occurs according to a simple first-order adjustment process as earlier. Consider now the impact effects of monetary expansion. The impact effects upon e, i, and y are given from the system

$$-\lambda di + \phi dy = dm,$$

$$\theta de + di = \theta,$$

$$-\mu\delta de + \mu\sigma di + dy = 0.$$

Denoting the Jacobian by

$$\Delta(\theta) \equiv \lambda\theta + \phi\mu[\delta + \sigma\theta],$$

the impact effects are given via

$$\frac{de}{dm} = 1 + \frac{1 - \phi\mu\delta}{\Delta(\theta)} \underset{<}{\overset{>}{=}} 1,$$

$$\frac{di}{dm} = \frac{-\theta(1 - \phi\mu\delta)}{\Delta(\theta)} \underset{<}{\overset{>}{=}} 0,$$

$$\frac{dy}{dm} = \frac{\mu\delta(1 + \lambda\theta) + \theta\sigma\mu}{\Delta(\theta)} > 0 \; (\equiv w). \tag{5.8}$$

Thus, exchange rate overshooting occurs as $(1 - \phi\mu\delta) \gtrless 0$ or as

$$(1 - \gamma) \gtrless \phi\delta. \tag{5.9}$$

Furthermore, if the exchange rate overadjusts, by necessity the domestic interest rate must have declined following the monetary expansion. During adjustment to the stationary state, the exchange rate and interest rate move in opposite directions (for example, if undershooting occurs, the exchange rate rises to the stationary state, while the interest rate, having risen, declines over time), and the level of income declines monotonically. Finally, one further interpretation of (5.9) is possible. Typical values of ϕ (the income elasticity of money demand) are in the neighborhood of unity, so that (5.9) would seem to dictate δ (the terms of trade elasticity of aggregate demand) be considerably less than unity if overshooting is to occur. For instance, if $\gamma = 0.8$, $\delta < 0.2$ is necessary for exchange rate overadjustment. Since δ is related to the degree of substitutability between domestic and foreign goods (the case of $\delta \to \infty$ representing purchasing power parity), it can be argued that a case for overshooting can be made for relatively closed rather than relatively open economies.

Next, consider briefly the implications of expenditure disturbances (a change in the term u) and of foreign price level shocks in this framework. Note, first, that the steady-state price level can again be obtained as

$$\bar{p} = m + \lambda i^* - \phi\bar{y} \qquad (5.10)$$

and is seen to be independent of both the foreign price level and the autonomous component of domestic expenditure. Utilizing this fact along with the assumption that the price level adjusts slowly, it is immediately clear from (5.6) that these exogenous disturbances do not imply any dynamics in the present framework. Rather, the system adjusts instantaneously from one steady state to the other.

The next section describes the alternative specification that permits richer adjustment patterns.

AN ALTERNATIVE FRAMEWORK FOR
INCOME ADJUSTMENT

The behavioral assumptions of the model on the money market and capital market side remain exactly the same as before. Hence, monetary equilibrium and covered interest arbitrage are again represented by

$$m - p = -\lambda i + \phi y \qquad (5.11)$$

and

$$i = i^* + \dot{e}^E. \qquad (5.12)$$

The commodity market is again characterized by the distributed lag specification of aggregate demand introduced in the previous chapter. However, both income and price are endogenous. Income at any instant is demand determined and is given by d_s^t (which is the only operational concept of aggregate demand).

Expectations now follow a two-dimensional scheme, that is,

$$\dot{e}^E = -\theta_1(e - \bar{e}) + \theta_2(p - \bar{p}), \qquad \theta_1, \theta_2 > 0. \qquad (5.13)$$

The scheme utilized earlier is a special case of (5.13) and will not (except by accident) be consistent with perfect foresight. Since actual depreciation is affected by movements in e, p, and y, and y can be written as a linear combination of e and p (see below), expected depreciation must take into account this structure—if there is to be perfect foresight. In earlier chapters first-order dynamics implied that e_t and p_t were proportional and not separate sources of information. Because of the underlying second-order dynamics, they are now separately useful.

Since income is demand determined, we can write

$$y_t = u_t + \delta_s(p_t^* + e_t - p_t) + \gamma_s y_t - \sigma_s i_t + v_t, \tag{5.14}$$

where v_t is an omnibus collection of time integrals that are fixed at t. And, as earlier,

$$d^L = u_t + \delta_L(p_t^* + e_t - p_t) + \gamma_L y_t - \sigma_L i_t. \tag{5.15}$$

Comparative Statics

The steady state is characterized by $e = \bar{e}$, $i = i^*$, $\dot{e}^E = \dot{e} = 0$, $\dot{p} = 0, p = \bar{p}, y = \bar{y}$, and $\dot{y} = 0$, and steady-state values $\bar{e}$ and $\bar{p}$ satisfy

$$\bar{e} = (m - p^*) + \left(\frac{1 - \gamma_L}{\delta_L} - \phi\right)\bar{y} + \left(\lambda + \frac{\sigma_L}{\delta_L}\right) i^* - \frac{u}{\delta_L} \tag{5.16}$$

and

$$\bar{p} = m + \lambda i^* - \phi\bar{y}. \tag{5.17}$$

It is also convenient to write the goods market clearing condition as

$$\bar{y} = \frac{1}{1 - \gamma_L}[u + \delta_L(p^* + \bar{e} - \bar{p}) - \sigma_L i^*]. \tag{5.18}$$

Instantaneous Responses: A Change in m (Monetary Policy)

Clearly $d\bar{e}/dm = d\bar{p}/dm = 1$, while $d\bar{y}/dm = 0$ again.[4] Also, it is assumed, as before, that $p_0(m_1) = p_0(m_0)$, that is, at the instant that m is changed, prices do not jump, while y may jump, the extent of which is constrained by the aggregate demand specification above.

The matrix system for m is

$$\begin{bmatrix} 0 & -\lambda & \phi \\ \theta_1 & 1 & 0 \\ -\mu_s\delta_s & \mu_s\sigma_s & 1 \end{bmatrix} \begin{bmatrix} de/dm \\ di/dm \\ dy/dm \end{bmatrix} = \begin{bmatrix} 1 \\ (\theta_1 - \theta_2) \\ 0 \end{bmatrix}.$$

The Jacobian will be denoted by

$$\Delta_s(\theta_1) = \theta_1\lambda + \phi\mu_s(\delta_s + \theta_1\sigma_s),$$

where $\mu_s = 1/1 - \gamma_s$. The value of $\Delta_s(\theta_1)$ when $\theta_1 = 0$ will be denoted by

$$\Delta_s(0) = \phi\mu_s\delta_s,$$

while

$$\Delta_s(\theta_2) = \theta_2\lambda + \phi\mu_s(\delta_s + \theta_2\sigma_s).$$

Given this notation,

$$\frac{de}{dm} = \frac{1 + (\theta_1 - \theta_2)(\lambda + \phi\mu_s\sigma_s)}{\Delta_s(\theta_1)}, \tag{5.19}$$

which must be strictly positive if $\theta_1 > \theta_2$.

In terms of our alternative notation (5.19) can be conveniently rewritten as

$$\frac{de}{dm} = 1 + \frac{1 - \Delta_s(\theta_2)}{\Delta_s(\theta_1)}. \tag{5.20}$$

Hence, the condition for overshooting (of e) is that $1 - \Delta_s(\theta_2) > 0$.[5] Further, note that

$$\frac{di}{dm} = \frac{-\theta_1 + \Delta_s(0)(\theta_1 - \theta_2)}{\Delta_s(\theta_1)} \tag{5.21}$$

and

$$\frac{dy}{dm} = \frac{\theta_1\mu_s\sigma_s + \mu_s\delta_s[\lambda(\theta_1 - \theta_2) + 1]}{\Delta_s(\theta_1)} \tag{5.22}$$

Note that a perverse income response is possible with an extremely high θ_2. An extremely high θ_2 may also cause exchange rate appreciation.[6]

The sensitivity of the exchange rate response (or elasticity of exchange rates with respect to nominal money) to the expectational parameters θ_1 and θ_2 is evidenced by inspection of (5.20):

$$\frac{d\left(\dfrac{de}{dm}\right)}{d\theta_1} = \frac{-[1 - \Delta_s(\theta_2)](\lambda + \mu_s\phi\sigma_s)}{\Delta_s(\theta_1)^2}, \tag{5.23}$$

the sign of which is determined by the condition for overshooting referred to earlier, while

$$\frac{d\left(\dfrac{de}{dm}\right)}{d\theta_2} = \frac{-\Delta_s(\theta_1)d\Delta_s(\theta_2)}{\Delta_s(\theta_1)^2} < 0.$$

Hence, we may write

$$\frac{de}{dm} = v(\theta_1, \theta_2) \tag{5.24}$$
$$(?) \ (-)$$

The sensitivity of exchange rate volatility to λ (interest semi-elasticity of money demand) is given by

$$\frac{d\left(\dfrac{de}{dm}\right)}{d\lambda} = \frac{-\Delta_s(\theta_1)\theta_2 - [1 - \Delta_s(\theta_2)]\theta_1}{[\Delta_s(\theta_1)]^2}. \tag{5.25}$$

Again, if there is overshooting, that is, $1 - \Delta_s(\theta_2) > 0$, then (5.25) is less than zero. Otherwise, it is ambiguous.

Finally, the $\lim\limits_{\lambda \to 0} \dfrac{d\left(\dfrac{de}{dm}\right)}{d\lambda}$ is a finite constant given by

$$\frac{1 + \phi\mu_s(\delta_s - \sigma_s\theta_2)}{\phi\mu_s(\delta_s + \sigma_s\theta_1)}.$$

Next, consider the effects of fiscal (expenditure) expansion (P). As in Chapter 4, fiscal policy is parameterized by writing

$$u = u_0 + u_1g,$$

where g is real government expenditure. The matrix system is given by

$$
\begin{bmatrix}
0 & -\lambda & \phi \\
\theta_1 & 1 & 0 \\
-\mu_s \delta_s & \mu_s \sigma_s & 1
\end{bmatrix}
\begin{bmatrix}
de/dg \\
di/dg \\
dy/dg
\end{bmatrix}
=
\begin{bmatrix}
0 \\
-\theta_1(u_1/\delta_L) \\
\mu_s u_1
\end{bmatrix},
\tag{5.26}
$$

whence

$$
\frac{de}{dg} = -\frac{u_1}{\delta_L} - \frac{\phi\mu_s(\delta_L - \delta_s)}{\Delta_s(\theta_1)} < 0 \text{ if } \delta_s < \delta_L,
\tag{5.27}
$$

$$
\frac{di}{dg} = \frac{\theta_1\mu_s u_1\phi\left(1 - \dfrac{\delta_s}{\delta_L}\right)}{\Delta_s\theta_1)} > 0 \text{ if } \delta_s < \delta_L,
\tag{5.28}
$$

$$
\frac{dy}{dg} = \frac{\dfrac{\lambda}{\phi}\theta_1\mu_s u_1\left(1 - \dfrac{\delta_s}{\delta_L}\right)}{\Delta_s(\theta_1)} > 0 \text{ if } \delta_s < \delta_L.
\tag{5.29}
$$

Hence, fiscal expansion implies all the standard results. Moreover, it is effective (in the sense of $dy/dg > 0$), and perverse possibilities cannot arise. Also note that

$$
\frac{d\bar{e}}{dg} = -\frac{u_1}{\delta_L}, \quad \frac{d\bar{p}}{dg} = 0.
$$

Three points should be noted. First,

$$
\left|\frac{de}{dg}\right| > \left|\frac{d\bar{e}}{dg}\right|,
$$

that is, there is exchange rate overshooting. Second, dynamic effects arise solely due to differences in short- and long-run demand elasticities. Third, all our results are independent of θ_2.

The dynamics of e, p, i, and y will be discussed in detail below.

Foreign Disturbances

A change in p^*, again, implies no dynamics, specifically

$$\frac{d\bar{p}}{dp^*} = \frac{dp}{dg} = 0$$

and

$$\frac{d\bar{e}}{dp^*} = \frac{de}{dp^*} = -1.$$

A change in i^* involves similar considerations, as in Chapter 4. First,

$$\frac{d\bar{p}}{di^*} = \lambda$$

and

$$\frac{d\bar{e}}{di^*} = \dot{\lambda} + \frac{\sigma_L}{\delta_L},$$

while

$$\frac{de}{di^*} = \frac{\left[1 + (\theta_1 - \theta_2)\lambda + \frac{\theta_1 \sigma_L}{\delta_L}\right](\lambda + \phi \mu_s \sigma_s)}{\Delta_s(\theta_1)} \tag{5.30}$$

Again, spot appreciation is possible for

$$\theta_2 > \frac{1}{\lambda} + \theta_1 + \frac{\theta_1 \sigma_L}{\delta_l \lambda}. \tag{5.31}$$

Dynamics and Perfect Foresight

This section derives the adjustment equations of the model. Aggregate demand is given by the distributed lag specification (5.32) below, which is equal to the actual level of income at any instant:

$$d_t^s = y_t = u + \int_{-\infty}^t \gamma_{t-\tau} y_\tau d\tau + \gamma_s y_t + \int_{-\infty}^t \delta_{t-\tau}(e_\tau + p^* - p_\tau) d\tau$$
$$+ \delta_s(e_t + p^* - p_t) - \int_{-\infty}^t \sigma_t -_{\tau} i_\tau d\tau - \sigma_s i_t, \tag{5.32}$$

while the fully adjusted level is

$$d^L = u + \gamma_L y + \delta_L(e + p^* - p) - \sigma_L i. \tag{5.33}$$

The interpretation of (5.33) is the same as before. Further, $\bar{y}$ satisfies

$$\bar{y} = u + \gamma_L \bar{y} + \delta_L(\bar{e} + p^* - \bar{p}) - \sigma_L i^*. \tag{5.34}$$

All weights are exponentially declining at the common rate α, that is,

$$\gamma_t = \gamma_0 \exp^{-\alpha(t-\tau)},$$

with similar expressions for δ_t and σ_t. It is easy to derive

$$d^L = u + \left(\frac{\gamma_0}{\alpha} + \gamma_s \right) y_t + \left(\frac{\delta_0}{\alpha} + \delta_s \right) (e_t + p^* - p_t)$$
$$- \left(\frac{\sigma_0}{\alpha} + \sigma_s \right) i_t. \tag{5.35}$$

Next, we obtain

$$\dot{d}_t^s = \dot{y}_t = -\alpha(d_t^s - d^L) + \gamma_s \dot{y}_t + \delta_s \dot{e}_t - \delta_s \dot{p}_t - \sigma_s i_t, \tag{5.36}$$

assuming no change in p^* or u. Utilizing

$$\dot{i}_t = \frac{\phi}{\lambda} \dot{y}_t + \frac{\dot{p}_t}{\lambda}$$

and

$$\dot{i}_t = -\theta_1 \dot{e}_t + \theta_2 \dot{p}_t,$$

we obtain

$$\left(1 - \gamma_s + \frac{\delta_s\phi}{\theta_1\lambda} + \frac{\sigma_s\phi}{\lambda}\right)\dot{y}_t = -\alpha(d_t^s - d^L)$$

$$+ \left[\delta_s\left(\frac{\theta_2\pi}{\theta_1} - \frac{\pi}{\theta_1\lambda}\right)\right.$$

$$\left. - \delta_s\pi - \frac{\sigma_s\pi}{\lambda}\right](y - \bar{y}), \qquad (5.37)$$

where we have imposed the adjustment equation

$$\dot{p} = \pi(y - \bar{y}), \qquad \pi > 0. \qquad (5.37')$$

Next, $(d_t^s - d^L)$ can be rewritten as

$$(d_t^s - d^L) = (1 - \gamma_L)(y - \bar{y}) - (\delta_L + \sigma_L\theta_1)(e - \bar{e})$$
$$+ (\delta_L + \sigma_L\theta_2)(p - \bar{p}), \qquad (5.38)$$

while

$$(e - \bar{e}) = -\frac{\phi}{\lambda\theta_1}(y - \bar{y}) - \left(\frac{1 - \lambda\theta_2}{\lambda\theta_1}\right)(p - \bar{p}), \qquad (5.39)$$

so that the dynamic system consists of

$$\left(1 - \gamma_s + \frac{\delta_s\phi}{\theta_1\lambda} + \frac{\sigma_s\phi}{\lambda}\right)\dot{y}_t = -\alpha\left[\frac{(\delta_L + \sigma_L\theta_1)(1 - \lambda\theta_2)}{\lambda\theta_1}\right.$$

$$\left. + \delta_L + \sigma_L\theta_2\right](P_t - \bar{p})$$

$$- \left\{\alpha\left[1 - \gamma_L + \frac{(\delta_L + \sigma_L\theta_1)\phi}{\lambda\theta_1}\right.\right.$$

$$+ \, \delta_s \pi + \frac{\sigma_s \pi}{\lambda}$$

$$- \, \delta_s \left(\frac{\theta_2}{\theta_1} \pi - \frac{\pi}{\theta_1 \lambda} \right) \Bigg\} (y_t - \bar{y})$$

$$(5.40)$$

and

$$\dot{p}_t = \pi(y_t - \bar{y}). \tag{5.37'}$$

If there are no new shocks, (5.37') and (5.40) represent the trend path to equilibrium (or the steady state).

The Form of the Solution

The dynamic system consists of the differential equations

$$\dot{y} = - b(y - \bar{y}) - c(p - \bar{p})$$

and

$$\dot{p} = \pi(y - \bar{y}),$$

where b and c are the expressions contained in (5.40). The solution to these equations thus follows a second-order path. Further, oscillations cannot be ruled out.

The characteristic equation is given by

$$r^2 + rb + c\pi = 0.$$

First note that if $c < 0$, then complex roots never arise in the solution, that is, there are no oscillations. A glance at the expression for c makes it clear that this is only possible for exceptionally large values of θ_2, specifically for

$$\theta_2 > \theta_1 \left(1 + \frac{\sigma_L}{\delta_L \lambda} \right) + \frac{1}{\lambda} \, .$$

For more moderate values of θ_2, in particular for those values that preclude perverse impact effects, there is the likelihood of oscillatory paths.

Further, for sufficiently small values of θ_2, b and c are both positive, which ensures stability. Assuming a price solution

$$p_t - \bar{p} = A_1 \exp^{r_1 t} + A_2 \exp^{r_2 t},$$

the corresponding income solution is

$$(y_t - \bar{y}) = \frac{A_1 r_1 \exp^{r_1 t}}{\pi} + \frac{A_2 \exp^{r_2 t}}{\pi},$$

while the time path of exchange rates is

$$e(t) = \bar{e} + \frac{\lambda \theta_2 - 1}{\lambda \theta_1} (A_1 \exp^{r_1 t} + A_2 \exp^{r_2 t})$$

$$- \frac{\phi}{\lambda \pi \theta_1} (r_1 A_1 \exp^{r_1 t} + r_2 A_2 \exp^{r_2 t}).$$

There is also an oscillatory path that is possible.

The Dynamics of Real Shocks

We now explicitly characterize the relevant path following a one-time real shock—such as a change in g. The analysis will assume stability and monotonicity.

The second-order system in y and p implies a price trajectory of the following general form:

$$p_t = \bar{p} + A_1 \exp^{r_1 t} + A_2 \exp^{r_2 t}. \tag{5.41}$$

From (5.41)

$$\dot{p} = r_1 A_1 \exp^{r_1 t} + r_2 A_2 \exp^{r_2 t}, \tag{5.42}$$

which implies the income solution as seen above:

$$(y_t - \bar{y}) = \frac{r_1 A_1 \exp^{r_1 t}}{\pi} + \frac{r_2 A_2 \exp^{r_2 t}}{\pi}. \tag{5.43}$$

Equation (5.41) implies that

$$A_1 + A_2 = 0. \tag{5.44}$$

Substituting from (5.44) into (5.43) at $t = 0$,

$$(y_0 - \bar{y}) = \frac{A_1}{\pi}(r_1 - r_2). \tag{5.45}$$

Assume A_1 is the positive constant in (5.44) (that is, $A_1 > 0, A_2 < 0$). Since $r_1 < 0$ and $r_2 < 0$ (in view of stability and monotonicity), then

$$|r_2| > |r_1|. \tag{5.46}$$

Equation (5.46) is true since $(y_0 - \bar{y}) > 0$ for a change in g (see [5.29]). In view of (5.45) and (5.46)

$$\frac{r_2 A_2}{\pi} > 0 \text{ while } \frac{r_1 A_1}{\pi} < 0 \text{ while } \left|\frac{r_2 A_2}{\pi}\right| > \left|\frac{r_1 A_1}{\pi}\right|.$$

Now from (5.41), again,

$$(p_t - \bar{p}) = A_1 \exp^{r_1 t} + A_2 \exp^{r_2 t}.$$

Since the root with larger absolute magnitude (that is, r_2) will decay faster, the negative term $A_2 \exp^{r_2 t}$ will decay to zero before $A_1 \exp^{r_1 t}$ (which is greater than zero). The price deviation is given by the sum of these countervailing forces and thus resembles an inverted U (see Figure 5.1).

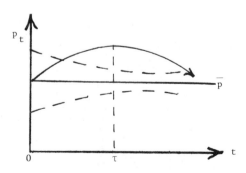

Figure 5.1

The corresponding income path is obtained with reference to

$$(y_t - \bar{y}) = \frac{r_1 A_1 \exp^{r_1 t}}{\pi} - \frac{r_2 A_2 \exp^{r_2 t}}{\pi}$$

or

$$(y_t - \bar{y}) = \frac{A_1}{\pi}(r_1 \exp^{r_1 t} - r_2 \exp^{r_2 t}). \tag{5.47}$$

Alternatively, it could be obtained from the price path above, since

$$(y_t - \bar{y}) = \frac{\dot{p}_t}{\pi}.$$

For example, at the stationary point where prices have attained their maximum level, $y_\tau = \bar{y}$. Over the interval $(0,\tau)$, $y_t > \bar{y}$ $(t < \tau)$, but since the rate of price increase (that is, $\dot{p}_t$) is declining, so is $(y_t - \bar{y})$. Over (τ, ∞) p is declining, so that $y_t < \bar{y}$.

It should be apparent that the maximum level of income is at 0; the minimum point occurs somewhere between τ and ∞, when prices are already declining (see Figure 5.2).

More specifically, the minimum point obtains at

$$t^* = \frac{\ln r_2^2 - \ln r_1^2}{r_1 - r_2}, \qquad \tau < t^* < \infty.$$

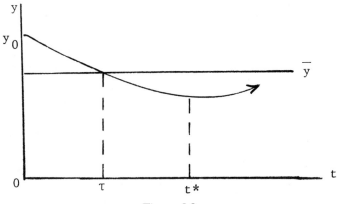

Figure 5.2

The interest rate and exchange rate paths are more difficult to characterize. The exchange rate solution is, for example,

$$(e_t - \bar{e}) = \left(\frac{\lambda\theta_2 - 1}{\lambda\theta_1} - \frac{r_1\phi}{\lambda\pi\theta_1} \right) A_1 \exp^{r_1 t}$$

$$+ \left(\frac{\lambda\theta_2 - 1}{\lambda\theta_1} - \frac{r_2\phi}{\lambda\pi\theta_1} \right) A_2 \exp^{r_2 t},$$

so that the exact nature of the path depends on whether $\theta_2 \gtrless 1/\lambda$. Two possibilities for the exchange rate path are suggested in Figures 5.3 and 5.4.

Figure 5.3 shows that the spot rate attains $\bar{e}(g_1)$ relatively early—that is, at t', when t' is given by

$$t' = \frac{\ln\left(\frac{\lambda\theta_2 - 1}{\lambda\theta_1} - \frac{r_2\phi}{\lambda\pi\theta_1} \right) - \ln\left(\frac{\lambda\theta_2 - 1}{\lambda\theta_1} - \frac{r_1\phi}{\lambda\pi\theta_1} \right)}{r_1 - r_2}.$$

At t', however, e is rising and attains a maximum somewhat later at t''. In Figure 5.4 there is smooth monotonic convergence to $\bar{e}(g_1)$. The corresponding interest rate paths can be obtained via reference to

$$i = i^* - \theta_1(e - \bar{e}) + \theta_2(p - \bar{p})$$

and will be left to the interested reader.

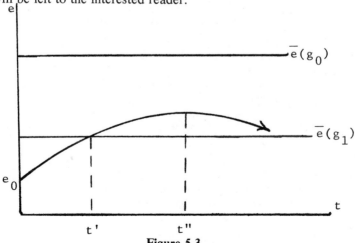

Figure 5.3

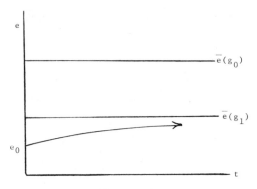

Figure 5.4

Perfect Foresight

We now impose perfect foresight. Since

$$\dot{e}^E = -\theta_1(e - \bar{e}) + \theta_2(p - \bar{p}),$$

the path of expected depreciation (for real roots) is

$$\dot{e}^E(t) = A_1 \exp^{r_1 t}\left(\frac{\phi r_1}{\lambda \pi} + \frac{1}{\lambda}\right) + A_2 \exp^{r_2 t}\left(\frac{\phi r_2}{\lambda \pi} + \frac{1}{\lambda}\right), \qquad (5.48)$$

while actual depreciation is given by

$$\dot{e}(t) = A_1 \exp^{r_1 t}\left(\frac{r_1(\lambda\theta_2 - 1)}{\lambda\theta_1} - \frac{\phi r_1^2}{\lambda\theta_1 \pi}\right)$$

$$+ A_2 \exp^{r_2 t}\left(\frac{r_2(\lambda\theta_2 - 1)}{\lambda\theta_1} - \frac{\phi r_2^2}{\lambda\theta_1 \pi}\right). \qquad (5.49)$$

For perfect foresight (5.48) and (5.49) must coincide, which can be enforced by choice of the speed parameters θ_1 and θ_2, subject to $\theta_1, \theta_2 > 0$. For example,

$$\theta_1 = \frac{-\dfrac{r_1\lambda r_2}{1 + \dfrac{r_1\phi}{\pi}} - r_1}{1 - \dfrac{r_1\lambda^2 r_2}{\left(1 + \dfrac{\phi r_1}{\pi}\right)\left(1 + \dfrac{\phi r_2}{\pi}\right)}} \qquad (5.50)$$

But since the eigenvalues r_1 and r_2 are obtained via a solution to

$$r_1 = r_1(\theta_1, \theta_2, \dots)$$

and

$$r_2 = r_2(\theta_1, \theta_2, \dots),$$

equation (5.50) is highly nonlinear in θ_1, with a similar statement being true for θ_2. This means that θ_1 and θ_2 must be obtained via nonlinear simultaneous equations of the form

$$f(\theta_1^2, \theta_1, \theta_2, \theta_2^2) = 0$$

and

$$g(\theta_1^2, \theta_1, \theta_2, \theta_2^2) = 0.$$

For imaginary solutions to the eigenvalues, perfect foresight values of θ_1 and θ_2 are computed in the same way.

NOTES

1. In Chapter 10 it will be seen that we introduce the supply side of the economy, so that income is determined by both demand and supply considerations.

2. It is possible to interpret this result (relating to the difficulty of obtaining the perfect foresight solutions) as being indicative of the implausibility of the perfect foresight hypothesis in a complex dynamic world.

3. In Chapter 4, it will be recalled, monetary disturbances implied instantaneous adjustment between steady states. Continuous price flexibility precluded dynamic adjustment for monetary shocks in that chapter.

4. We are considering arbitrary quasi-rational values of θ_1 and θ_2 below.

5. This condition is seen to be stricter than the analogous condition in the earlier (Dornbusch) framework.

6. It should be pointed out that once θ_1 and θ_2 are properly constrained in accordance with perfect foresight, that these perverse responses may cease to be a possibility.

REFERENCE

Dornbusch, R. 1976. "Expectations and Exchange Rate Dynamics." *Journal of Political Economy*, 84, (December): 1161–76.

6

ANNOUNCEMENT EFFECTS

This chapter is concerned with an important extension of the previous framework. Specifically, the policy and other exogenous changes we have hitherto examined have consisted of one-time unanticipated shocks that occur at the present instant. Such was the nature of shocks in m, g, p^*, i^*, and so on, in Chapters 2, 3, 4, and 5. Here we are concerned with the effects of anticipated (to occur at some time in the foreseeable future) one-time shocks in m^1.

ANTICIPATED SHOCKS

It is a well-established proposition in monetary theory that inflation anticipated to occur sometime in the future will cause prices to start rising now. The standard account of this phenomenon is as follows. Suppose that at time $t = 0$, (that is, today) the government (or the Federal Reserve) announces that, in contrast to currently prevailing zero monetary growth, monetary growth will occur at x percent per annum, starting at time $T(> 0)$. An economically sophisticated public has learned from experience that x percent monetary growth over a long-run trend path will cause x percent price inflation (assuming away real growth for simplicity). This expected erosion in purchasing power will imply that the public will tend to substitute commodities for money in their wealth portfolios today—that is, the resulting excess demand in the commodity market will drive up prices now, well before inflation actually occurs.

The moral of this account is that quite apart from the well-publicized lags in transmittal of monetary policy there may in fact be leads involved, if expectations are held with certainty.

This chapter is concerned with an analogous issue. Specifically, we ask, What is the entire time path of exchange rates (and prices), given that the public knows with certainty (or expects with certainty) that a policy change represented by a change in, say, m will occur at some future date? The merit of this approach is to disentangle the effects of the announcement from the effects of the actual policy change.

Announcement Effects in the Basic Model

Consider first the basic (benchmark) model of Chapter 2. The exchange rate solution corresponding to the adjustment process is

$$e_t - \bar{e} = A\exp^{s_1 t} + B\exp^{s_2 t}, \tag{6.1}$$

where A and B are arbitrary constants and $s_2 < 0$, while $s_2 > 0$. The corresponding price solution is

$$p_t - \bar{p} = \lambda s_1 A \exp^{s_1 t} + \lambda s_2 B \exp^{s_2 t}. \tag{6.2}$$

Examine now the effects of an announcement of a change in m. More concretely, assume that the initial state is a steady state with $m = m_0$, and the Federal Reserve announces at $t = 0$ that it will increase $m = m_1$, at $t = T$. The question is, What are the paths of all relevant variables from 0 to T and from T to ∞?

Consider first the effects following the actual policy change, that is, the interval (T, ∞). Confining ourselves to the stable arm of the saddle (where $B = 0$),

$$\dot{e} = s_1 A \exp^{s_1 t},$$

or using (6.1),

$$\dot{e} = s_1 [e_t - \bar{e}(m_1)]. \tag{6.3}$$

Equation (6.3) describes adjustment after the shock has occurred. Meanwhile, recall that the steady-state solutions $\bar{p}(m)$ and $\bar{e}(m)$ are such that $d\bar{p} = d\bar{e} = d\bar{m}$. Further, from (6.2)

$$p_t - \bar{p}(m_1) = \lambda s_1 [e_t - \bar{e}(m_1)] \ \forall_{t \geq T}. \tag{6.4}$$

The original overshooting result followed from (6.4). Since $p_0 = \bar{p}(m_0)$ because of sluggish price adjustment), the jump in e is, when $T = 0$,

$$\frac{de_0^+}{dm} = 1 - \frac{1}{s_1\lambda} > 1$$

in view of $s_1 < 0$. At the same time there is a discrete downward jump in the interest rate (to maintain monetary equilibrium).

Now consider the interval $(0,T)$. Since the economy is initially in a stationary state, $p_0 = \bar{p}(m_0)$. From (6.2) and (6.1)

$$\frac{p_t - \bar{p}(m_0)}{e_t - \bar{e}(m_0)} = \frac{\lambda(s_1 A\exp^{s_1 t} + s_2\exp^{s_2 t})}{A\exp^{s_1 t} - B\exp^{s_2 t}},$$

and noting that $s_1 A + s_2 B = 0$,

$$\frac{p_t - \bar{p}(m_0)}{e_t - \bar{e}(m_0)} = \lambda s_1 s_2 \left(\frac{\exp^{s_1 t} - \exp^{s_2 t}}{s_2\exp^{s_1 t} - s_1\exp^{s_2 t}}\right) = v(t)$$

The value of the v function at $t = T$ then defines a relation between p_T, e_T, $\bar{p}(m_0)$, and $\bar{e}(m_0)$—that is, it is independent of m_1. It can be shown that

$$v(\infty) < 1 \text{ and } \frac{dv}{dt} > 0 \text{ while } v(0) = 0.$$

Let $m_1 - m_0 \equiv \Delta m$. From the steady-state solutions it follows that

$$\bar{p}(m_1) = \bar{p}(m_0) + \Delta m$$

and

$$\bar{e}(m_1) = \bar{e}(m_0) + \Delta m.$$

Further, since (6.4) must hold at $t = T$, it can be transformed as follows:

$$p_T - \bar{p}(m_0) - \Delta m = \lambda s_1[e_T - \bar{e}(m_0) - \Delta m]$$

or

$$\frac{p_T - \bar{p}(m_0)}{e_T - \bar{e}(m_0)} = \lambda s_1 + \frac{\Delta m(1 - \lambda s_1)}{e_T - \bar{e}(m_0)} \equiv w(\Delta m, e_T). \qquad (6.5)$$
$$ (+) \quad (-)$$

Consistency requires that

$$v(T) - w(e_T, \Delta m) = 0. \tag{6.6}$$

Equation (6.6) determines e_T as a function of T and m. e_T can be written as

$$e_T = \bar{e}(m_1) - \Delta m + \frac{\Delta m(1 - \lambda s_1)}{v(T) - \lambda s_1}, \tag{6.7}$$

and since $v(t) < 1$, it is clear that $e_T > \bar{e}(m_1) > \bar{e}(m_0)$. This result means that, regardless of what happens during $(0, T)$, at the instant m is increased, the exchange rate will exceed its long-run value $\bar{e}(m_1)$. Correspondingly, $p_T < \bar{p}(m_1)$.

Now, note that since $dv/dT > 0$,

$$\frac{de_T}{dT} < 0$$

and

$$\frac{d[e_T - \bar{e}(m_0)]}{d\Delta m} = \frac{1 - \lambda s_1}{v(T) - \lambda s_1} > 1.$$

Further, for $T = 0$ (that is, no lead time)

$$e_0 - \bar{e}(m_0) = \left(1 - \frac{1}{\lambda s_1}\right)\Delta m$$

—the familiar overshooting result. It remains to establish $e_0 > \bar{e}(m_0)$ for $T > 0$. From (6.1) evaluating at $t = 0$ and $t = T$, we obtain

$$e_0 - \bar{e}(m_0) = \frac{(s_2 - s_1)[e_T - \bar{e}(m_0)]}{s_2 \exp^{s_1 T} - s_1 \exp^{s_2 T}}, \tag{6.8}$$

which is greater than zero for $t < T$. Since $e_T > \bar{e}(m_1) > \bar{e}(m_0)$ and $s_1 < 0$ and $s_2 > 0$, (6.8) clearly brings out the effect of the announcement on the current spot rate. The extent of this effect can be seen via

$$e_0 - \bar{e}(m_0) = \frac{(s_2 - s_1)\left[\dfrac{\Delta m(1 - \lambda s_1)}{v(T) - \lambda s_1}\right]}{s_2 \exp^{s_1 T} - s_1 \exp^{s_2 T}} > 0. \qquad (6.9)$$

Clearly $de_0/dT < 0$ in view of $dv/dT > 0$. Again, (6.9) confirms that for $t = T = 0$

$$e(0) - \bar{e}(m_0) = \frac{\Delta m(1 - \lambda s_1)}{-\lambda s_1} = \left(1 - \frac{1}{\lambda s_1}\right)\Delta m,$$

while for $T \to \infty$, $e_0 - \bar{e}(m_0) \to 0$.

The critical lead time for which $e_0 = \bar{e}(m_1)$ is a solution T^* such that

$$\frac{e_0 - \bar{e}(m_0)}{\Delta m} = 1$$

(see [6.9]) and is a function of Δm.

What are the paths of p_t and i_t? For convenience assume $T > T^*$. We know that the announcement causes a discrete jump in e_0. But there is no discrete jump in i, since money supply has not yet changed. The spot depreciation in exchange rates generates excess demand at home and, hence, rising prices, which lead now to increasing interest rates and therefore further depreciation. This continues until $t = T$. At this point the money supply increases, causing a discrete drop in i. Excess demand is further stimulated, so that prices continue to rise, but arbitrage now implies, in conjunction with perfect foresight, that the exchange rate be falling. The relevant time paths are illustrated by Figure 6.1 ($T > T^*$ assumed).

Effects on Real Income

So far we have assumed that real income is fixed at $y = \bar{y}$. What is the path of income and other endogenous variables when this assumption is relaxed? To answer this question a framework like that in the first half of Chapter 5 must be developed. Specifically, income is demand determined, and there is no distinction between short- and long-run demand elasticities.

Income is determined via

$$y_t = \mu[u + \delta(p^* + e_t - p_t) - \sigma i_t],$$

where

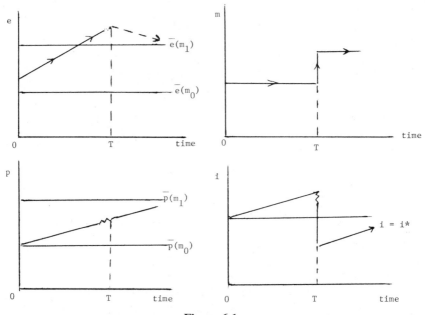

Figure 6.1

$$\mu = \frac{1}{1 - \gamma}.$$

Since

$$i\dagger = \frac{p_t - m}{\lambda} + \frac{\phi}{\lambda} y_t$$

and

$$i^* = \frac{\bar{p} - m}{\lambda} + \frac{\phi}{\lambda} \bar{y},$$

$$\dot{e} = \frac{p_t - \bar{p}}{\lambda} + \frac{\phi}{\lambda} (y_t - \bar{y}). \tag{6.10}$$

Next, note that

$$(y_t - \bar{y}) = \mu\delta(e_t - \bar{e}) - \mu\delta(p_t - \bar{p}) - \mu\sigma\dot{e}. \tag{6.11}$$

Substituting from (6.11) into (6.10), we obtain

$$\dot{e} = \left(\frac{1 - \mu\delta\phi}{\lambda + \phi\mu\sigma}\right)(p_t - \bar{p}) + \left(\frac{\phi\mu\delta}{\lambda + \phi\mu\sigma}\right)(e_t - \bar{e}). \tag{6.12}$$

The other dynamic equation of the model is as earlier

$$\dot{p} = \pi(y_t - \bar{y}), \tag{6.12'}$$

which can be written as

$$\dot{p} = \frac{\pi\mu\delta\lambda}{\lambda + \mu\sigma\phi}(e_t - \bar{e}) - \frac{(\lambda\delta + \sigma)\pi\mu}{\lambda + \mu\sigma\phi}(p_t - \bar{p}). \tag{6.12''}$$

Equations (6.12) and (6.12'') form a second-order dynamical system, the general solution to which is

$$(e_t - \bar{e}) = A \ \exp^{s_1 t} + B \ \exp^{s_2 t}.$$

At this point it should be recalled that this model exhibits saddle point instability as well. Therefore, $s_1 < 0$ and $s_2 > 0$.

The price solution corresponding to the exchange rate solution is

$$(p_t - \bar{p}) = \frac{(\lambda + \phi\mu\sigma)}{1 - \phi\mu\delta}\dot{e} - \frac{\phi\mu\delta}{1 - \phi\mu\delta}(e_t - \bar{e}),$$

which after substituting for $(e_t - \bar{e})$ and $\dot{e}$ from the general form of the exchange rate solution yields

$$(p_t - \bar{p}) = \frac{\lambda + \phi\mu\sigma}{1 - \phi\mu\delta}(s_1 A \ \exp^{s_1 t} + s_2 B \ \exp^{s_2 t})$$

$$- \frac{\phi\mu\delta}{1 - \phi\mu\delta}(A \ \exp^{s_1 t} + B \ \exp^{s_2 t}). \tag{6.13}$$

The above equations hold for t belonging to $(0, T)$, that is, they are only relevant for the lead time interval length. As before the interval (T, ∞) involves first-order adjustment if stability is to be ensured. It should also be understood that $\bar{e}$ denotes the steady-state exchange rate corresponding to the original unchanged stock of money; when necessary we will use $\bar{e}(m_0)$ to denote this.

Now consider the effects of the announcement at $t = 0$ that m_0 will increase to m_1 at $t = T$. Again, it is necessary to consider the subintervals $(0, T)$ and (T, ∞) separately. Over the interval (T, ∞), confining ourselves to, the stable arm of the saddle,

$$\dot{e} = s_1 A \exp^{s_1 t} \qquad (t \geq T)$$

is still true. Noting that $A \exp^{s_1 t} = e_t - \bar{e}(m_1)$, one can derive the price path over this interval as

$$p_t - \bar{p}(m_1) = \frac{A \exp^{s_1 t}[s_1 \lambda + \phi\mu(s_1\sigma - \delta)]}{1 - \phi\mu\delta} \qquad (6.14)$$

for $t \geq T$ or alternatively,

$$p_t - \bar{p}(m_1) = [e_t - \bar{e}(m_1)]\left[\frac{s_1\lambda + \phi\mu(s_1\sigma - \delta)}{1 - \phi\mu\delta}\right]. \qquad (6.14')$$

This equation was already implied in the analysis in Chapter 5 where we considered the interval $(t > T)$ only and, in particular, brings out the fact that exchange rate overshooting need not occur once income is variable. Specifically, since prices cannot jump, $(p_0 - \bar{p}(m_1)) = -dm$, for $T = 0$, if the initial state is a steady state. Hence, evaluating $(6.4')$ at $T = 0$,

$$-dm = [e_0 - \bar{e}(m_1)]\left[\frac{s_1\lambda + \phi\mu(s_1\sigma - \delta)}{1 - \phi\mu\delta}\right],$$

whence,

$$\frac{de_0}{dm} = 1 - \frac{1}{A},$$

where

$$A \equiv \frac{s_1\lambda + \phi\mu(s_1\sigma - \delta)}{1 - \phi\mu\delta} \lesseqgtr 0.$$

This demonstrates that overshooting (with no lead time) will occur if $(1 - \phi\mu\delta) > 0$ and conversely, since $s_1 < 0$. This aspect of the model has been emphasized in Chapter 5 and will not be pursued further here.

Our interest here is to consider the interval $(0, T)$ when income is endogenous.

Evaluating (6.13) at $t = 0$ and noting $p_0 = \bar{p}(m_0)$, notice that

$$A\ [s_1\lambda + \phi\mu(s_1\sigma - \delta)] + B[s_2\lambda + \phi\mu(s_2\sigma - \delta)] = 0 \qquad (6.15)$$

Next obtain a function $v(t)$ as defined earlier:

$$v(t) \equiv \frac{p_t - \bar{p}(m_0)}{e_t - \bar{e}(m_0)}$$

$$= \frac{A\ \exp^{s_1 t}\left[\dfrac{s_1\lambda + \phi\mu(s_1\sigma - \delta)}{1 - \phi\mu\delta}\right] + B\ \exp^{s_2 t}\left[\dfrac{s_2\lambda + \phi\mu(s_2\sigma - \delta)}{1 - \phi\mu\delta}\right]}{A\ \exp^{s_1 t} + B\ \exp^{s_2 t}},$$

which upon simplification and use of (6.15) is

$$v(t) =$$

$$\frac{[s_1\lambda + \phi\mu(s_1\sigma - \delta)][s_2\lambda + \phi\mu(s_2\sigma - \delta)](\exp^{s_1 t} - \exp^{s_2 t})}{(1 - \phi\mu\delta)\{[s_2\lambda + \phi\mu(s_2\sigma - \delta)]\exp^{s_1 t} - [s_1\lambda + \phi\mu(s_1\sigma - \delta)]\exp^{s_2 t}\}}$$

$$(6.16)$$

for $t \leq T$.

Note that $v(0) = 0$, while $dv/dt > 0$ if $(1 - \phi\mu\delta) > 0$ and for the same condition $v(\infty) < 1$. This implies that the v function now is similar to the previous one with expressions like

$$\frac{s_1\lambda + \phi\mu(s_1\sigma - \delta)}{1 - \phi\mu\delta}$$

replacing $s_1\lambda$, and so on. The analysis below will assume for expositional purposes.

that $(1 - \phi\mu\delta) > 0$, so that overshooting of exchange rates ultimately occurs.

Now derive the function $w(e_T, \Delta m)$ as noted earlier. Since (6.14) also holds at $t = T$, and noting that

$$\bar{p}(m_1) = \bar{p}(m_0) + \Delta m$$

and

$$\bar{e}(m_1) = \bar{e}(m_0) + \Delta m,$$

tedious calculations show that

$$\frac{p_T - \bar{p}(m_0)}{e_T - \bar{e}(m_0)} = \frac{s_1\lambda + \phi\mu(s_1\sigma - \delta)}{1 - \phi\mu\delta}$$

$$+ \frac{\Delta m}{e_T - \bar{e}(m_0)} \left[\frac{1 - s_1\lambda - \phi\mu(s_1\sigma - \delta)}{1 - \phi\mu\delta} \right] \equiv w(e_T, \Delta m).$$

$$(6.17)$$

Again, for consistency it is necessary that

$$v(T) - w(e_T, \Delta m) = 0.$$

This equation determines $e_T - \bar{e}(m_0)$, which is

$$e_T = \bar{e}(m_1) - \Delta m + \frac{\Delta m[1 - s_1\lambda - \phi\mu(s_1\sigma - \delta)]}{v(T)(1 - \phi\mu\delta) - [s_1\lambda + \phi\mu(s_1\sigma - \delta)]}.$$

Compare (6.18) with (6.7) above. Notice that $e_T > \bar{e}(m_1)$ is still true if $(1 - \phi\mu\delta) < 0$—that is, at the time the announcement goes into effect, the exchange rate overshoots its long-run equilibrium valve. But, if $(1 - \phi\mu\delta) < 0$, $e_T \gtrless \bar{e}(m_1)$ is possible. Also, unless $(1 - \phi\mu\delta) > 0$, it is not true that $de_T/dT < 0$.

It now remains to establish the sign of $e_0 - \bar{e}(m_0)$ for $T > 0$. This will determine what effect the announcement (to go into effect at $t = T$) will have on the spot rate now. With income fixed we saw that $e_0 - \bar{e}(m_0) > 0$ and was a decreasing function of lead time T.

Recall that

$$e_t - \bar{e}(m_0) = A \exp^{s_1 t} + B \exp^{s_2 t},$$

which at $t = 0$ is

$$e_0 - \bar{e}(m_0) = A + B. \tag{6.19}$$

Next,

$$e_T - \bar{e}(m_0) = A \exp^{s_1 t} + B \exp^{s_2 t}, \tag{6.20}$$

so that

$$\frac{e_0 - \bar{e}(m_0)}{e_T - \bar{e}(m_0)} = \frac{A + B}{A \exp^{s_1 t} + B \exp^{s_2 t}}. \tag{6.21}$$

Then substitute for B from (6.15) as

$$B = \frac{-A[s_1\lambda + \phi\mu(s_1\sigma - \delta)]}{s_2\lambda + \phi\mu(s_2\sigma - \delta)}$$

into (6.21) and obtain

$$\frac{e_0 - \bar{e}(m_0)}{e_T - \bar{e}(m_0)} =$$

$$\frac{(s_2 - s_1)(\lambda + \phi\mu\sigma)}{[s_2\lambda + \phi\mu(s_2\sigma - \delta)]\exp^{s_1 T} - [s_1\lambda + \phi\mu(s_1\sigma - \delta)]\exp^{s_2 T}}, \tag{6.22}$$

which can be rewritten as

$$e_0 - \bar{e}(m_0) =$$

$$\frac{(s_2 - s_1)(\lambda + \phi\mu\sigma)[e_T - \bar{e}(m_0)]}{[s_2\lambda + \phi\mu(s_2\sigma + \delta)]\exp^{s_1 T} - [s_1\lambda + \phi\mu(s_1\sigma - \delta)]\exp^{s_2 T}}. \tag{6.23}$$

Now recall that

$$e_T - \bar{e}(m_0) = \frac{\Delta m[1 - s_1\lambda - \phi\mu(s_1\sigma - \delta)]}{v(T)(1 - \phi\mu\delta) - [s_1\lambda + \phi\mu(s_1\sigma - \delta)]}, \tag{6.18}$$

so that (6.23) may be rewritten as

$$e_0 - \bar{e}(m_0) =$$

$$\frac{(s_2 - s_1)\lambda + \phi\mu\delta}{\{[s_2\lambda + \phi\mu(s_2\sigma - \delta)]\exp^{s_1 T} - [s_1\lambda + \phi\mu(s_1\sigma - \delta)]\exp^{s_2 T}\}}$$

$$\frac{\Delta m[1 - s_1\lambda + \phi\mu(s_1\sigma - \delta)]}{\{v(T)(1 - \phi\mu\delta) - [s_1\lambda + \phi\mu(s_1\sigma - \delta)]\}}$$

From (6.24) it is clear that if $(1 - \phi\mu\delta) > 0$ and $s_2 > \phi\mu\sigma/(\lambda + \phi\mu\delta)$, $e_0 - \bar{e}(m_0) > 0$. But even if both conditions are not fulfilled, it is not necessary that perverse announcement effects emerge, that is, $e_0 - \bar{e}(m_0) < 0$. Also note that under both conditions $\lim_{T \to \infty} e_0 - \bar{e}(m_0) \to 0$.

Our conclusions for the exchange rate are:

1. If the structural parameters of the system are such that exchange rate overshooting occurs at time T, the effects of the announcement over the interval $(0, T)$ are very similar to the fixed-income case.
2. If overshooting does not eventually occur (that is, at $t = T$), nothing conclusive can be said about the exchange rate path, and pathological outcomes are possible.

Coming now to the effects on y_t and i_t, we know from Chapter 5 that over (T, ∞), y_t declines to $\bar{y}$, and if $(1 - \phi\mu\delta) > 0$, i_t rises to i^* and e_t falls toward $\bar{e}(m_1)$. Consider now the interval $(0, T)$. Since

$$y_t = \mu\left[u + \delta(e_t + p^* - p_t) - \sigma\left(\frac{p_t - m}{\lambda} + \frac{\sigma}{\lambda}y_t\right)\right],$$

then

$$y_t = \frac{\lambda\mu}{\lambda + \phi\mu\sigma}\left[u + \delta e_t - \left(\delta + \frac{\sigma}{\lambda}\right)p_t + \frac{\sigma}{\lambda}m\right].$$

(We have dropped the constant p^*.) At $t = 0$, p_0 is fixed at $\bar{p}(m_0)$, while m_0 itself is fixed. Hence, the effect on income at $t = 0$ is determined completely by the behavior of the exchange rate. Specifically,

$$dy_0 = \left(\frac{\lambda\mu\delta}{\lambda + \mu\phi\sigma}\right)de_0,$$

which is greater than zero in the normal case. Next, note that over the interval $(0, T)$, e_t rises to e_T regardless of $e_0 - \bar{e}(m_0) \gtrless 0$. Further monetary equilibrium dictates that $(m_0 - p_t) = -\lambda i_t \neq \phi y_t$. Hence, at $t = 0$, if $y_0 > \bar{y}$, then $i_0 > i^*$ is necessary. Over time the exchange rate depreciates, generating excess demand. Hence, p_t increases over $(0, T)$. The effect on income over $(0, T)$ is determined by

$$\frac{\partial y_t}{\partial e_t} + \frac{\partial y_t}{\partial p_t}$$

at each instant $t \leq T$. Reference to the earlier equation indicates that

$$\frac{\partial y_t}{\partial e_t} = \frac{\lambda \mu \delta}{\lambda + \phi \mu \sigma}$$

and

$$\frac{\partial y_t}{\partial p_t} = -\frac{\lambda \mu}{\lambda + \phi \mu \sigma} \left(\delta + \frac{\sigma}{\lambda} \right) \, ,$$

so that y_t declines until T. At that point m_0 increases to m_1. The path of i_t over $(0, T)$ depends upon the magnitude of ϕ. Specifically,

$$\frac{\partial i}{\partial p} + \frac{\partial i}{\partial y} = \frac{1}{\lambda} + \frac{\phi}{\lambda}$$

at each instant, so that if $\phi > 1$, then i declines over $(0, T)$ and conversely for $\phi < 1$. The effects over (T, ∞) are known from Chapter 5.

NOTE

1. This account is based on Wilson (1979).

REFERENCE

Wilson, C. 1979. "Anticipated Shocks and Exchange Rate Dynamics", *Journal of Political Economy* 87 (June): 639–47.

7

ALTERNATIVE MONETARY POLICIES IN AN INFLATIONARY EQUILIBRIUM MODEL OF THE OPEN ECONOMY

The latter part of the 1970s has seen a growing literature analyzing the effects of monetary policy under flexible exchange rates. Much of the emphasis of this literature has been directed at exchange rate expectations, with a general conclusion being that many of the propositions of the traditional static Fleming-Mundell model (see Fleming 1962; Mundell 1968) of the 1960s are subject to substantial modifications once such expectations are taken into account.[1]

Most of the existing literature, including the previous six chapters, deals with a noninflationary environment in the sense that the system, if stable, converges to an equilibrium in which the domestic and foreign price levels, as well as the domestic exchange rate, remain constant. Yet the current prevailing international experience is one of more or less sustained inflation, and indeed a major reason for the recent worldwide adoption of more flexible exchange rates is the accommodation of long-run differences in national inflation rates. Accordingly, it seems more fruitful to analyze monetary policies in such a context of secular inflation, which is the objective of this chapter.

While, as noted, most of the literature is presented in terms of economies having stable price levels, some authors have developed inflationary models (see, for example, Turnovsky and Kingston 1977, 1979). These papers, however, suffer from several difficulties. First, they incorporate several dynamic processes into the model (asset accumulation, sluggishly evolving inflationary expectations, gradually changing terms of trade), rendering an explicit analysis of the dynamic properties rather difficult. Indeed, it is by no means certain that these models are dynamically stable, in which case, an

---

This chapter is based on joint work with Stephen J. Turnovsky.

analysis of their steady state is irrelevant. Second, and perhaps more important, the short-run implications of monetary expansion are unsatisfactory. For example, they show that an increase in the domestic rate of monetary growth does not immediately raise the rate of exchange depreciation. On the contrary, it will temporarily reduce the rate of exchange depreciation before eventually leading to a proportionate increase in the long-run rate of exchange depreciation. This perverse short-run result is a direct consequence of the two assumptions of interest rate parity and perfect myopic foresight. Taken together, these assumptions make the rate of exchange depreciation play the role of the domestic interest rate so that it therefore responds inversely to a monetary expansion. In technical terms the result is bound up with problems of saddle point instability, familiar in models of perfect foresight; to eliminate it it is necessary to allow the level of exchange rate to undergo an initial jump at the time the monetary disturbance occurs (see, for example, Gray and Turnovsky 1979). While this is easily accomplished in a stable price model, it is much more difficult to incorporate within a model of secular inflation.

The model we shall develop and analyze in the present chapter differs from the existing literature in several important respects. First, to avoid these perverse implications for monetary policy, an alternative expectations hypothesis is introduced. Specifically, we shall assume that expectations of both the rate of exchange depreciation and the rate of inflation are generated by an inflation-adjusted form of the regressive expectations hypothesis (see, for example, Frankel 1979).

Second, a much wider range of passive monetary policies than is normally considered in the literature is discussed. For example, a typical analysis involves pegging the money supply (or its rate of growth) and determining the implications for the exchange rate (or the rate of exchange depreciation). In connection with this, issues such as whether short-run movements in the exchange rate overshoot or undershoot their long-run adjustment have been discussed at length (see, for example, Dornbusch 1976a; Niehans 1977; etc.). In practice, and particularly in an inflationary environment, a number of alternative passive monetary policies merit consideration.[2] For example, the literature on the crawling peg suggests that fixing the rate of exchange depreciation is an important alternative form of passive monetary policy (see, for example, Mathieson 1976). Other possible passive policies include pegging the rate of inflation of domestic goods, or of the domestic cost of living, and so on. The relationships between such policies both in the steady-state equilibrium and in the short run are discussed at length.[3] For example, it is shown how overshooting of the short-run rate of exchange depreciation in response to an increase in the rate of growth of the domestic money supply implies undershooting of the rate of growth of the money supply in response to changes in the rate of exchange depreciation and vice versa. For expository purposes the model is kept as simple as possible, enabling us to solve explicitly for the dynamic adjustment. Furthermore, in each case the chosen passive monetary policy is combined with a short-run monetary intervention rule, so that the regime we consider is more properly regarded as one of a managed float.

THE MODEL

The economy we shall consider is assumed to produce a single (composite) commodity, part of which is consumed domestically, the remainder of which is exported. The price of this commodity is determined in the market for domestic output, so that the price of exports is endogenously determined. On the other hand, we assume that the country is sufficiently competitive in the market for its imports to take the (foreign) price of imports as given. Second, the domestic bond market is assumed to be perfectly integrated with that in the rest of the world. The model is described by the following relationships:

$$Y = d_1 Y - d_2(r - c^*) + d_3 \sigma \qquad 0 < d_1 < 1$$
$$d_2 > 0, d_3 > 0 \qquad\qquad \text{(7.1a)}$$

$$C = \delta P + (1 - \delta)(Q + E) \qquad 0 < \delta < 1 \qquad\qquad \text{(7.1b)}$$

$$\sigma = Q + E - P \qquad\qquad \text{(7.1c)}$$

$$M - C = \alpha_1 Y - \alpha_2 r \qquad \alpha_1 > 0, \alpha_2 > 0 \qquad\qquad \text{(7.1d)}$$

$$r = \bar{r} + e^* \qquad\qquad \text{(7.1e)}$$

$$\dot{M} = \mu - v\dot{\sigma} \qquad v \geq 0 \qquad\qquad \text{(7.1f)}$$

$$p = \beta(Y - \bar{Y}) + c^* \qquad \beta > 0 \qquad\qquad \text{(7.1g)}$$

$$e^* = \theta_1(\tilde{E} - E) + \tilde{e} \qquad \theta_1 > 0 \qquad\qquad \text{(7.1h)}$$

$$c^* = \theta_2(\tilde{C} - C) + \tilde{c} \qquad \theta_2 > 0, \qquad\qquad \text{(7.1i)}$$

where

Y = real domestic output, expressed in logarithms,
$\bar{Y}$ = full-employment level of real domestic output, expressed in logarithms,
r = domestic nominal interest rate,
$\bar{r}$ = foreign nominal interest rate, taken to be exogenous,

$P =$ price of domestic output (in terms of domestic currency), expressed in logarithms,

$Q =$ price of imported good (in terms of foreign currency), expressed in logarithms,

$E =$ logarithm of the current exchange rate (measured in units of the domestic currency per unit of foreign currency),

$C =$ domestic cost of living (measured in domestic currency), expressed in logarithms,

$\sigma =$ relative price of foreign to domestic goods, expressed in logarithms,

$M =$ logarithm of the domestic nominal money supply,

$\mu = \dot{M}/M =$ rate of domestic nominal monetary expansion,

$p = \dot{P}, q = \dot{Q}, e = \dot{E}, c = \dot{C}$; that is, p denotes the actual rate of inflation of P, etc.,

$p^*, q^*, e^*,$ and c^* denote the instantaneous expected rates of inflation of P, Q, E, and C, respectively,

denotes steady state; hence $\tilde{E}$ is the steady state level of the exchange rate; $\tilde{p}, \tilde{q}, \tilde{e},$ and $\tilde{c}$ are the steady-state actual (and expected) rates of inflation of P, Q, E, and C, respectively, and

denotes time derivative.

Equation (7.1a) describes the domestic economy's (IS) curve. The demand for domestic output varies positively with domestic income and the relative price of foreign to domestic goods. It varies inversely with the real rate of interest, which is defined to be the domestic nominal rate, less the expected rate of inflation of the domestic cost of living. Equation (7.1b) defines the domestic cost of living, the consumer price index (CPI), to be a multiplicatively weighted average of the price of domestic goods and the domestic price of foreign goods. While this form is chosen primarily for convenience, it does have some theoretical merit. It is the "true" cost of living index if the domestic residents' utility function, defined with domestic goods and foreign goods as arguments, is of the Cobb-Douglas form. The relative weight δ can be used to parameterize the economy; the larger δ, the less open the economy and vice versa. The next equation, (7.1c), simply defines the relative price σ.

The monetary sector is summarized by equations (7.1d) through (7.1f). The first of these describes the domestic (LM) curve, making the usual assumption that all domestic money is held by domestic residents who also hold no foreign currency.[4] Note that the domestic stock of money is deflated by the overall domestic CPI, reflecting the fact that part of the transactions demand for money is for imports. The assumption of perfect capital market integration is embodied in (7.1e), which defines the domestic interest rate so as to equal the exogenous world rate plus the expected rate of exchange depreciation.

The rate of change of the domestic money supply is governed by (7.1f) and consists of two components. The first of these is the growth rate μ, and it may be exogenously determined by policy, provided all other monetary magnitudes in the system are free to accommodate. Alternatively, if the rate of growth of some other monetary magnitude—such as the rate of exchange depreciation e—is pegged by policy, μ must adjust endogenously to accommodate to the chosen policy. The second term describes the short-run intervention rule, whereby the monetary authorities seek to counteract movements in the relative price of foreign to domestic goods. If this relative price increases, the domestic monetary authorities engage in monetary contraction and vice versa. It is therefore essentially a policy of leaning against the world and as such is similar to the "optica" rule suggested for the European Economic Community.[5] Other modifications to (7.1f) are possible and are briefly discussed below.

The rate of change of the price of domestic output is described by the expectations-augmented Phillips curve (7.1d). It can be viewed as a reduced form for the wage-price sector in which the rate of money wage inflation depends in part upon the expected rate of inflation of the domestic CPI (see, for example, Buiter 1979).

Two expectational variables, e^* and c^*, appear directly in the model, and these are generated by the final two equations. These are, in effect, inflationary-augmented versions of the regressive hypothesis proposed recently by Frankel (1979).[6] According to (7.1h), in the short run the expected rate of exchange depreciation is expected to regress at a rate θ_1 toward its equilibrium level $\tilde{E}$. But in the long run when $E = \tilde{E}$ (with both growing at a steady rate), the exchange rate is expected to depreciate at its long-run rate $\check{e}$. The equation describing inflationary expectations c^* can be interpreted similarly.

While this completes the description of the model, in addition the following conditions must also clearly hold:

$$\tilde{C} = \delta\tilde{P} + (1 - \delta)(\tilde{Q} + \tilde{E}), \tag{7.2a}$$

$$\tilde{c} = \delta\tilde{p} + (1 - \delta)(\check{q} + \check{e}), \tag{7.2b}$$

$$c^* = \delta p^* + (1 - \delta)(q^* + e^*). \tag{7.2c}$$

To reduce the system to a form convenient for analysis, we begin by taking the time derivatives of equations (7.1a) through (7.1e) and (7.1g) through (7.1i). In doing so we assume that all steady-state rates of change in monetary variables are constant, so that

$$\dot{\check{e}} = \dot{\check{c}} = 0.$$

Thus, we obtain

$$\dot{Y} = d_1\dot{Y} - d_2(\dot{r} - \dot{c}^*) + d_3\dot{\sigma}, \tag{7.1a'}$$

$$c = \delta p + (1 - \delta)(q + e), \tag{7.1b'}$$

$$\sigma = q + e - p, \tag{7.1c'}$$

$$\mu - c = \alpha_1 \dot{Y} - \alpha_2 \dot{r}, \tag{7.1d'}$$

$$\dot{r} = \dot{e}*, \tag{7.1e'}$$

$$\dot{p} = \beta \dot{Y} + c*, \tag{7.1f'}$$

$$\dot{e} = \theta_1(\tilde{e} - e), \tag{7.1g'}$$

$$\dot{c}* = \theta_2(\tilde{c} - c), \tag{7.1h'}$$

where in deriving these relationships we are invoking the definitions of c, p, and others. Using equations (7.1a') through (7.1h'), together with the money supply rule (7.1f), the system may be reduced to the following set of relationships, which forms the basis for our subsequent analysis:

$$(1 - d_1)\dot{Y} = -d_2[\theta_1(\tilde{e} - e) - \theta_2(\tilde{c} - c)] + d_3(q + e - p), \tag{7.3a}$$

$$c = \delta p + (1 - \delta)(q + e), \tag{7.3b}$$

$$\mu - v(q + e - p) = \alpha_1 \dot{Y} - \alpha_2 \theta_1(\tilde{e} - e) + c, \tag{7.3c}$$

$$\dot{p} = \beta \dot{Y} + \theta_2(\tilde{c} - c). \tag{7.3d}$$

This system is in effect the original system in time-differentiated form. Loosely speaking, it behaves as follows. Given the steady-state values of e and c, equations (7.3a) through (7.3c) provide three relationships involving the four variables e, c, μ, and Y, together with the dynamically evolving variable p. Once a policy specification—typically postulated in terms of one of the variables e, c, or μ—is chosen, these three equations determine the short-run equilibrium for the remaining three in terms of p and the parametaized fourth variable. These solutions can then be inserted into the fourth equation, (7.3d), to determine the evolution of the rate of inflation of domestic output and, hence, the system over time.[7]

THE STEADY STATE

We begin by considering the steady-state equilibrium of the system. This is attained when

$$\dot{\sigma} = \dot{r} = \dot{e}* = \dot{c} = \dot{p} = \dot{Y} = 0. \tag{7.4}$$

Substituting these conditions into (7.1c′) and (7.3a) through (7.3d), it follows that steady state is generally characterized by

$$\tilde{\mu} = \tilde{c} = \tilde{p} = \tilde{q} + \tilde{e}. \tag{7.5}$$

That is, all domestic monetary magnitudes grow at the same rate. The last equality in (7.5) is of course just a statement of purchasing power parity. Equation (7.5) serves to highlight the long-run constraints on domestic monetary policy. In effect the domestic monetary authorities can, in the long run, choose to peg only one of the monetary growth rates μ, c, p, or e. Whichever one is chosen, the rest are tied to it by virtue of the steady-state relationship contained in (7.5).

In the next section we shall analyze the short-run and transitional behavior of the following four passive monetary policies:

Pegging the monetary growth rate, that is, $\mu = \bar{\mu}$;
Pegging the rate of exchange depreciation, that is $e = \bar{e}$;
Pegging the overall domestic rate of inflation, that is, $c = \bar{c}$; and
Pegging the rate of inflation of domestic output, that is $p = \bar{p}$.

SHORT-RUN RESPONSE TO ALTERNATIVE POLICIES

We now turn to a consideration of the short-run behavior of the system under alternative monetary policies.

Peg $\mu = \bar{\mu}$

The policy of pegging the nominal rate of monetary growth is undoubtedly the most familiar in the literature and leads to the following characterization of the steady rate:

$$\tilde{\mu} = \tilde{c} = \tilde{p} = \tilde{q} + \tilde{e}, \tag{7.6}$$

that is, the rates of inflation of the domestic good and the domestic CPI are both tied to the monetary growth rate; the rate of exchange depreciation is equal to the difference between the domestic monetary growth rate and the foreign rate of inflation.

Substituting the steady-state relationships corresponding to the present monetary policy into (7.3a) through (7.3d), the short-run behavior of the system is now described by

$$(1 - d_1)z = -d_2[\theta_1(\bar{\mu} - q - e) - \theta_2(\bar{\mu} - c)] + d_3(q + e - p),$$
$$\tag{7.7a}$$

$$c = \delta p + (1 - \delta)(q + e),\tag{7.7b}$$

$$\bar{\mu} - v(q + e - p) = \alpha_1 z - \alpha_2 \theta_1(\bar{\mu} - q - e) + c,\tag{7.7c}$$

$$\dot{p} = \beta z + \theta_2(\bar{\mu} - c),\tag{7.7d}$$

where for convenience we define $z = \dot{Y}$. Equations (7.7a) through (7.7c) determine the short-run solutions for the rate of exchange depreciation e, the domestic rate of inflation c, and the rate of change of domestic output z, as functions of the rate of inflation of domestic output p and the pegged monetary growth rate $\bar{\mu}$. Having determined these, the dynamics of p, and therefore the evolution of the system, is governed by (7.7d).

The characteristic equation for the first-order differential equation determined by (7.7a) through (7.7d) is

$$\{(1 - \delta)[(1 - d_1) - \alpha_2 d_1 \theta_2] + (\alpha_2 \theta_1 + v)(1 - d_1)$$
$$+ \alpha_1(d_2 \theta_1 + d_3)\}\lambda + \delta \theta_1[d_2 \beta(1 + \alpha_2 \theta_2) + \alpha_2 \theta_2(1 - d_1)$$
$$+ \alpha_1 d_2 \theta_2] + d_3[\beta(1 + \alpha_2 \theta_1) + \alpha_1 \theta_2] + v[\beta d_2(\theta_2 - \theta_1)$$
$$+ d_2 \theta_1 \theta_2(1 - d_1)] = 0;\tag{7.8}$$

for stability the coefficient of λ and the constant should be of the same sign. From inspection of (7.8) it is seen that these two coefficients are almost certainly both positive, although this is not unambiguously the case. A simple sufficient condition that ensures that stability is met is

$$1 > \frac{\theta_1}{\theta_2} > (1 - \delta).\tag{7.9}$$

That is, the ratio of the regressive coefficient in exchange depreciation expectations to that in inflationary expectations lies between 1 and the fraction of the domestic CPI consisting of imports. But this condition is not necessary and weaker, but more complicated conditions ensuring stability can also be found. At the same time instability cannot be ruled out. For example, if $\theta_2 > \theta_1$ and the income elasticity of the demand for money, α_1, is sufficiently large, the system may indeed become unstable. Also, while the short-run intervention rule (7.1f) is generally stabilizing, it may also generate instability if, for example, $\theta_1 > \theta_2$, and the coefficient βd_2 is sufficiently large.

The short-run effects of an increase in the monetary growth rate on the system are given by the following expressions:

$$\frac{dz}{d\bar{\mu}} = \frac{d_2\theta_1\delta(1 + \alpha_2\theta_2) + d_3(1 + \alpha_2\theta_1) + vd_2(\theta_2 - \theta_1)}{\Delta},$$

$$\tag{7.10a}$$

$$\frac{de}{d\bar{\mu}} = \frac{(1 - d_1)(1 + \alpha_2\theta_1) + \alpha_1 d_2(\theta_1 - \theta_2)}{\Delta}, \tag{7.10b}$$

$$\frac{dc}{d\bar{\mu}} = \frac{(1 - \delta)[\alpha_1 d_2(\theta_1 - \theta_2) + (1 - d_1)(1 + \alpha_2\theta_1)]}{\Delta}, \tag{7.10c}$$

where

$$\Delta \equiv (1 - \delta)[(1 - d_1) - \alpha_1 d_2\theta_2] + (\alpha_2\theta_1 + v)(1 - d_1)$$
$$+ \alpha_1(d_2\theta_1 + d_3)$$

and is assumed to be positive to ensure stability. While none of these expressions can be signed unambiguously, provided θ_1 and θ_2 are comparable in magnitude, one would expect an increase in the monetary growth rate to lead to increases in the rate of growth of output, the rate of inflation of the domestic CPI, and the rate of exchange depreciation. In particular the perverse short-run response of the rate of exchange depreciation, previously obtained by Turnovsky and Kingston (1977), is eliminated. Indeterminateness is introduced into the above expressions through the term $(\theta_1 - \theta_2)$. This measures the effect of an increase in $\bar{\mu}$ on the real rate of interest. If $\theta_1 > \theta_2$, the increase in $\bar{\mu}$ increases the real rate of interest, which causes an offsetting contractionary effect on z. And similarly for the other responses.

To compare with long-run responses, it is convenient to write equations (7.10b) and (7.10c) as

$$\frac{de}{d\bar{\mu}} - 1 = \frac{(\delta - v)(1 - d_1) - \alpha_1(d_2\theta_2\delta + d_3)}{\Delta} \tag{7.10b'}$$

and

$$\frac{dc}{d\bar{\mu}} - 1 = \frac{-(1 - d_1)(v + \delta d_2\theta_1) - \alpha_1(\delta d_2\theta_1 + d_3)}{\Delta} > 0, \tag{7.10c'}$$

respectively. From the latter of these two equations it is immediately apparent that an increase in the monetary growth rate leads to a short-run undershooting of the domestic rate of inflation. The short-run response of the rate of exchange depreciation is, however, more complex. In the absence of short-run monetary intervention ($v = 0$) and if output is fixed (so in effect $d_1 = \alpha_1 = 0$), (7.10b′) implies that we get short-run overshooting of the rate of exchange depreciation to the rate of monetary growth. This result parallels the well-known Dornbusch (1976a) proposition obtained for levels, and the explanation is broadly similar. At the initial rate of inflation a 1 percent monetary expansion exerts a downward pressure on the domestic interest rate and generates expectations of an expected rate of exchange appreciation in the long run. To compensate for the imminent reduction in the rate of interest on domestic assets, the instantaneous increase in the rate of exchange depreciation must exceed the 1 percent long-run increase; otherwise, interest rate parity cannot hold on the path to long-run equilibrium. To the extent that the domestic currency equivalent of foreign inflation impinges directly on the domestic inflation rate, that rate will rise, thereby squeezing the percentage rate of change of domestic real balances. This dampens the overshooting of the exchange depreciation rate, although it does not eliminate it.

To the extent that some of the expansion in the monetary growth rate is accompanied by a rate of growth in the demand for money resulting from an increase in output (in effect $\alpha_1 > 0$), the short-run overshooting is tempered and indeed may be reversed. And this is further dampened by the short-run intervention rule. Indeed, a simple, sufficient condition to ensure short-run undershooting of the exchange rate is

$$v > \delta, \tag{7.11}$$

that is, the degree of intervention in response to short-run movements in the relative price should exceed the proportion of domestic goods contained in the domestic CPI; the more open the economy (the smaller δ), the less intervention is required to eliminate overshooting.

Peg $e = \bar{e}$

Let us now suppose that the domestic monetary authorities peg the rate of exchange depreciation $e = \bar{e}$. Assuming this is known, it follows that $e^* = \bar{e}$, so that such a policy also amounts to pegging the domestic nominal rate of interest. The steady state under the present policy is now characterized by

$$\tilde{\mu} = \tilde{c} = \tilde{p} = q + \bar{e}, \tag{7.12}$$

and substituting from (7.12) into the basic model (7.3), the short-run behavior of the system is now described by

$$(1 - d_1)z = d_2\theta_2(q + \bar{e} - c) + d_3(q + \bar{e} - p), \qquad (7.13a)$$

$$c = \delta p + (1 - \delta)(q + \bar{e}), \qquad (7.13b)$$

$$\mu - v(q + \bar{e} - p) = \alpha_1 z + c, \qquad (7.13c)$$

$$\dot{p} = \beta z + \theta_2(q + \bar{e} - c). \qquad (7.13d)$$

With the rate of exchange depreciation pegged, equations (7.13a) through (7.13c) now determine the short-run solutions for μ, c, and z as functions of p and $\bar{e}$. In particular note that the rate of monetary growth is now required to accommodate to the chosen rate of exchange depreciation.

The characteristic equation is now

$$(1 - d_1)\lambda + \beta(d_3 + d_2\theta_2\delta) + (1 - d_1)\delta\theta_2 = 0, \qquad (7.14)$$

from which the stability of the system is immediately inferred. The short-run effects of an increase in the pegged rate of exchange depreciation are

$$\frac{dz}{d\bar{e}} = \frac{d_2\theta_2\delta + d_3}{1 - d_1}, \qquad (7.15a)$$

$$\frac{dc}{d\bar{e}} = 1 - \delta, \qquad (7.15b)$$

$$\frac{d\mu}{d\bar{e}} = 1 + (v - \delta) + \frac{\alpha_1(d_2\theta_2\delta + d_3)}{1 - d_1}. \qquad (7.15c)$$

That is, an increase in the rate of exchange depreciation will increase the rate of domestic output growth and raise the domestic rate of inflation partially to the extent that foreign goods contribute toward the domestic CPI. It will also probably lead to an increase in the rate of domestic monetary growth, a sufficient condition for this to be so being $v > \delta$.

From (7.15c) it is seen that precisely the same factors that contribute to the short-run overshooting of $de/d\bar{\mu}$, under a pegged monetary growth policy, contribute to an *undershooting* of $d\mu/d\bar{e}$ under a pegged exchange rate depreciation (or pegged interest rate) policy. For example, if output is fixed, the fact that an increase in the rate of exchange depreciation leads to a less-than-proportionate increase in the short-run rate of inflation implies that it leads to a less-than-proportionate increase in the demand for, and hence the growth of, the money supply. More generally, a comparison of (7.10c') and

(7.15c) highlights an interesting comparison between the short-run effects of these two forms of monetary policy, namely,

$$ sign\left(\frac{de}{d\bar{\mu}} - 1 \right) = -sign\left(\frac{d\mu}{d\bar{e}} - 1 \right) , \qquad (7.16) $$

that is, the response of the short-run rate of exchange depreciation to an increase in the monetary growth rate overshoots its long-run response if and only if the response of the short-run rate of monetary growth in response to an increase in the rate of exchange depreciation undershoots its long-run response. Put another way, if there is short-run overshooting in one response, there must necessarily be short-run undershooting in the other. It is impossible for both responses to approach their respective long-run equilibrium changes without overshooting.

Peg $c = \bar{c}$

The third policy we shall consider is one where the monetary authorities peg the domestic rate of inflation. Assuming this is known, this implies $c^* = c = \bar{c}$, and the steady state is now characterized by

$$ \tilde{\mu} = \bar{c} = \tilde{p} = q + \tilde{e}. \qquad (7.17) $$

Substituting from (7.17) into the basic model (7.3), the short-run behavior corresponding to the present policy is

$$ (1 - d_1)z = -d_2\theta_1(\bar{c} - q - e) + d_3(q + e - p), \qquad (7.18a) $$

$$ \bar{c} = \delta p + (1 - \delta)(q + e), \qquad (7.18b) $$

$$ \mu - \nu(q + e - p) = \alpha_1 z - \alpha_2\theta_1(\bar{c} - q - e) + \bar{c}, \qquad (7.18c) $$

$$ \dot{p} = \beta z, \qquad (7.18d) $$

the first three equations of which determine z, e, and μ in terms of $\bar{c}$ and p. The characteristic equation is now

$$ (1 - \delta)(1 - d_1)\lambda + \beta[\delta d_2\theta_1 + d_3] = 0 \qquad (7.19) $$

and, again, the system is unambiguously stable.

The short-run effects of an increase in the pegged rate of inflation are

$$\frac{dz}{d\bar{c}} = \frac{\delta d_2 \theta_1 + d_3}{(1 - d_1)(1 - \delta)}, \tag{7.20a}$$

$$\frac{de}{d\bar{c}} = \frac{1}{1 - \delta} > 0, \tag{7.20b}$$

$$\frac{d\mu}{d\bar{c}} = 1 + \frac{v + \alpha_2 \theta_1 \delta}{1 - \delta} + \frac{\alpha_1(\delta d_2 \theta_1 + d_3)}{(1 - \delta)(1 - d_1)} > 1. \tag{7.20c}$$

Thus, an increase in the fixed rate of inflation leads to a short-run over-shooting of both the rate of exchange depreciation and the accommodating rate of monetary growth. Moreover, the kinds of symmetries in short-run response we have just been discussing with respect to monetary growth apply here as well. Comparing (7.20b) and (7.15b), it is seen that whereas an increase in $\bar{e}$ leads to an undershooting in c, an increase in $\bar{c}$, causes a short-run overshooting in e. The same applies with respect to the rate of monetary growth, as can be seen by comparing (7.20c) with (7.10c). The reasons for these effects are straightforward. For example, the overshooting of the exchange rate follows directly from the fact that p is predetermined in the short run and imported goods make up only a fraction of the domestic CPI. The overresponses in the short run of e and μ are both expansionary and are the reason for the short-run rate of increase in the rate of growth of output.

Peg $p = \bar{p}$

The final policy we shall consider is one where the domestic monetary authorities peg the rate of inflation of the domestic good. With $p = \bar{p}$ it follows that $\dot{p} = 0$. The steady state is now

$$\tilde{\mu} = \tilde{c} = \bar{p} = q + \tilde{e}, \tag{7.21}$$

while the short-run system may be written as

$$(1 - d_1)z = -d_2[\theta_1(\bar{p} - q - e) - \theta_2(\bar{p} - c)] + d_3(q + e - \bar{p}), \tag{7.22a}$$

$$c - \bar{p} = (1 - \delta)(q + e - \bar{p}), \tag{7.22b}$$

$$(\mu - c) - v(q + e - \bar{p}) = \alpha_1 z - \alpha_2 \theta_1(\bar{p} - q - e). \tag{7.22c}$$

$$b_2 + \theta_2(\bar{p} - c) = 0 \tag{7.22d}$$

It is readily apparent that (7.22) constitutes a set of four homogenous equations in the four variables z, $(\mu - c)$, $(\bar{p} - c)$, $(q + e - \bar{p})$. The matrix of coefficients is nonsingular, so that the solution is simply

$$z = 0, \mu = c = \bar{p} = q = e. \tag{7.23}$$

That is, there are no dynamics; the system adjusts instantaneously to the exogenously pegged rate of inflation of the domestic good. In other words the system is driven instantly to steady state.

SOME OTHER ISSUES

To conclude we briefly deal with two further issues. These relate to modifications to the the intervention function and consistency of the expectations schemes with perfect myopic foresight.

Alternative Short-Run Intervention Functions

The short-run monetary intervention rule (7.1f) focuses only on the change in relative price as determining the degree of intervention. In addition it would be quite reasonable to suppose that the monetary authorities in determining their intervention are also concerned with some notion of output stability. There are several ways that this might be formulated, one of the most obvious being

$$\dot{M} = \mu - v_1\dot{\sigma} - v_2(Y - \bar{Y}), \quad v_1 > 0_1, v_2 > 0, \tag{7.24}$$

according to which the monetary authorities increase or decrease the rate of monetary growth according to whether income is below or above its long-run level. Replacing (7.1f) by (7.24) has little effect on the analysis. The short-run effects all remain unchanged. The only difference is that the dynamics now consist of a pair of differential equations involving p and y, but the stability properties of the alternative policies remain virtually unaltered.

An alternative modification is

$$\dot{M} = \mu - v_1\sigma - v_2\dot{Y}, \quad v_1 > 0, v_2 > 0, \tag{7.24'}$$

according to which the rate of monetary growth is varied inversely with the rate of growth of output. This rule, in fact, turns out to be identical with the case we have considered; all that happens is that the coefficient α_1 is replaced by $(\alpha_1 + v_2)$ and everything remains unchanged. Thus, our conclusions appear to be reasonably robust with respect to the specifications of intervention function.

Consistency of Expectations Scheme with Perfect Myopic Foresight

One of the attractive features of the regressive expectations hypothesis argued by Dornbusch is that his model yields consistent expectations in the sense of actual and expected rates of change being equal. As noted by Gray and Turnovsky (1979), this property turns out to be critically dependent upon the structure of his model and the fact that the dynamics can be reduced to a single first-order differential equation.

We shall briefly consider this issue in the present context. In doing so we shall restrict our attention to the case of zero short-run intervention ($v = 0$) and the first policy of pegging the rate of growth of the nominal money supply. Under such a policy the dynamics of the system, described by (7.7), can be expressed as the following differential equation in p:

$$\dot{p} = \lambda(\bar{\mu} - p), \tag{7.25}$$

where λ is the root to the characteristic equation (7.8). Because of the linearity of the system, the differential equation (7.25) can be expressed equivalently in terms of e and c, namely, as

$$\dot{e} = \lambda(\bar{\mu} - q - e) \tag{7.26a}$$

and

$$\dot{c} = \lambda(\bar{\mu} - c). \tag{7.26b}$$

The expectations hypothesis generating e^* and c^* are

$$\dot{e}^* = \theta_1(\bar{\mu} - q - e)$$

and

$$\dot{c}^* = \theta_2(\bar{\mu} - c).$$

For perfect myopic foresight to hold we require $e^* = e$ and $c^* = c$, that is,

$$\lambda = \theta_1 = \theta_2 = \theta, \tag{7.27}$$

say, so that the rates of regression in exchange rate expectations and inflationary expectations must be the same. The expression for λ given in (7.8) involves θ, so that the issue of consistent expectations reduces to determining whether there is a value of $\theta > 0$ that is consistent with (7.27). Using (7.8), this reduces to finding whether there exists a $\theta > 0$, which solves the quadratic equation

$$[\alpha_2(1 - d_1)(1 - \delta) - \alpha_2 d_2 \delta]\theta^2 + [(1 - \delta)(1 - d_1)$$
$$- \beta(\alpha_2 d_3 + d_2)]\theta - \beta d_3 = 0. \tag{7.28}$$

The answer to this question is that there may either be zero, one, or two values of θ that are consistent, depending upon other parameters of the system. Should there be more than one stable root, the question would arise as to which path the economy actually follows to equilibrium. Presumably, the choice between alternative stable paths would depend upon individual maximizing behavior. Such an inquiry is outside the scope of this chapter.

CONCLUSION

This chapter has constructed and analyzed a simple inflationary equilibrium model of the open economy under floating exchange rates. An innovative feature of the model is the treatment and analysis of alternative monetary options. Specifically, we have analyzed four kinds of passive monetary rules (1) pegging the monetary growth rate, (2) pegging the rate of exchange depreciation (which amounts to a pegged interest rate policy), (3) pegging the overall domestic rate of inflation and (4) pegging the rate of inflation of the price of domestic output. In each case the passive monetary rule is combined with an activist intervention policy based on dynamic purchasing power parity.

Our results may be summarized as follows. an increase in the monetary growth rate leads to a less-than-proportionate increase in the domestic rate of inflation. For fixed output and no activist intervention the response of the rate of exchange depreciation is more than proportional. This is thus the moving equilibrium analogue to the overshooting result popularized by Dornbusch (1976a). An increase in the pegged rate of exchange depreciation—or equivalently, the nominal interest rate target—under a regime of exchange depreciation stabilization implies an increase in the rate of growth of domestic output, the rate of monetary growth, and the rate of inflation of the domestic price index. An interesting result here is the inverse relationship between the reaction of the rate of short-run exchange depreciation under a pegged monetary growth rate policy and the response of short-run monetary growth under a policy of exchange depreciation stabilization. More specifically, if there is overshooting in one response, there is necessarily undershooting in the other. A regime of pegging that rate of domestic inflation involves similar symmetries. Finally, the policy of stabilizing the price of domestic output results in instantaneous adjustment. These results appear reasonably robust with respect to the precise form of the activist intervention function.

NOTES

1. See, for example, Argy and Porter (1972), Niehans (1975), Dornbusch (1976b), and Turnovsky and Kingston (1977), among others.

2. A brief discussion of alternative monetary policies in an open inflationary economy is given by Turnovsky and Kingston (1979).

3. Alternative forms of monetary policies in the context of a closed economy have received some attention in the literature, especially with reference to the "target-indicator" debate.

4. This means that we are abstracting from the possibility of currency substitution, an issue that is receiving increasing attention in the international monetary literature. For example, see Miles (1979).

5. See, for example, Basevi and de Grauwe (1977). The "optica" rule is based on dynamic purchasing power parity and is asymmetrical.

6. In terms of our notation the hypothesis as postulated by Frankel (1979) is

$$e^* = \theta_1(\bar{E} - E) + (\bar{c} - q).$$

Using the steady-state relationships given in equation (7.5) this is equivalent to our formulation.

7. It should be pointed out that our model abstracts from the accumulation of wealth and the dynamic process that imposes on the system. As noted, the analysis of such processes for a small open inflationary economy operating under flexible exchange rates is contained in Turnovsky and Kingston (1977, 1979).

REFERENCES

Argy, V., and M. Porter. 1972. "Foreign Exchange Markets and the Effects of Domestic and External Disturbances under Alternative Exchange Rate Systems." *IMF Staff Papers* 19 (November): 503–28.

Basevi, G., and P. de Grauwe. 1977. "Vicious and Virtuous Circles." *European Economic Review* 10 (December): 277–301.

Buiter, W. H. 1979. "Unemployment-Inflation Trade-Offs with Rational Expectations in an Open Economy." *Journal of Economic Dynamics and Control* 1 (February): 117–41.

Dornbusch, R. 1976a. "Expectations and Exchange Rate Dynamics." *Journal of Political Economy* 84 (December): 1161–76.

———. 1976b. "The Theory of Flexible Exchange Rate Regimes and Macroeconomic Policy." *Scandinavian Journal of Economics* 78 (2): 254–75.

Fleming, J. M. 1962. "Domestic Financial Policies under Fixed and Floating Exchange Rates." *IMF Staff Papers* 9: 369–79.

Frankel, J. A. 1979. "On the Mark: A Theory of Floating Exchange Rates Based on Real Interest Differentials." *American Economic Review* 69 (September): 610–22.

Gray, M. R., and S. J. Turnovsky. 1979. "The Stability of Exchange Rate Dynamics under Perfect Myopic Foresight." *International Economic Review* 20 (October): 643–60.

Mathieson, D. J. 1976. "Is There an Optimal Crawl?" *Journal of International Economics* 6 (May): 183–202.

Miles, M. 1979. "Currency Substitution, Flexible Exchange Rates and Monetary Independence." *American Economic Review* 68 (June): 428–36.

Mundell, R. A. 1968. *International Economics*. New York: Macmillan.

Niehans, J. 1977. "Exchange Rate Dynamics with Stock/Flow Interaction," *Journal of Political Economy* 85 (December): 1245–57.

Niehans, J. 1975. "Some Doubts about the Efficiency of Monetary Policy under Flexible Exchange Rates." *Journal of International Economics* 5 (August): 275–82.

Turnovsky, S. J., and G. H. Kingston. 1979. "Government Policies and Secular Inflation under Flexible Exchange Rates." *Southern Economic Journal* 47 (October): 389–412.

_____. 1977. "Monetary and Fiscal Policies under Flexible Exchange Rates and Perfect Myopic Foresight in an Inflationary World." *Scandinavian Journal of Economics* 79 (4): 424–41.

8

EXCHANGE RATE DYNAMICS IN LARGE OPEN ECONOMIES

The recent rapidly growing literature on exchange rate dynamics (which, for the most part has stemmed from Dornbusch's [1976] seminal contribution) can be roughly divided into two main categories. One category emphasizes the asset market view of exchange rate determination, wherein the instantaneous exchange rate is determined by the condition of continuous financial market equilibrium, its dynamics being governed by slowly evolving prices. This is the view taken, for example, in the original contribution by Dornbusch (1976) as well as by Mathieson (1977), Bilson (1979), Witte (1979a), and Dornbusch (1979). An alternative approach to exchange rate determination and dynamics may be termed the *portfolio balance approach*. This approach is primarily concerned with imperfect substitutability between domestic and foreign assets. The spot exchange rate is determined by the requirement of balance between actual and desired portfolio compositions. Differential speeds of adjustment between asset and goods markets are not stressed in this approach; instead, exchange rate (and other) dynamics result from wealth accumulation, which, in turn, is due to accumulated current account imbalances. Chief among the contributions along this line of inquiry have been Kouri (1976), Branson (1976), Dornbusch and Fischer (1978), and, to some extent, Rodriguez (1977) and Dooley and Isard (1979). A comparison and synthesis of these two approaches is attempted in Henderson (1979).

An assumption that is universally employed by the above authors is the small-country assumption. Specifically, the country under question is small in commodity import markets (but not in export markets) as well as in the security market to the extent that the world price of importables as well as the world yield on international securities is parametrically given. Such a setting might indeed be appropriate for describing certain situations (for example, the international economic relations between Denmark and the United States) but is completely inapplicable as a framework characterizing trade (in goods and securities) between countries of roughly equal economic size (such as France and Germany). The major portion of international trade in any European country is conducted with other European countries; and while there are some economic dwarfs in Europe, most are not, so that, for a variety of instances at least, the small open economy paradigm is inappropriate.

To be sure there is no dearth of two-country static models in the literature; the lacuna in the literature is in the two-country (or multicountry) extension of the recent work on exchange rate dynamics pioneered by Dornbusch (1976).[1] This chapter is an attempt to bridge this gap. Specifically, we construct a two-country analogue (except for some minor modifications) to Dornbusch (1976). The analysis thus emphasizes rapid clearing of money markets in relation to slowly adjusting commodity markets. The two-country extension to the portfolio balance approach mentioned earlier is to be regarded as unfinished business. The present framework may be taken as being applicable to two economies of roughly equal economic size that conduct most of their trade with one another. The emphasis is on the mutual interdependencies (or feedback considerations) that exist in such a setting. To highlight these, some of the differences between these countries will be deliberately suppressed. It will thus be possible to examine the robustness of some of the well-known small-country results (especially, the exchange rate overshooting result) when the framework involves feedback considerations.

In what follows the first section describes the model, the second obtains instantaneous and equilibrium solutions, and the third derives the dynamic equations of the model and discusses stability. In the fourth section a specific disturbance is analyzed in detail as an example of the applicability of this approach. The fifth section briefly addresses some policy issues, and the conclusion summarizes the main results and suggests some avenues for future research.

SETUP OF THE MODEL

The hypothetical world of this model consists of two countries. Each produces a single final commodity. Both goods enter into consumption in each country as imperfect substitutes. Each country supplies bonds denominated in its own currency to the world market. These assets are assumed to be perfect substitutes on an "uncovered" basis, so that, effectively, there is a single internationally traded bond. Domestic residents in any country have the option of holding domestically issued money or the international bond. They may not hold foreign currency.[2] All considerations of intermediate products, capital formation, and the labor market are deliberately suppressed. Income is exogenously fixed at its respective full-employment supply level in each country.[3] The model to be detailed below contains a description of the money and commodity markets in each country, along with the specification of uncovered interest arbitrage. The bond market is omitted via Walras's law. Continuous monetary stock equilibrium prevails in each country. By contrast commodity markets are sluggish, and prices respond over time to continue disequilibrium in the goods markets. There are other simplifying assumptions, and these will be introduced as the analysis is presented.

The following notation is employed:

i: domestic nominal interest rate,
e: log domestic exchange rate (number of domestic currency units per unit of foreign currency
$\bar{y}$: log domestic (full-employment) income level,
m: log domestic money supply,
p: log domestic price level,
d: log domestic (real) aggregate demand, and
g: log domestic government purchases of the domestically produced good.

A dot denotes a time derivative, overbars denote equilibrium or steady-state levels, and starred variables refer to the foreign country. The structural parameters of the model are each defined as positive. These are $\theta, \lambda, \phi, \delta, \gamma, \sigma, \alpha$, and π with corresponding analogues for the foreign country (except when assumed to be the same for both countries). Reduced-form parameters will be introduced below.

Since domestic and foreign assets are viewed (ex ante) by residents of each country as being perfect substitutes on an uncovered basis, net yields on these two assets must be equal, that is,

$$i = i^* + z \tag{8.1}$$

must hold, where z is the expected rate of depreciation of home currency vis-à-vis foreign currency. The rest of the model is log-linear.

Expected depreciation is given by

$$z = -\theta(e - \bar{e}), \quad \theta > 0. \tag{8.2}$$

Equation (8.2) states that the equilibrium exchange rate is known to market participants in each country and a fraction of the gap between current and equilibrium exchange rates is expected by market participants in each country to be monotonically closed each period.[4] Equations (8.1) and (8.2) also imply the assumption that expectations about the future course of exchange rates are identical in both countries. Such an assumption would be borne out in practice if forward exchange markets in the two countries were sufficiently homogenous, since forward arbitrage would otherwise lead speculators to rearrange their portfolios at the given interest yields until a single arbitrage relation such as (8.2) were satisfied.[5] While the analysis of systematically divergent expectations may be of interest in describing short-term disequilibrium situations, it would lead to considerable complexity in the current framework and will not be pursued.

Continuous monetary equilibrium prevails in each country. Nominal money supplies are exogenously determined, while real money demand depends upon the nominal interest rate and output level. The model ignores wealth accumulation that occurs through accumulated trade surpluses, and wealth effects on money demand or consumption demand are also neglected. Equation (8.3) expresses the conditions for monetary equilibrium in each country:

$$m - q = -\lambda i + \phi \bar{y} \tag{8.3a}$$

and

$$m^* - q^* = -\lambda i^* + \phi \bar{y}^*, \tag{8.3b}$$

where q and q^* are (log) price indexes in the home and foreign country, respectively, and the simplifying assumptions $\lambda = \lambda^*$ and $\phi = \phi^*$ have been made.[6] These price indexes are assumed to be multiplicatively weighted averages of the price of domestic goods and foreign goods (in each country). Hence, real balances in (8.3) are real in the sense of expressing purchasing power over two goods, which is the essence of the open economy framework. If the consumers' underlying utility functions are of the Cobb-Douglas type, the fixed weight price index is in fact the true cost of living index (see Samuelson and Swamy [1974]). The weights are fractions of expenditure falling on the two goods in each country and thus characterize the degree of openness. If α is the fraction expended by the domestic country on foreign goods and α^* the analogous fraction for the foreign country, it follows that

$$q = (1 - \alpha)p + \alpha(p^* + e) \tag{8.4a}$$

and

$$q^* = (1 - \alpha^*)p^* + \alpha^*(p - e). \tag{8.4b}$$

Aggregate demand in each country is given by

$$d = u + g + \delta(e + p^* - p) + \gamma \bar{y} - \sigma r + \alpha^* d^* \tag{8.5a}$$

and

$$d^* = u^* + g^* - \delta^*(e + p^* - p) + \gamma^* \bar{y}^* - \sigma^* r^* + \alpha d, \quad (8.5b)$$

where r and r^* are real interest rates and u and u^* are autonomous components of expenditure. The interpretation of (8.5) is fairly standard. An increase in the relative price of importables switches aggregate demand toward the domestic good in each country. An increase in own-interest rates reduces aggregate demand. Fractions α and α^* of aggregate demand in each country fall on the home good of the other. Thus equations (8.1) and (8.5) stress two channels of mutual interdependence between countries. These result from trade in securities and in commodities.

Substituting for d^* and d in (8.5a) and (8.5b), respectively, the latter can be expressed as

$$d = \frac{1}{1 - \alpha \alpha^*} [u + \alpha^* u^* + g + \alpha^* g^* + (\delta - \alpha^* \delta^*)(e + p^* - p)$$
$$+ \gamma \bar{y} + \alpha^* \gamma^* \bar{y}^* - \sigma r - \alpha^* \sigma^* r^*] \quad (8.6a)$$

and

$$d^* = \frac{1}{1 - \alpha \alpha^*} [u^* + \alpha u + \alpha g + g^* - (\delta^* - \alpha \delta)(e + p^* - p)$$
$$+ \alpha \gamma \bar{y} + \gamma^* \bar{y}^* - \alpha \sigma r - \sigma^* r^*]. \quad (8.6b)$$

Since α and α^* are fractions, it is clear that $(1 - \alpha \alpha^*) > 0$. Next, $(\delta - \alpha^* \delta^*)$ and $(\delta^* - \alpha \delta)$ will each be positive if $\alpha^* < (\delta/\delta^*) < 1/\alpha$. In what follows it is assumed that this is indeed the case.[7] The equations in (8.6) can now be expressed in reduced form as

$$d = a_1 g + a_2 g^* - a_3 r - a_4 r^* + a_5 (e + p^* - p) + a_6 \bar{y}$$
$$+ a_7 \bar{y}^*$$

and

$$d^* = b_1 g + b_2 g^* - b_3 r - b_4 r^* - b_5 (e + p^* - p) + b_6 \bar{y}$$
$$+ b_7 \bar{y}^*, \quad (8.7b)$$

where all $a_i, b_j > 0$ and the autonomous terms have been suppressed.

In terms of structural parameters the reduced-form coefficients are given by

$$a_1 \equiv \frac{1}{1 - \alpha\alpha^*}, a_2 \equiv \frac{\alpha^*}{1 - \alpha\alpha^*}, a_3 \equiv \frac{\sigma}{1 - \alpha\alpha^*}, a_4 \equiv \frac{\alpha^*\sigma^*}{1 - \alpha\alpha^*},$$

$$a_5 \equiv \frac{\delta - \alpha^*\delta^*}{1 - \alpha\alpha^*}, a_6 \equiv \frac{\gamma}{1 - \alpha\alpha^*}, a_7 \equiv \frac{\alpha^*\gamma^*}{1 - \alpha\alpha^*},$$

$$b_1 \equiv \frac{\alpha}{1 - \alpha\alpha^*}, b_2 \equiv \frac{1}{1 - \alpha\alpha^*}, b_3 \equiv \frac{\alpha\sigma}{1 - \alpha\alpha^*}, b_4 \equiv \frac{\sigma^*}{1 - \alpha\alpha^*},$$

$$b_5 \equiv \frac{\delta^* - \alpha\delta}{1 - \alpha\alpha^*}, b_6 \equiv \frac{\alpha\gamma}{1 - \alpha\alpha^*}, \text{ and } b_7 \equiv \frac{\gamma^*}{1 - \alpha\alpha^*}.$$

Since α and $\alpha^* < 1$, it is clear that

$$a_1 > a_2, b_2 > b_1, a_1 > b_1, b_2 > a_2, a_3 > b_3, b_4 > a_4, a_6 > b_6,$$
$$b_7 > a_7, a_1 = b_2.$$

Equation (8.7) emphasizes the international effects of monetary of fiscal operations conducted in any one country. An increase in either home or foreign government spending increases home aggregate demand, although the effect of increased foreign spending must operate via increased foreign imports. An increase in the domestic nominal money supply reduces the domestic interest rate (at the given level of prices) and stimulates home aggregate demand. Part of the latter increase falls upon the foreign commodity via increased home imports. The secondary or feedback responses are fractions of the initial responses. An increase in the relative home currency price of foreign goods $(e + p^* - p)$ involves conflicting effects. First, the increase in the relative price diverts home demand toward home goods. The increase in home aggregate demand spills over partially onto increased imports, thus stimulating d^*. However, at the same time the increase in the relative price implies that foreign demand is switched toward home goods as well. Thus, home exports are stimulated, with a consequential increase in d and a decline in d^*. The standard assumption is made that the net effect of an increase in home terms of trade is to stimulate home demand and depress foreign demand.

The next step in the model is to describe the determination of the real interest rates r and r^*. Specifically, it is assumed that these are determined in Fisherian fashion by the difference between the nominal interest rate and expected inflation rate. Expectations of the rate of inflation of the price of domestically produced goods in each country are defined in a manner symmetrical to exchange rate expectations, that is,

$$\dot{p}^E = -\beta(p - \bar{p}), \quad \beta > 0, \tag{8.8a}$$

and

$$\dot{p}^{*E} = -\beta^*(p^* - \bar{p}^*), \quad \beta^* > 0, \tag{8.8b}$$

where $\bar{p}$ and $\bar{p}^*$ are equilibrium price levels, which are known to market participants. Solutions for these will be obtained below. Thus, the expected rates of inflation of the respective price indexes are given by (using [8.2], [8.4], and [8.8])

$$\dot{q}^E = -\beta(1 - \alpha)(p - \bar{p}) - \alpha\beta^*(p^* - \bar{p}^*) - \alpha\theta(e - \bar{e}) \tag{8.9a}$$

and

$$\dot{q}^E = -\beta^*(1 - \alpha^*)(p^* - \bar{p}^*) - \alpha^*\beta(p - \bar{p}) + \alpha^*\theta(e - \bar{e}). \tag{8.9b}$$

Real interest rates can now be obtained from

$$r = i - \dot{q}^E \tag{8.10a}$$

and

$$r^* = i^* - \dot{q}^{*E}. \tag{8.10b}$$

The final equations of the model describe price adjustment. Specifically, prices of the domestic good in each country adjust according to a measure of excess demand in the home goods markets:

$$\dot{p} = \pi(d - \bar{y}), \quad \pi > 0 \tag{8.11a}$$

and

$$\dot{p}^* = \pi^*(d^* - \bar{y}^*), \quad \pi^* > 0. \tag{8.11b}$$

The steady state of the model is described by a constant level of prices and exchange rates, that is $p = p^* = \bar{p}^*$, $e = \bar{e}$, and $i = i^* = \bar{\imath} = \bar{r}$. This completes the specification of the model.

INSTANTANEOUS AND EQUILIBRIUM SOLUTIONS

Is Overshooting a Small-Country Result?

This section derives a number of instantaneous relations as well as explicit steady-state (or equilibrium) solutions. The impact effects of shocks in nominal money supply or in government spending will also be analyzed here.

According to the asset market approach, the instantaneous exchange rate is determined entirely in asset markets, while its evolution over time is governed by both monetary and real considerations. Solving for nominal interest rates from the money market equilibrium conditions (8.3) and using (8.1) and (8.2), we obtain

$$(e - \bar{e}) = -\frac{(q - q^*)}{\lambda\theta} + \frac{(m - m^*)}{\lambda\theta} - \frac{\phi}{\lambda\theta}(\bar{y} - \bar{y}^*). \qquad (8.12)$$

Equation (8.12) represents combined monetary equilibrium in addition to uncovered interest arbitrage. According to (8.12), for a given equilibrium exchange rate the higher the domestic nominal money supply relative to the foreign money supply, the higher the domestic exchange rate. Further, the exchange rate (relative to its equilibrium level) is related inversely to the home price index relative to the foreign price index. Since

$$(q - q^*) = (p - p^*) + (\alpha + \alpha^*)(e + p^* - p),$$

(8.12) can be rewritten as

$$(e - \bar{e}) = \frac{-(p - p^*)}{\lambda\theta} - \frac{(\alpha + \alpha^*)}{\lambda\theta}(e + p^* - p) + \frac{(m - m^*)}{\lambda\theta}$$

$$-\frac{\phi}{\lambda\theta}(\bar{y} - \bar{y}^*). \qquad (8.13)$$

Equation (8.13) shows the inverse dependence of the exchange rate deviation on the home terms of trade ($T = e + p^* - p$). Equation (8.13) is (superficially at least) consistent with conventional accounts of the balance of payments, wherein increased terms of trade result in improved balance of payments and consequently in an appreciating exchange rate. Equation (8.13) can also be solved for the terms of trade as

$$T = \left(\frac{\lambda\theta}{\lambda\theta + \alpha + \alpha*} \right) \bar{e} - \left(\frac{1 + \lambda\theta}{\lambda\theta + \alpha + \alpha*} \right) (p - p*)$$

$$+ \frac{m - m*}{\lambda\theta + \alpha + \alpha*} - \left(\frac{\phi}{\lambda\theta + \alpha + \alpha*} \right) (\bar{y} - \bar{y}*). \qquad (8.14)$$

For given $\bar{e}$ the relative price differential $(p - p*)$ does not affect the current terms of trade equiproportionately, as may have been implied by the definition of T, but by a factor of $(1 + \lambda\theta)/(\lambda\theta + \alpha + \alpha*)$, which could exceed or fall short of unity. The equilibrium exchange rate affects the current terms of trade less than proportionately. Next, (8.12) can also be written in terms of price index deviations as

$$(e - \bar{e}) = \frac{-(q - \bar{q})}{\lambda\theta} + \frac{(q* - \bar{q}*)}{\lambda\theta} \qquad (8.12')$$

or as

$$(e - \bar{e}) = \frac{-(1 - \alpha - \alpha*)}{\lambda\theta + \alpha + \alpha*} (p - \bar{p})$$

$$+ \frac{1 - \alpha - \alpha*}{\lambda\theta + \alpha + \alpha*} (p* - \bar{p}*) \qquad (8.12'')$$

upon substituting from the definitions in (8.4). [8] Finally, an expression for equilibrium terms of trade $\bar{T}$ can be derived as

$$\bar{T} = \frac{\bar{e}}{1 - \alpha - \alpha*} - \frac{m - m*}{1 - \alpha - \alpha*} + \frac{\phi}{1 - \alpha - \alpha*} (\bar{y} - \bar{y}*),$$
$$(8.14')$$

which shows that the equilibrium exchange rate may even be inversely related to $\bar{T}$ if $(1 - \alpha - \alpha*) < 0$.[9] Some of these expressions will be useful in examining the comparative static properties of the model and in deriving adjustment equations. Prior to this, explicit solutions for steady-state values of interest rates, exchange rates, and terms of trade will be obtained.

Now the full-employment income levels must satisfy

$$\bar{y} = a_1 g + a_2 g* - (a_3 + a_4)\bar{r} + a_5 \bar{T} + a_6 \bar{y} + a_7 \bar{y}*$$

and

$$\bar{y}^* = b_1g + b_2g^* + (b_3 + b_4)\bar{r} - b_5\bar{T} + b_6\bar{y} + b_7\bar{y}^*,$$

which can be written as

$$K - (a_3 + a_4)\bar{r} + a_5\bar{T} = 0, K = a_1g + a_2g^* + (a_6 - 1)\bar{y} + a_7y^*,$$

and

$$K^* - (b_3 + b_4)\bar{r} - b_5\bar{T} = 0, K^* = b_1g + b_2g^* + b_6\bar{y} + (b_7 - 1)\bar{y}^*,$$

where K and K^* are purely exogenous and are assumed to be positive, by a suitable choice of units. These equations may be solved as

$$\bar{i} = \bar{r} = \frac{b_5K + a_5K^*}{b_5(a_3 + a_4) + a_5(b_3 + b_4)} \tag{8.15}$$

and

$$\bar{T} = \frac{(a_3 + a_4)K^* - (b_3 + b_4)K}{b_5(a_3 + a_4) + a_5(b_3 + b_4)}. \tag{8.16}$$

Next, using (8.14′) and (8.16),

$$\bar{e} = \frac{(1 - \alpha - \alpha^*)[(a_3 + a_4)K^* - (b_3 + b_4)K]}{b_5(a_3 + a_4) + a_5(b_3 + b_4)} + (m - m^*)$$
$$- \phi(\bar{y} - \bar{y}^*). \tag{8.17}$$

Finally, using the solutions for $\bar{q}$ and $\bar{q}^*$ from the money markets and (8.15),

$$\bar{q} = \lambda\left[\frac{b_5K + a_5K^*}{b_5(a_3 + a_4) + a_5(b_3 + b_4)}\right] + m - \phi\bar{y} \tag{8.18a}$$

and

$$\bar{q}^* = \lambda\left[\frac{b_5K + a_5K^*}{b_5(a_3 + a_4) + a_5(b_3 + b_4)}\right] + m^* - \phi\bar{y}^*. \tag{8.18b}$$

A glance at (8.15) and (8.16) shows that the steady-state interest rate and terms of trade level are independent of monetary factors and are determined entirely by real considerations. The equilibrium exchange rate and domestic price level are affected equiproportionately by domestic nominal monetary expansion, while the equilibrium foreign price level is independent of domestic monetary policy. It is also easy to show that $\bar{p}$ (the equilibrium price level of domestic goods) exhibits a unitary elasticity with respect to m, while $\bar{p}^*$ is independent of it.

Consider now the impact and steady-state effects of an increase in domestic money supply. The increase in m affects the equilibrium exchange rate as well as $\bar{q}$ and $\bar{p}$ equiproportionately as seen above, with no effects on the equilibrium terms of trade or interest rate. The effect on the spot exchange rate can be obtained from (8.12) (or [8.12′] or [8.12″]) or (8.13) and is seen to be

$$\frac{de}{dm} = \frac{\lambda\theta + 1}{\lambda\theta + \alpha + \alpha^*} \underset{<}{\overset{>}{=}} 1. \tag{8.19}$$

According to (8.19), the spot exchange rate may overshoot or undershoot its equilibrium level in response to a monetary expansion. Overshooting occurs as $1 > (\alpha + \alpha^*)$ and conversely. If the two countries under consideration are highly open, so that imports form a sizable fraction of total spending, exchange rate overshooting will not occur. By contrast, for a small country, Dornbusch's (1976) framework yields

$$\frac{de}{dm} = \frac{1 + \lambda\theta}{\alpha + \lambda\theta}.^{10} \tag{8.19′}$$

Comparing (8.19) and (8.19′), it is clear that the exchange rate response is clearly dampened for large economies.

Next, consider the response to an increase in domestic real spending, as characterized by an increase in g. Recalling the definitions of K and K^*, the effect on the equilibrium interest rate is positive (as may be expected):

$$\frac{d\bar{r}}{dg} = \frac{d\bar{i}}{dg} = \frac{a_1 b_5 + b_1 a_5}{b_5(a_3 + a_4) + a_5(b_3 + b_4)} > 0.$$

The long-run terms of trade unambiguously decline by

$$\frac{d\bar{T}}{dg} = \frac{(a_3 b_1 - b_3 a_1) + (a_4 b_1 - b_4 a_1)}{b_5(a_3 + a_4) + a_5(b_3 + b_4)} < 0,$$

since $(a_3b_1 - b_3a_1) = 0$ and

$$a_4b_1 - b_4a_1 = \frac{\alpha^*\sigma^*\alpha}{(1 - \alpha\alpha^*)^2} - \frac{\sigma^*}{(1 - \alpha\alpha^*)^2} < 0.$$

The increase in government spending must, in final equilibrium, be accommodated by an equivalent decline in private spending on home goods, which occurs through a combination of expenditure reduction (via increase in $\bar{r}$) and an expenditure switch in favor of the foreign good (via a decline in $\bar{T}$). The effect on the equilibrium exchange rate is given by

$$\frac{d\bar{e}}{dg} = \frac{(a_4b_1 - b_4a_1)(1 - \alpha - \alpha^*)}{b_5(a_3 + a_4) + a_5(b_3 + b_4)}$$

and is ambiguous without a knowledge of the sign of $(1 - \alpha - \alpha^*)$. Specifically, if $(1 - \alpha - \alpha^*) < 0$, there is equilibrium depreciation, as in the case of monetary expansion.

The effects of the real disturbance on the spot exchange rate may be obtained by reference to (8.12):

$$\frac{d(e - \bar{e})}{dg} = -\frac{1}{\lambda\theta} \frac{d(q - q^*)}{dg},$$

which, using the definitions of q and q^*, can be reduced to

$$\frac{de}{dg} = \frac{\dfrac{d\bar{e}}{dg}}{\dfrac{(\lambda\theta + \alpha + \alpha^*)}{\lambda\theta}}.$$

This equation makes it clear that the spot rate unambiguously undershoots the equilibrium exchange rate in response to a real disturbance. Comparison with the small-country framework of Dornbusch[11] indicates that in the latter the spot exchange rate response is equal to the equilibrium response—that is, there is neither overshooting nor undershooting for a real disturbance. Hence, in the case of real disturbances as well, the large-country framework yields reduced volatility of the spot exchange rate.

DYNAMICS AND STABILITY

Here, the final-form adjustment equations of the model are derived. First note that

$$(d - \bar{y}) = -a_3(r - \bar{r}) - a_4(r^* - \bar{r}) + a_5(e - \bar{e}) + a_5(p^* - \bar{p}^*)$$
$$- a_5(p - \bar{p})$$

and

$$(d^* - \bar{y}) = -b_3(r - \bar{r}) - b_4(r^* - \bar{r}) - b_5(e - \bar{e}) - b_5(p^* - \bar{p}^*)$$
$$- b_5(p - \bar{p}).$$

Recalling the definition of the real interest rate and using the solutions for i, i^*, and T from the money market along with (8.9), it can be shown that

$$(r - \bar{r}) = (1 - \alpha)\left(\frac{1}{\lambda} + \beta\right)(p - \bar{p}) + \alpha\left(\frac{1}{\lambda} + \beta^*\right)(p^* - \bar{p}^*)$$
$$+ \alpha\left(\frac{1}{\lambda} + \theta\right)(e - \bar{e}) \qquad (8.20)$$

and

$$(r^* - \bar{r}) = \alpha^*\left(\frac{1}{\lambda} + \beta\right)(p - \bar{p}) + (1 - \alpha^*)\left(\frac{1}{\lambda} - \beta^*\right)(p^* - \bar{p}^*)$$
$$- \alpha^*\left(\frac{1}{\lambda} + \theta\right)(e - \bar{e}). \qquad (8.20a)$$

Using (8.20) along with (8.12″) yields the adjustment equations

$$\dot{p} = -\pi\left[a_5 + \left(\frac{1}{\lambda} + \theta\right)(a_4\alpha^* - a_3\alpha)\right] \qquad (8.21a)$$

$$\times \left(\frac{1 - \alpha - \alpha^*}{\lambda\theta + \alpha + \alpha^*}\right)(p - \bar{p}) + \pi\left[a_5\right.$$

$$+ \left(\frac{1}{\lambda} + \theta\right)(a_4\alpha^* - a_3\alpha)\right]\left(\frac{1 - \alpha - \alpha^*}{\lambda\theta + \alpha + \alpha^*}\right)(p^* - \bar{p}^*)$$

$$- \pi\left\{a_5 + \left(\frac{1}{\lambda} + \beta\right)[a_4\alpha^* - a_3(1 - \alpha)]\right\}(p - \bar{p})$$

$$+ \pi\left\{a_5 - \left(\frac{1}{\lambda} + \beta^*\right)[a_3\alpha + a_4(1 - \alpha)]\right\}(p^* - \bar{p}^*)$$

and

$$\dot{p}* = -\pi*\left\{ b_5 + \left(\frac{1}{\lambda} + \beta*\right)[b_3\alpha + (1-\alpha)b_4]\right\}(p* - \bar{p}*)$$

$$- \pi*\left(\frac{1-\alpha-\alpha*}{\lambda\theta+\alpha+\alpha*}\right)\left[\left(\frac{1}{\lambda}+\theta\right)(b_4\alpha* - b_3\alpha) - b_5\right]$$

$$\times (p - \bar{p}) + \pi*\left(\frac{1-\alpha-\alpha*}{\lambda\theta+\alpha+\alpha*}\right)\left[\left(\frac{1}{\lambda}+\theta\right)(b_4\alpha* - b_3\alpha)\right.$$

$$\left. - b_5\right](p* - \bar{p}*) + \pi*\left\{ b_5 - \left(\frac{1}{\lambda}+\beta\right)[b_4\alpha* + b_3(1-\alpha)]\right\}$$

$$\times (p - \bar{p}). \tag{8.21b}$$

Note that $(a_4\alpha* - a_3\alpha) = [1/(1 - \alpha\alpha*)](\alpha^{*2}\sigma* - \alpha\sigma)$, and is most likely negative (if the parameters for the two countries are not too different), while $(b_4\alpha* - b_3\alpha) = [1/(1 - \alpha\alpha*)](\alpha*\sigma* - \alpha^2\sigma)$ is likely to be > 0. In order for the system to be stable, it is sufficient that the coefficients on $(p - \bar{p})$ and $(p* - \bar{p}*)$ each be negative in (8.21a) and (8.21b), respectively. Sufficient conditions to ensure that this is indeed the case are

$$a_5 + \left(\frac{1}{\lambda}+\theta\right)(a_4\alpha* - a_3\alpha) > 0 \tag{8.22a}$$

and

$$b_5 + \left(\frac{1}{\lambda}+\theta\right)(b_3\alpha - b_4\alpha*) > 0.^{12} \tag{8.22b}$$

Substituting for the definitions of these coefficients in terms of structural parameters, it can be seen that equations (8.22) require that

$$\delta > \left(\frac{1}{\lambda}+\theta\right)(\alpha\sigma - \alpha^{*2}\sigma*) + \alpha*\delta*$$

and

$$\delta* > \left(\frac{1}{\lambda}+\theta\right)(\alpha*\sigma* - \alpha^2\sigma) + \alpha\delta. \tag{8.23b}$$

Equations (8.23) are completely consistent with the requirement that $\alpha* < \delta/\delta* < 1/\alpha$, and in what follows it will be assumed that (8.23) is satisfied. Thus, adjustment can be described by the following second-order system:

$$\dot{p} = -f_1(p - \bar{p}) + f_2(p* - \bar{p}*) \tag{8.24}$$

and

$$\dot{p}* = g_2(p - \bar{p}) - g_1(p* - \bar{p}*),$$

where $f_1, g_1 > 0$,[13] under the stability requirement (8.23). The cross coefficients are given by

$$f_2 \equiv \pi \left(\left[a_5 + \left(\frac{1}{\lambda} + \theta\right)(a_4\alpha* - a_3\alpha)\right]\left(\frac{1 - \alpha - \alpha*}{\lambda\theta + \alpha + \alpha*}\right)\right.$$

$$\left. + \left\{ a_5 - \left(\frac{1}{\lambda} + \beta*\right)[a_3\alpha + a_4(1 - \alpha)]\right\}\right)$$

and

$$g_2 \equiv \pi* \left(\left[b_5 + \left(\frac{1}{\lambda} + \theta\right)(b_3\alpha - b_4\alpha*)\right]\left(\frac{1 - \alpha - \alpha*}{\lambda\theta + \alpha + \alpha*}\right)\right.$$

$$\left. + \left\{ b_5 - \left(\frac{1}{\lambda} + \beta\right)[b_4\alpha* + b_3(1 - \alpha)]\right\}\right).$$

Both f_2 and g_2 are ambiguous in sign, without further restrictions, but if the two economies are similar in terms of parameter magnitudes, f_2 and g_2 may be expected to be of the same sign (recall that $a_3\alpha$ in the home country plays the role of $b_4\alpha*$ in the foreign economy). In any case it is clear that $f_1 > f_2$ and $g_1 > g_2$. The characteristic equation from (3.24) is

$$s^2 + s(f_1 + g_1) + (f_1g_1 - f_2g_2) = 0,$$

whence the solution for the two roots is

$$s_1, s_2 = \frac{(f_1 + g_1) \pm [(f_1 + g_1)^2 - 4(f_1g_1 - f_2g_2)]^{1/2}}{2}.$$

Since f_1 and g_1 are each positive if (8.23) holds and $f_1g_1 > f_2g_2$, stability is ensured.[14] It can be seen that monotonic adjustment will result if $(f_1 - g_1)^2 >$

$-4f_2g_2$. Thus, if f_2 and g_2 are of the same sign, adjustment will be monotonic. If the two economies under question are dissimilar in terms of parameter magnitudes, f_2 and g_2 will be of differing signs, resulting in oscillatory adjustment.

ADJUSTMENT FOLLOWING A MONETARY DISTURBANCE ORIGINATING IN ONE COUNTRY

In this section we investigate the precise nature of the adjustment process following an unanticipated (and one-shot) monetary expansion in the home country, while the foreign country remains completely passive. Possible retaliation (or reaction by the foreign country is briefly discussed in the next section.

It has already been demonstrated that monetary expansion in the home country causes the spot exchange rate to depreciate by a factor of $(1 - \alpha - \alpha^*)/(\lambda\theta + \alpha + \alpha^*)$, while the equilibrium exchange rate and domestic price level ($\bar{p}$ as well as $\bar{q}$) are affected equiproportionately. The equilibrium level of foreign prices ($\bar{p}^*$) is, however, unchanged by this disturbance.[15] Immediately following the disturbance, adjustment occurs according to (8.24). Assuming monotonic adjustment for expository purposes, the general form of the solution to p_t is

$$(p_t - \bar{p}) = A_1 \exp^{-s_1 t} + A_2 \exp^{-s_2 t}. \qquad (8.25a)$$

Using (8.24) again, foreign prices adjust according to

$$(p_t^* - \bar{p}^*) = \frac{A_1(f_1 - s_1)}{f_2} \exp^{-s_1 t} + \frac{A_2(f_1 - s_1)}{f_2} \exp^{-s_2 t}. \qquad (8.25b)$$

It is easy to show that the stability conditions (8.22) or (8.23) ensure $\dot{p}_0$ and $\dot{p}_0^* > 0$. Thus, at the instant of the shock both price levels are rising. Next, evaluating (8.25a) at $t = 0$ yields

$$(p_0 - \bar{p}) = (A_1 + A_2) < 0 \qquad (8.26)$$

in view of the fact that $\bar{p}$ increases with m, while prices are initially sticky. Assume that $A_1 > 0$, so that $A_2 < 0$ and $|A_2| > A_1$. Further, since $\bar{p}^*$ is unaffected by m, and foreign prices are also sticky, (8.25b) yields (for $t = 0$)

$$A_1(f_1 - s_1) = -A_2(f_1 - s_2). \qquad (8.27)$$

From (8.27)

$$\frac{-(f_1 - s_2)}{(f_1 - s_1)} \left(\frac{A_2}{A_1} \right) = 1.$$

Recalling that $|A_2| > A_1$ and $A_2 < 0$, it follows that

$$1 > \frac{f_1 - s_2}{f_1 - s_1} > 0,$$

which in turn implies that

$$s_2 > s_1. \tag{8.28}$$

From (8.25a), evaluating at $t = 0$,

$$\dot{p}_0 = -(s_1 A_1 + s_2 A_2) > 0,$$

while

$$\ddot{p}_0 = (s_1^2 A_1 + s_2^2 A_2) < 0.$$

Thus, initially at least, the domestic price path is concave upward. Equation (8.25b) along with (8.27), at $t = 0$, yields

$$\dot{p}_0{}^* = \frac{A_1(f_1 - s_1)}{f_2} (s_2 - s_1)$$

and

$$\ddot{p}_0^* = \frac{A_1(f_1 - s_1)}{f_2} (s_1^2 - s_2^2).$$

Since the stability condition ensures that $\dot{p}_0^* > 0$, it follows that $(f_1 - s_1)/f_2 > 0$. Consequently, $\ddot{p}_0^* < 0$, that is, the path of foreign prices is also initially concave. Both domestic and foreign prices continue to rise until a turning point is reached. The turning point for p_t^* occurs at $t = t^*$, for which

$$\dot{p}^* = A_1 \left(\frac{f_1 - s_1}{f_2} \right) \left(s_2 \exp^{-s_2 t} - s_1 \exp^{-s_1 t} \right) = 0,$$

from which

$$t^* = \frac{\ln s_2 - \ln s_1}{s_2 - s_1}.$$ (8.29)

The turning point for domestic prices occurs at $t = \hat{t}$, such that

$$\dot{p} = -s_1 A_1 \exp^{-s_1 t} - s_2 A_2 \exp^{-s_2 t} = 0,$$

whence

$$\hat{t} = \frac{\ln(-s_2 A_2) - \ln(s_1 A_1)}{s_2 - s_1}.$$ (8.30)

Since $|A_2| > A_1$, it is clear that $\hat{t}$ occurs after t^*. These considerations imply that the adjustment paths for p_t and p_t^* are of the shapes depicted in Figure 8.1. Over the time interval $(0, t^*)$ both price levels are observed to be increasing (following the one-time domestic monetary expansion), while over $(t^*, \hat{t})$ the domestic price level continues to rise, overshooting its equilibrium level, while the foreign price level declines. Finally, over the third period following $\hat{t}$ both price levels are observed to be declining. Thus, three distinct phases of price behavior can be recognized.

A phase-space representation of these processes is also easily constructed as shown in Figure 8.2. Assuming $f_2, g_2 > 0$ as an illustrative case (the reader can easily construct the appropriate diagram for $f_1, g_1 < 0$), both the $\dot{p} = 0$ and $\dot{p}^* = 0$ lines are positively sloped, the latter line being steeper.

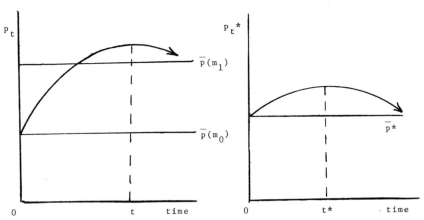

Paths for Domestic and Foreign Price Level Following Monetary Expansion in the Domestic Economy

Figure 8.1

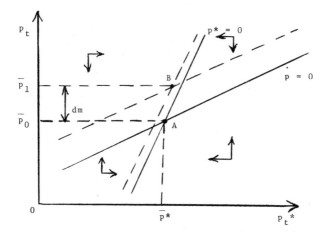

Paths for Domestic and Foreign Price Level Following Monetary Expansion in the Domestic Economy

Figure 8.2

Initial equilibrium occurs at A, and the directions of movement follow from
the stability requirement. An increase in m shifts both lines to the left, the
$\dot{p} = 0$ locus shifting more than the $\dot{p}^* = 0$ locus. The new equilibrium B lies
vertically above A. The heavy shaded line shows the movement of both price
levels.

Coming now to the nature of the exchange rate path, the latter is
obtained from (8.12''). Note that

$$\dot{e}_0 = \frac{1 - \alpha - \alpha^*}{\lambda\theta + \alpha + \alpha^*} (\dot{p}_0^* - \dot{p}_0),$$

which can be reduced to

$$\dot{e}_0 = \left(\frac{1 - \alpha - \alpha^*}{\lambda\theta + \alpha + \alpha^*} \right) [A_1(s_2 - s_1)] \left(\frac{f_1 - s_1}{f_2} - \frac{f_1}{f_1 - s_2} \right).$$
$$(8.31)$$

There are two sources of ambiguity in (8.31). First is the factor
$(1 - \alpha - \alpha^*)/(\lambda\theta + \alpha + \alpha^*)$, which determines whether there is overshooting
or undershooting and hence whether the exchange rate rises or falls to its new
equilibrium. Second, the third term in brackets in (8.31) is ambiguous unless
$f_1 < s_2$, in which case the entire third term is positive. This second source of
ambiguity raises an interesting possibility. Specifically, it is entirely possible
for the spot rate (after an initial, discrete jump) to deviate away from its new

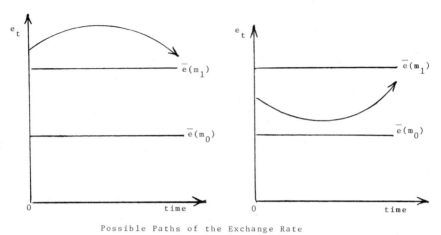

Possible Paths of the Exchange Rate

Figure 8.3

equilibrium value for a while before turning direction toward its steady state. Figure 8.3 depicts the possibility for both overshooting and undershooting. Another possibility is that of initial undershooting followed by delayed overshooting as in Figure 8.4. Clearly, direct unidirectional adjustment to the steady state is also possible, and without a knowledge of the precise magnitudes involved it is impossible to determine a priori the precise form of the exchange rate path. All that can be said is that if a positive solution for t^{**} can be found such that $\dot{e} = 0$, the exchange rate path is characterized by a turning point. Such a point t^{**}, if it exists, must satisfy

$$t^{**} = \frac{\ln s_1 + \ln s_2 + \ln(f_1 - s_1) + \ln\left[\dfrac{f_1 - s_2 - f_2}{f_2(f_1 - s_2)}\right] + \ln\left(\dfrac{f_2 - f_1 + s_1}{f_1}\right)}{s_1 + s_2}.$$

A final comment on the expectational behavior assumed in this chapter is in order. Specifically, the analysis of the previous sections has resulted in

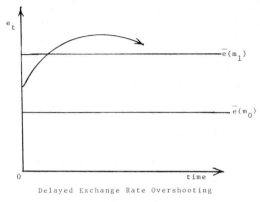

Delayed Exchange Rate Overshooting

Figure 8.4

second-order adjustment paths for the prices and exchange rate, while expected values of the same variables were assumed to follow simple exponential first-order paths (resulting from the use of [8.2] and [8.8]). The implication is that expectations will not, except by accident, be consistent with perfect foresight. This author is unpersuaded that this represents a fatal flaw in the analysis. While not conforming for perfect foresight, expectations in this model will still be semirational, that is, on average expectations will be approximately borne out. Further, a modification to (8.2), for example, to accommodate perfect foresight is easy enough. Specifically, an expectational scheme such as

$$x = -\theta_1(e - \bar{e}) + \theta_2(p - \bar{p}) \tag{8.32}$$

will, for appropriately chosen θ_1 and θ_2, result in perfectly forecast exchange rates. Formally, the state of the economy is completely described by three states: $(e - \bar{e})$, $(p - \bar{p})$, and $(p^* - \bar{p}^*)$. Only two of these complete independent sources of information as shown by (8.12″). Consequently, speculators basing their forecasts upon (8.32) will have utilized all the available and relevant information on the structure of the economy. This procedure was utilized in Chapter 5. Similar statements hold for $\dot{p}^E$ and $\dot{p}^{*E}$. The use of the more detailed expectational schemes will not alter any of the qualitative properties of the model.

The results of this section have implications for the international transmission of economic disturbances. The domestic monetary expansion results in inflation in the domestic economy, and this is associated with an initial period of rising foreign prices to be followed by a later period during which the foreign price level recedes to its original level. Thus, the foreign country is seen to import inflation, but only over the period $(0,t^*)$. Real disturbances will also be transmitted internationally. However, detailed analysis of the dynamics resulting from a real disturbance originating in one country is considerably more difficult (since equilibrium prices in both countries are affected) and is beyond the scope of the present chapter.

POLICY IMPLICATIONS

It was shown above that monetary policy pursued by one country will force the other into a long and possibly painful adjustment process if the latter remains completely inactive. Rather than passively accept the consequences of domestic monetary policy, the foreign country may attempt to offset its effects. What is clear is that a one-shot adjustment in foreign money supply will not succeed in eliminating all the imported effects.

Consider Figure 8.5, for example. In the absence of any action by the foreign country foreign prices follow an inverted U-shaped path. Suppose that foreign policy makers, unwilling to accept the externally imposed price increase engage in monetary contraction. Such an action would superimpose a downward path for p_t^* on the existing trajectory, and the resulting path is the heavily shaded path in Figure 8.5.

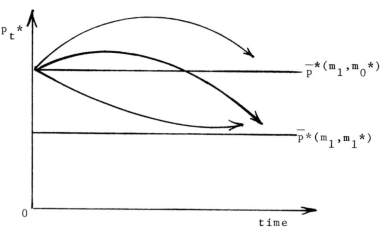

A Possible Attempt at Insulation in the Foreign Country

Figure 8.5

In general terms the path would be given by

$$p_t^* - \bar{p}(m_1, m_1^*) = B_1 \exp^{-s_1 t} + B_2 \exp^{-s_2 t} + \frac{A_1(f_1 - s_1)}{f_2}$$

$$\exp^{-s_1 t} + \frac{A_2(f_1 - s_2)}{f_2} \exp^{-s_2 t}.$$

Formally, the problem occurs because monetary adjustment alters the equilibrium price level in the country in which it occurs but not in the other. Thus, not only do flexible exchange rates fail to insulate the economy from an external (nominal) disturbance, but no simple policy (such as a one-time discretionary monetary adjustment) exists that will ensure insulation. A heavy burden of adjustment is placed upon the foreign country, the escape from which requires a costly policy of continual monetary adjustment. The precise form of this policy can be obtained from (8.24) by setting $\dot{p}^* = 0$. Thus, the policy requires $g_1(p^* - \bar{p}^*) = g_2(p - \bar{p})$, which can be related to foreign money supply changes by

$$(m^* - \bar{m}^*) = -\alpha(i^* - \bar{i}) + \left(\alpha^* \frac{g_2}{g_1} + 1 - \alpha^*\right)(p - \bar{p})$$

$$- (1 - \alpha^*)(e - \bar{e}), \qquad (8.33)$$

where $(i^* - \bar{i})$ replicates $(p^* - \bar{p})$, and $(p - \bar{p})$ and $(e - \bar{e})$ are as obtained in the previous section. Equation (8.33) can be reduced, for $t = 0$, to

$$\frac{(m_0^* - \bar{m}^*)}{\Delta m} = -\alpha^* \frac{g_2}{g_1} - (1 - \alpha^*)\left(\frac{\lambda\theta + 1}{\lambda\theta + \alpha + \alpha^*}\right).[16]$$

Thus, if $g_2 > 0$, the optimal rule calls for initial deflation of foreign money supply, but if $g_2 < 0$, the possibility cannot be ruled out that foreign money supply should initially be increased.

Once foreign authorities embark upon the optimal policy (8.33), actual domestic prices will no longer follow (8.24) but instead

$$\dot{p} = -\left(f_1 - \frac{f_2 g_2}{g_1}\right)(p - \bar{p}).$$

Since, $f_1 > f_2$ and $g_1 > g_2$, it is clear that domestic prices follow a simple first-order (exponential) path to the new equilibrium, and delayed (price) overshooting now does not occur.[17] The actual (realized) exchange rate path is also a simple exponential under the rule (8.33) and can be computed by using (8.31).

Hence, unlike the traditional framework wherein the independence of national monetary policies under floating rates is stressed, the analysis of this section suggests the need for coordination of such policies.

CONCLUSION

This chapter has constructed and analyzed a simple macrodynamic model of two interdependent economies. It is precisely within such a framework that fears about imported inflation are conventionally expressed. The analysis of this chapter has shown that if there is inflation in one country (resulting from monetary expansion), the other country, if it remains passive, will experience periods of both rising and falling prices. Furthermore, the scope for retaliation in order to offset the effects of the external disturbance may be quite limited in that a one-shot discretionary monetary adjustment cannot succeed. This underscores the need for coordinating certain economic policies even in a flexible exchange rate framework.

A rich variety of possibilities exists for the exchange rate in this framework. Specifically, the instantaneous exchange rate overshooting result popularized by Dornbusch (1976) is not robust for large economies. Several new possibilities with respect to monetary disturbances arise here; one of these is that of delayed overshooting. Finally, real disturbances were seen to invariably result in exchange rate undershooting on impact, although, here again, overshooting may occur as a delayed response.

Several extensions of this framework are clearly possible. One of these would seem to be to account for wealth accumulation, although this would place the framework outside the class of asset market (or speeds of adjustment) type of models, as mentioned earlier. What is clear, however, is that the incorporation of another dynamic relation describing wealth adjustments will considerably complicate the analysis in that the transition paths will now be of the third-order variety. How much additional insight will be gained by this piece of descriptive realism remains unclear. A more fruitful line of inquiry might be to extend this framework to allow for steady-state inflation. Such a framework could then properly analyze changes in the rates of growth of money supply or the effects of alternative monetary rules pursued in isolation in one country or simultaneously in both countries. A literature on the subject of alternative stabilization rules is already emerging. Turnovsky (1979a) discusses various "neutral" monetary rules in the context of a closed economy; in another paper (1979b) he derives and analyzes the "optimal monetary rule" in the context of the Dornbusch small economy framework. A small open economy framework is also utilized in Bilson (1979), Dornbusch (1979), and Witte (1979b) in their analyses of monetary rules.

NOTES

1. A two-country model is provided by Aoki and Canzoneri (1978). The latter is not within the asset market view of exchange rate determination. In addition the emphasis is on state controllability of prices and income, and, to this end, a state-space representation is employed.

2. As Miles (1978) points out, the existence of currency substitution may be an important channel of transmission of economic disturbances between countries.

3. It is possible to extend the framework below to incorporate demand determination of income.

4. The period length is that over which interest rates are defined in (8.1).

5. Consider the following example: suppose $i = 3$ percent and $i^* = 5$ percent, while expected depreciation from the point of view of home residents is 3 percent per period. Then, domestic residents are indifferent between assets denominated in either currency. Now suppose that foreigners expect appreciation at 4 percent rather than 3 percent, per period. From the point of view of the latter the return on foreign assets is $i^* = 5$ percent, with the ex ante net yield on domestic assets being 4 percent. Hence, foreign investors will shift out of domestic assets into foreign assets. Only if foreigners expect appreciation at 3 percent will there be no incentive for speculators in either country to shuffle their portfolios.

6. Empirical estimates of the interest rate and income elasticities of money demand do not exhibit great intercountry variation.

7. This restriction will necessarily be satisfied if δ and δ^* are not too different.

8. This follows from $(\bar{q} - \bar{q}^*) = (m - m^*) - \phi(\bar{y} - \bar{y})$. The latter, in turn, is based upon the solutions for $\bar{\imath}$ from the money markets.

9. This is based on

$$(\bar{q} - \bar{q}^*) = (\bar{p} - \bar{p}^*) + (\alpha + \alpha^*)\bar{T} = (m - m^*) - \phi(\bar{y} - \bar{y}^*).$$

10. Actually, Dornbusch does not use a deflator based on prices of both goods. His procedure is equivalent to setting $\alpha = 0$. In any case, since $\alpha < 1$, overshooting is certain to occur in a small country.

11. Dornbusch did not specifically analyze a real shock, although such an analysis follows directly from his framework. See Chapter 2.

12. For example, if (8.22a) is satisfied, then the coefficient on $(p - \bar{p})$ in (8.21a) can be shown to be negative if

$$-a_5\left(\frac{1 - \alpha - \alpha^*}{\lambda\theta + \alpha + \alpha^*}\right) - \left(\frac{1}{\lambda} + \theta\right)(a_4\alpha^* - a_3\alpha)\left(\frac{1 - \alpha - \alpha^*}{\lambda\theta + \alpha + \alpha^*}\right) - a_5$$

$$-\left(\frac{1}{\lambda} + \beta\right)[a_4\alpha^* + a_3(1 - \alpha)] < 0,$$

which requires that

$$-\left[\frac{1 - \alpha - \alpha^*}{\lambda\theta + \alpha + \alpha^*}\right] < \frac{a_5 + \left(\frac{1}{\lambda} + \beta\right)(a_4\alpha^* - a_3\alpha + a_3)}{a_5 + \left(\frac{1}{\lambda} + \theta\right)(a_4\alpha^* - a_3\alpha)}.$$

Let the right-hand side be called $G(>1)$. Then the condition reduces to $1 - \alpha - \alpha^*/\lambda\theta + \alpha + \alpha^* > -G$ (where $G > 1$), which, in turn, can be reduced to $1 > -G\lambda\theta + (1 - G)(\alpha + \alpha^*)$. Since $G > 1$, this last condition is trivially satisfied. A similar argument holds true for (8.22b).

13.

$$f_1 \equiv \pi \left(\left[a_5 + \left(\frac{1}{\lambda} + \theta \right) (a_4\alpha^* - a_3\alpha) \right] \left(\frac{1 - \alpha - \alpha^*}{\lambda\theta + \alpha + \alpha^*} \right) \right.$$

$$\left. + \left\{ a_5 + \left(\frac{1}{\lambda} + \beta \right) [a_4\alpha^* + a_3(1 - \alpha)] \right\} \right)$$

and

$$g_1 \equiv \pi^* \left(\left[b_5 + \left(\frac{1}{\lambda} + \theta \right) (b_3\alpha - b_4\alpha^*) \right] \left(\frac{1 - \alpha - \alpha^*}{\lambda\theta + \alpha + \alpha^*} \right) \right.$$

$$\left. + \left\{ b_5 + \left(\frac{1}{\lambda} + \beta^* \right) [b_3\alpha + (1 - \alpha)b_4] \right\} \right).$$

14. The stability condition (8.23) is strongly sufficient in that it requires both $f_1, g_1 > 0$. Weaker conditions will also result in stability as long as $(f_1 + g_1) > 0$.

15. Recall (8.18b), which shows that $\bar{q}^*$ is not affected by m and the definition $\bar{q}^* = (1 - \alpha^*)\bar{p}^* + \alpha(\bar{p} - \bar{e})$. Since $d\bar{q}/dm = 0$, while $d\bar{p}/dm = d\bar{e}/dm = 1$, it follows that $d\bar{p}^*/dm = 0$.

16. Recall that i^* and p are initially fixed, at $t = 0$.

17. Again, the domestic economy derives benefits from the foreign policy action in that domestic prices adjust somewhat quicker than if the foreign authorities had remained inactive.

REFERENCES

Aoki, M., and M. Canzoneri. 1978. "Macroeconomic Policy in Dynamic Two-Country Model." *Annals of Economic and Social Measurement* 6(Spring): 631–50.

Bilson, J. 1979. "The Vicious Circle Hypothesis." *IMF Staff Papers* 26(March): 1–37.

Branson, W. 1976. "Asset Markets and Relative Prices in Exchange Rate Determination." *Seminar Paper no. 66.* Institute for International Economic Studies, Stockholm, Sweden, December.

Dooley, M., and P. Isard. 1979. "The Portfolio Balance Model of Exchange Rates." Discussion Paper. Washington, D.C.. Federal Reserve Board, International Finance Section.

Dornbusch, R. 1979. "Monetary Stabilization, Intervention and Real Appreciation. Mimeographed. Rio de Janeiro, Brazil, October.

———. 1976. "Expectations and Exchange Rate Dynamics." *Journal of Political Economy* 84(December) 1161–76.

Dornbusch, R., and S. Fischer. 1978. "Exchange Rates and the Current Account." Mimeographed. Cambridge, Mass.: MIT.

Henderson, D. 1979. "The Dynamic Effects of Exchange Market Intervention Policy: Two Extreme Views and a Synthesis." Discussion Paper. Federal Reserve Board, International Finance Section, Washington, D.C..

Kouri, P. 1976. "The Exchange Rate and Balance of Payments in the Short Run and in the Long Run: A Monetary Approach." *Scandinavian Journal of Economics* 78(2): 208–304.

Mathieson, D. 1977. "The Impact of Monetary and Fiscal Policy under Flexible Exchange Rates and Alternative Expectations Structures." *IMF Staff Papers* 24(November): 535–68.

Miles, M. 1978. "Currency Substitution, Flexible Exchange Rates and Monetary Independence." *American Economic Review* 68(June): 428–36.

Rodriguez, C. 1977. "The Role of Trade Flows in Exchange Rate Determination: A Rational Expectations Approach." Mimeographed. New York: Columbia University.

Samuelson, P. A., and S. Swamy. 1974. "Invariant Economic Index Numbers and Canonical Duality: Survey and Synthesis." *American Economic Review* 64(September): 566–93.

Turnovsky, S. 1979a. "Alternative Neutral Monetary Policies in an Inflationary Economy." *Journal of Macroeconomics* (1): 33–63.

———. 1979b. "Optimal Monetary Policy under Flexible Exchange Rates." *Journal of Economic Dynamics and Control* 1(February): 85–99.

Witte, W. 1979a. "Dynamic Adjustment in an Open Economy with Flexible Exchange Rates." *Southern Economic Journal* 45(April): 1072–90.

———. 1979b. "Expectations, Monetary Policy Rules and Macroeconomic Stability." Mimeographed. University Park, Pennsylvania, November.

9

TOWARD A MULTI-COUNTRY MODEL OF EXCHANGE RATE DETERMINATION

Recent work on flexible exchange rates has emphasized the short-run volatility of exchange rates. A strong statement of this view is embodied in the exchange rate overshooting hypothesis popularized by Dornbusch (1976, 1979) and discussed extensively in Chapters 2 and 3. Specifically, in a small economy characterized by floating exchange rates, short-run price inflexibility, money market equilibrium, and perfect capital mobility, Dornbusch shows that an increase in nominal money supply implies a more-than-proportional short-run exchange rate response. This result is not modified if steady-state inflation is incorporated (Frankel 1979), although qualifications result if (1) income is endogenously determined (Dornbusch 1976, app.), (2) continuous money market equilibrium does not prevail (Bhandari, in press; Niehans 1977), (3) price expectations are introduced (Arndt 1976), (4) a short-run monetary intervention rule is incorporated (Bilson 1979; Bhandari and Turnovsky 1980), or (5) other sources of dynamics (such as income dynamics) are permitted (Bhandari 1981; Witte 1979). Further modifications to this result emerge if the short-run price stickiness assumption is dropped and imperfect substitutability of domestic and foreign assets is permitted (Branson 1976; Turnovsky, in press),[1] and a useful anatomy of the exchange rate overshooting hypothesis is provided by Frenkel and Rodriguez (1980).

A common theme to all of the above analysis is the small-country assumption. Such an assumption, while analytically convenient, is hardly realistic in describing most bilateral trade relations.[2]

The two-country framework discussed in a previous chapter imposes a certain symmetry between these countries—for example, if one country's exchange rate or terms of trade improve, the other's must necessarily deteriorate, and so on. Consequently, this chapter constructs a model of three interdependent economies. The approach may be viewed as an extension of the simple but elegant framework proposed by Dornbusch (1976). To keep the analysis tractable it is assumed that the three economies in question are structurally similar.

The next section specifies the analytical framework, while the second section investigates the impact effects of an increase in nominal money originating in one country on the two independent bilateral exchange rates. The principal result of this section is that the exchange rate overshooting result is not necessarily robust in this multicountry framework, although there may be a presumption in favor of the result based on reasonable parameter values, provided that money demand functions do not exhibit great intercountry variation. The consequences of the disturbance for the bilateral exchange rate between the other two countries are also investigated.

SETUP OF THE MODEL

The hypothetical world of this model consists of three countries, A, B, and C, each of which is specialized in the production of a distinct, homogenous commodity. Universal free trade prevails, so that consumers in each country have access to each of the three goods, and these are regarded by agents everywhere as being imperfectly substitutable on the demand side. Instantaneous money market equilibrium obtains in each country, and there is no currency substitution—that is, the money stock in any country is held entirely by domestic agents. The capital markets of all countries are perfectly integrated, and triangular arbitrage ensures that security yields expressed in any currency are equal, net of anticipated exchange rate movements. Thus, in addition to the local money market wealth owners in each country have access to worldwide capital market dealing in homogenous risk-free securities. Output is fixed at its respective full-employment level in each country.

The model to be detailed below contains a description of the money market and aggregate demand in each country. Although the real sector is irrelevant for determining the instantaneous exchange rates, the dynamic evolution of the latter is governed by the interaction of real and monetary phenomena. In addition to money market and commodity market specifications, certain consistency relations necessitated by direct and cross arbitrage between currencies and securities must hold. The model is log-linear in all variables introduced below except nominal interest rates.

Denote by e^{AB} the (log) exchange rate between the currencies of A and B (that is, the A currency price of one unit of B currency) and by e^{BC} the (log) exchange rate between B and C (the B currency price of one unit of C currency). Spot arbitrage will ensure that in the absence of exchange controls and transactions costs the exchange rate between A and C is given by

$$e^{AC} = e^{AB} + e^{BC}. \tag{9.1}$$

Next, let p^A, p^B, and p^C denote the (log) own-currency price of domestic output in A, B, and C, respectively. From the point of view of A's residents then, the consumer price index (CPI) is given by

$$Q^A = W_A^A p^A + W_A^B (p^B + e^{AB}) + W_A^C (p^C + e^{AB} + e^{BC}), \tag{9.2}$$
$$\sum_j W_A^j = 1, j = A, B, C,$$

where W_A^j is the weight allocated to the A currency price of good j by A's residents. It will be supposed that the underlying utility functions are of the Cobb-Douglas variety, so that the weights correspond to real expenditures shares (for example, W_A^C is the share of C's expenditure falling on good A). Equation (9.3) expresses the condition of money market equilibrium in country A:

$$\bar{M}^A - Q^A = l_1^A \bar{y}^A - l_2^A i^A, \tag{9.3}$$

where $\bar{y}^A$ is the full-employment output in A, and i^A is the nominal yield on securities denominated in A's currency. Similar considerations imply that the price index and money market conditions in countries B and C are given by (9.4) through (9.7).

$$Q^B = W_B^A (p^A - e^{AB}) + W_B^B p^B + W_B^C (p^C + e^{BC}), \tag{9.4}$$
$$\sum_j W_B^j = 1, j = A, B, C,$$

$$\bar{M}^B - Q^B = l_1^B \bar{y}^B - l_2^B i^B, \tag{9.5}$$

$$Q^C = W_C^A (p^A - e^{AB} - e^{BC}) + W_C^B (p^B - e^{BC}) + W_C^C p^C, \tag{9.6}$$

$$\sum_j W_C^j = 1, j = A, B, C,$$
$$\bar{M}^C - Q^C = l_1^C \bar{y}^C - l_2^C i^C. \tag{9.7}$$

Triangular arbitrage ensures that net interest rates are equalized across countries, that is,

$$i^A = i^B + \varepsilon^{AB} \tag{9.8}$$

and

$$i^B = i^C + \varepsilon^{BC}, \tag{9.9}$$

where ε^{AB} is the expected rate of depreciation of currency A vis-à-vis B, and ε^{BC} is the expected rate of depreciation between currencies B and C. It is assumed that expectations are uniform across agents in all countries.[3] Expectational consistency requires that

$$\varepsilon^{AC} = \varepsilon^{AB} + \varepsilon^{BC}. \tag{9.10}$$

If (9.10) did not hold, exploitable arbitrage profit possibilities would remain. Finally, expectations are described by the simple regressive schemes

$$\varepsilon^{AB} = -\theta(e^{AB} - \bar{e}^{AB}), \tag{9.11}$$

and

$$\varepsilon^{BC} = -\theta(e^{BC} - \bar{e}^{BC}), \qquad \theta > 0, \tag{9.12}$$

$\bar{e}^{AB}$ and $\bar{e}^{BC}$ being the steady-state values of the relevant exchange rates and assumed known to market participants. The speed of adjustment of expectations is assumed to be the same for both bilateral exchange rates, but no substantive difference would be made if this assumption were not retained.

The real sector of the model is described by three relations characterizing aggregate demand in each country. Specifically, aggregate demand (for the domestic good) is given by the sum of total domestic absorption and the net trade balance. Total absorption in any country is determined by domestic income as well as aggregate demand in the other two countries (since a part of the latter falls on the domestic good), while the net trade balance depends upon the relevant terms of trade between exportables and the two importables. In the interest of analytic simplicity and to avoid specifying price expectations, we assume that real interest rates do not enter the aggregate demand functions. As far as the present chapter is concerned, this concession makes no difference at all; and even with respect to the dynamic properties of the model, the difference is only quantitative not qualitative. Consequently,

$$d^A = u^A + \delta^{AB}(e^{AB} + p^B - p^A) + \delta^{AC}(e^{AB} + e^{BC} + p^C - p^A)$$
$$+ W_B^A d^B + W_C^A d^C + \gamma^A \bar{y}^A, \tag{9.13}$$

$$d^B = u^B + \delta^{BA}(p^A - e^{AB} - p^B) + \delta^{BC}(e^{BC} + p^C - p^B)$$
$$+ W_A^B d^A + W_C^B d^C + \gamma^B \bar{y}^B, \tag{9.14}$$

$$d^C = u^C + \delta^{CA}(p^A - e^{AB} - e^{BC} - p^C) + \delta^{CB}(p^B - e^{BC} - p^C)$$
$$+ W_A^C d^A + \bar{W}_B^C d^B + \gamma^C \bar{y}^C, \tag{9.15}$$

all coefficients being defined positively. The terms u^j and $j = A,B,C$ denote autonomous components of expenditure in each country. Consider (9.13), for example: total demand for good A is given by the sum of an autonomous component u^A, the net trade surplus with respect to the rest of the world, which is determined by the terms of trade terms, total spending by domestic residents on good A (determined by $\bar{y}^A$), and that part of foreign aggregate demand that impinges on this commodity. Thus, fractions W_B^A of aggregate demand in B and W_C^A in C fall upon good A; the same fractions were utilized in constructing the price index in (9.2). Similar considerations apply to (9.12) and (9.15).

Equations (9.13) through (9.15) can now be converted to reduced form by eliminating the terms involving foreign aggregate demand in each equation using recursive substitution and ignoring terms involving the "second order of smalls." From (9.13)

$$d^A = (u^A + W_B^A u^B + W_C^A u^C) + (\delta^{AB} - W_B^A \delta^{BA})(e^{AB} + p^B - p^A)$$
$$+ (\delta^{AC} - W_C^A \delta^{CA})(e^{AB} + e^{BC} + p^C - p^A)$$
$$+ (W_B^A \delta^{BC} - W_C^A \delta^{CB})(p^B - e^{BC} - p^C) + \gamma^A \bar{y}^A + W_B^A \gamma^B \bar{y}^B$$
$$+ W_C^A \gamma^C \bar{y}^C,$$

where the terms $W_B^A W_A^B \delta^A$, $W_B^A W_C^B \delta^C$, $W_C^A W_A^C \delta^A$, and $W_C^A W_B^C \delta^B$ involve second-round feedbacks and have been ignored. (Recall that W_j^i is a fraction.)

Similarly,

$$d^B = (u^B + W_A^B u^A + W_C^B u^C) + (\delta^{BA} - W_A^B \delta^{AB})(p^A - e^{AB} - p^B)$$
$$+ (\delta^{BC} - W_C^B \delta^{CB})(e^{BC} + p^C - p^B) + (W_A^B \delta_C^A - W_C^B \delta^{CA})$$
$$(e^{AB} + e^{BC} + p^C - p^A) + \gamma^B \bar{y}^B + W_A^B \gamma^A \bar{y}^A$$
$$+ W_C^B \gamma^C \bar{y}^C$$

and

$$d^C = (u^C + W_A^C u^A + W_B^C u^B) + (\delta^{CA} - W_A^C \delta^{AC})$$
$$(p^A - e^{AB} - e^{BC} - p^C) + (\delta^{CB} - w_B^C \delta^{BC})(p^B - e^{BC} - p^C)$$
$$+ (W_A^C \delta^{AB} - W_B^C \delta^{BA})(e^{AB} + p^B - p^A) + \gamma^C \bar{y}^C + W_A^C \gamma^A \bar{y}^A$$
$$+ W_B^C \gamma^B \bar{y}^C.$$

Equations (9.13) through (9.15) highlight the mutual interdependencies that exist between the three countries. These interdependencies result from trade in commodities and securities. The terms-of-trade expressions make clear the fact that conventionally expected effects are conditional upon certain constraints upon parameter magnitudes. Consider (9.13), for example. An increase in the (domestic currency) price of B relative to that of A will switch total demand in favor of A only if the term $(\delta^{AB} - W_B^A \delta^{BA})$ is positive. Since W_j^i is a fraction, the latter term will be positive provided that the structural elasticities δ^{AB} and δ^{BA} are of roughly similar magnitudes. Similar considerations apply to the terms of trade between A and C. The explanation of the ambiguity is straightforward: an increase in p^B, for example, has a direct terms-of-trade effect from (9.13) and increases d^A. At the same time, however, aggregate demand in B declines, and a part of this decline is reflected in an induced reduction in net foreign demand for A. The net effect is thus given by the term $(\delta^{AB} - W_B^A \delta^{BA})$. By contrast a small-country framework ignores feedback considerations, and the secondary term $W_B^A \delta^{BA}$ is not considered. One other feature of (9.13) that merits attention is that aggregate demand for A is influenced not only by the direct terms of trade between A and B and A and C (the second and third terms) but also by the terms of trade between B and C (the fourth term), since the latter affects d^B and d^C and hence d^A. The direction of the effect of this last influence is, however, quite ambiguous without knowledge of the structural parameters of the model. Identical considerations are operative for equations (9.14) and (9.15).

The dynamic relations of the model are described by (9.16) through (9.18) and posit, as in Dornbusch (1976), that domestic prices slowly adjust according to commodity market excess demand:

$$\dot{p}^A = \pi^A(d^A - \bar{y}^A), \qquad \pi^A > 0, \tag{9.16}$$

$$\dot{p}^B = \pi^B(d^B - \bar{y}^B), \qquad \pi^B > 0, \tag{9.17}$$

$$\dot{p}^C = \pi^C(d^C - \bar{y}^C), \qquad \pi^C > 0. \tag{9.18}$$

In the steady state prices and exchange rates have attained their equilibrium values $(\bar{p}^A, \bar{p}^B, \bar{p}^C, \bar{e}^{AB}, \bar{e}^{BC})$, and expectational phenomena are eliminated, implying in turn that all interests are equalized worldwide—that is, $\bar{\imath}^A = \bar{\imath}^B = \bar{\imath}^C = \bar{\imath}$.

AN INCREASE IN NOMINAL MONEY IN ONE COUNTRY

Consider now an unanticipated permanent increase in nominal money supply in country A. It will become clear that the effects of an increase in $\bar{M}^A$ are not symmetrical with those of an increase in, say $\bar{M}^B$. It is readily apparent at the outset that the increase in $\bar{M}^A$ will result in equiproportionate increases in $\bar{p}^A$ and $\bar{e}^{AB}$, while other steady-state price levels and $\bar{e}^{BC}$ are totally unaffected. This feature will clearly be present in any model that preserves the long-run neutrality properties of money and that is not specific to the present framework. The reader may verify that

$$\frac{d\bar{e}^{AB}}{d\bar{M}^A} = \frac{d\bar{p}^A}{d\bar{M}^A} = 1, \frac{d\bar{p}^B}{d\bar{M}^A} = \frac{d\bar{p}^C}{d\bar{M}^A} = \frac{d\bar{e}^{BC}}{d\bar{M}^A} = \frac{d\bar{\imath}}{d\bar{M}^A} = 0$$

is indeed a solution to the steady state of the model by substituting these solutions in the steady-state version of equations (9.1) through (9.18).

Next, given the national price levels are initially fixed, equations (9.3), (9.5), and (9.7) yield, after substitution from (9.2), (9.4), (9.6), (9.8), and (9.9), the short-run matrix equation

$$\begin{bmatrix} (W_A^B + W_A^C) & W_A^C & -l_2^A \\ (W_B^A + l_2^B\theta) & -W_B^C & l_2^B \\ (W_C^A + l_2^C\theta) & (W_C^A + W_C^B + l_2^C\theta) & l_2^C \end{bmatrix} \begin{bmatrix} \dfrac{de^{AB}}{d\bar{M}^A} \\[2ex] \dfrac{de^{BC}}{d\bar{M}^A} \\[2ex] \dfrac{di^A}{d\bar{M}^A} \end{bmatrix} = \begin{bmatrix} 1 \\ l_2^B\theta \\ l_2^C\theta \end{bmatrix},$$

(9.19)

which involves the two bilateral exchange rates and one nominal interest rate. Given the latter, the other interest rates are residually determined as shown below.

Considerable interest attaches to determining whether e^{AB} overshoots its long-run equilibrium value and whether the other bilateral exchange rate (that is, e^{BC}) depreciates or appreciates. Thus, manipulating (9.19), we obtain

$$\Delta \frac{de^{AB}}{d\bar{M}^A} = -[l_2^C W_B^C + l_2^B(W_C^A + W_C^B + l_2^C\theta)]$$
$$- l_2^B \theta[l_2^A(W_C^A + W_C^B + l_2^C\theta)]$$
$$- l_2^C \theta W_B^C l_2^A, \tag{9.20}$$

where

$$\Delta = -W_A^B[l_2^C W_B^C + l_2^B(W_C^A + W_C^B + l_2^C \theta)]$$
$$- W_A^C(l_2^C W_B^C + l_2^B W_C^B)$$
$$- (W_B^A + l_2^B \theta)[l_2^C W_A^C + l_2^A(W_C^A + W_C^B + l_2^C \theta)]$$
$$- (W_C^A + l_2^C \theta) W_B^C l_2^A < 0.$$

Hence, e^{AB} depreciates unambiguously. Overshooting occurs if $\Delta(de^{AB}/d\bar{M}^A < \Delta$ and conversely (recall that Δ is negative). It can be shown that the overshooting condition can be written as

$$W_A^A(l_2^C W_B^C + W_C^A l_2^B + l_2^B l_2^C \theta + W_C^B l_2^B) + W_C^A W_A^C l_2^B >$$
$$l_2^A(W_C^A W_B^C + W_C^B W_B^A + W_B^A W_C^A + W_B^A l_2^C \theta) + W_A^C W_B^A l_2^C.[4]$$

$$\tag{9.21}$$

Examination of (9.21) demonstrates that the overshooting condition depends in a complicated way upon asset market parameters of the entire world, and overshooting of the spot exchange rate need not necessarily result from the monetary expansion. This ambiguity notwithstanding, there are similarities between equation (9.21) and the results obtainable from the small-country framework utilized by Dornbusch (1976). Specifically, the extent of overshooting in the latter framework is (in or notation)

$$\frac{W_A^A}{1 - W_A^A + l_2^A} > 0.[5] \tag{9.22}$$

Certain similarities between (9.21) and (9.22) are apparent. For example, as W_A^A (the weight attached to domestic prices in the price index of A) increases, the likelihood of overshooting is seen to increase in (9.21), or the extent of overshooting, if any, increases. A similar statement is true of (9.22). An increase in l_2^A (income elasticity money demand) has precisely the opposite effects in both (9.21) and (9.22). The symmetry ends here, however, and a contrast is provided by an increase in θ (adjustment speed of exchange rate expectation). While in the small-country case an increase in the latter leads to an unambiguous decline in the extent of overshooting, this is not true in a multicountry world, and the net effect depends upon $l_2^C (W_A^A l_2^B - l_2^A W_B^A) \gtrless 0$. The contribution of other parameters appearing in (9.21) can be similarly assessed. For instance, an increase in W_B^A (the share of A's good in B's consumption) will diminish the likelihood of overshooting, but an increase in l_2^B (interest rate semielasticity of money demand in the other country) will have precisely the opposite effect.

Next consider the extent to which the result contained in (9.21) is dependent upon intercountry differences in money demand functions. If world money demand functions were identical, (9.21) would become

$$W_A^A (l_2 W_B^C + W_C^A l_2 + l_2 \theta + W_C^B l_2) + W_C^A W_A^C l_2 >$$
$$l_2(W_C^A W_B^C + W_C^B W_B^A + W_C^A W_B^A + W_B^A l_2 \theta) + W_A^C W_B^A l_2,$$

$$(9.21')$$

where

$$l_2^A = l_2^B = l_2^C = l_2.$$

Some further insight can be gained by expressing (9.21') alternatively as

$$1 > (W_A^B + W_B^A + W_A^C) + \frac{(W_C^A - W_B^A)(W_B^C - W_A^C)}{W_B^C + W_C^A + W_C^B + l_2 \theta}. \qquad (9.23)$$

Since the terms W_i^j are each fractions, the last term on the right-hand side of (9.23) involves the "second order of smalls" and may safely be ignored. Thus, exchange rate overshooting (assuming identical world money demand functions) requires that the shares of expenditure in countries B and C allocated to good A plus the share of good B in country A's expenditure fall short of unity. Empirical analysis alone can definitively settle this question, although it may be argued that unless one considers "banana republics," there appears to be a presumption in favor of overshooting based on (9.23). For example, assume that each country allocates half its expenditure to its own product, the other half being divided equally between goods from the other two countries. Then each of W_A^B, W_B^A, and W_A^C is one-quarter, implying that overshooting occurs.[6]

It has been seen, therefore, that provided taste patterns in countries B and C are not severely biased in favor of the good produced in country A (see [9.23]), there appears to be a case for overshooting subject to the further qualification that there is not substantial variation in cross-country money demand functions. To see the role of the latter more clearly, consider for a moment the two-country case (A and B only). A straightforward application of the above framework demonstrates that

$$\frac{de^{AB}}{d\bar{M}^A} = \frac{1 + l_2^A \theta}{1 + l_2^A \theta + (1 - W_B^B)\dfrac{l_2^A}{l_2^B} - W_A^A},$$

whence overshooting requires that

$$\frac{W_A^A}{1 - W_B^B} > \frac{l_2^A}{l_2^B}. \tag{9.24}$$

If l_2^A and l_2^B are of a similar order of magnitude, the case for overshooting is clearly very strong and requires only that the sum of fractions of expenditure of A and B on their own goods exceed unity (that is, $W_A^A + W_B^B > 1$). The case is made even stronger if $l_2^A > l_2^B$, but complications result in the opposite circumstance, and there exists a critical positive value of ($l_2^B - l_2^A$) for which overshooting will not occur even if $(W_A^A + W_B^B) > 1$. Similar (but clearly more complicated considerations) apply to equation (9.21).

The above digression into the two-country world provides another valuable insight into the effects of increasing the number of countries. It is clear that (9.21) is a far more stringent condition than (9.24). Further, if money demand functions are assumed identical, overshooting in the three-country world requires (9.23), while in a two-country world this requires that $(W_A^A + W_B^B) > 1$, which is the same as

$$W_B^A + W_A^B < 1.[7] \tag{9.25}$$

Equation (9.23) is seen to be a stricter condition than (9.25). It can be argued, therefore, that as the number of countries considered increases, the likelihood of overshooting diminishes.[8]

A final special case is provided by the situation where all countries are identical to the extent that $l_2^A = l_2^B = l_2^C$ and $W^{ij} = W, i, j = A, B, C$. Substituting these magnitudes into (9.21), it follows that both sides of the expression are precisely equal—there can be neither overshooting nor undershooting in this case (that is,

$$\frac{de^{AB}}{d\bar{M}^A} = \frac{d\bar{e}^{AB}}{d\bar{M}^A} = 1).$$

Consider now the effects of A's monetary expansion upon the bilateral exchange rate between B and C, that is, e^{BC}. From (9.19) it can be shown that

$$\Delta \frac{de^{BC}}{d\bar{M}^A} = (1 + l_2^A \theta)(W_C^A l_2^B - W_B^A l_2^C) \overset{>}{\underset{<}{}} 0. \tag{9.26}$$

Since $\Delta < 0$, for e^{BC} to depreciate it is necessary that $W_B^A/W_C^A > l_2^B/l_2^C$—that is, the ratio of A's share in the consumption of B to its share in C must exceed the ratio between the interest rate semielasticity of money demand in B to that in C. The ambiguity in e^{BC} notwithstanding, the exchange rate between A and C ($e^{AC} = e^{AB} + e^{BC}$) can also be seen to unambiguously depreciate.[9]

Coming now to the effects of the monetary expansion in A on the interest rates in B and C, (9.6) indicates that if e^{BC} depreciates, C's price index Q^C declines, necessitating a decline in i^C. The effect upon B's price index—and hence i^B—does not, however, depend upon the direction of change in e^{BC} and is unambiguously negative.[10] These considerations make it clear that if e^{BC} appreciates, interest rates in B and C move in opposite directions; if e^{BC} depreciates, the movement is in the same direction. Finally, A's price index increases following the monetary expansion, but the effect on i^A depends upon whether e^{AB} overshoots. If there is overshooting, (9.8) makes it clear that i^A declines unambiguously. Otherwise, the effect on i^A is not immediately obvious and depends upon specific parameter magnitudes.

Once the impact effects have worked themselves out, the world begins a transition to the new steady state as governed by the dynamic relations (9.16) through (9.18) and the aggregate demand equations (9.13) through (9.15). A precise investigation of the dynamic behavior of the three economies is outside the scope of the present work. It is clear, however, that adjustment will occur according to a third-order differential equation system. Thus, a considerable variety of price (and exchange rate) movement is likely, and phases of rising and falling prices in some or all countries are quite possible.[11] In the end price levels in B and C and the exchange rate e^{BC} will have returned to their predisturbance levels.

The policy implications of this section are straightforward. Despite freely floating exchange rates, the effects of a policy action instituted in one country are not limited to that country alone. In general every country is forced into a prolonged adjustment process. Consequently, there may be pressures upon individual countries to coordinate their monetary policies. This prescription is somewhat at variance with traditional accounts of flexible exchange rate systems that stress autonomy of national economic policies.

CONCLUSION

This chapter has constructed a rudimentary model of bilateral exchange rate determination in a three-country trading world. The approach is based on an extension of the sticky-price monetary model proposed by Dornbusch (1976). The results of the investigation indicate that exchange rate over-shooting need not necessarily occur, although there is a presumption in favor of this result based on reasonable parameter values, provided that money demand functions do not exhibit great cross-country variation. The chapter also reveals that increasing the number of countries is likely to diminish this presumption. Although the present discussion focuses on the impact effects of an increase in nominal money in one country on the two bilateral exchange rates, the dynamic implications of such a disturbance are far more complex than in a one-country model. The model also lends support to the argument that national economic policies, even in a floating exchange rate world, may need to be coordinated rather than autonomous.

NOTES

1. Another line of inquiry has been to incorporate announcement effects. See Wilson (1979), Gray and Turnovsky (1979), Bhandari and Hanson (1980), and Dornbusch and Fischer (1978).

2. For example, the major proportion of trade of any Western European nation is conducted with a few trade partners within this area rather than with the United States. Even if, say, Belgium could regard its actions as not affecting the United States, trade relations between Belgium and Holland are much more important for both their economies than their relations with the United States.

3. The basis for this assumption is the fact that there is a single worldwide capital market and the further assumption that all agents have access to the same information set, regardless of national origin.

4. We have chosen this form of the condition to highlight the role of A country parameters such as W_A^A and l_2^A.

5. Actually, Dornbusch does not use a price index but, rather, the domestic price level to deflate nominal money balances. This procedure is equivalent to setting $W_A^A = 1$ in (9.22). In any case overshooting remains.

6. If, however, B and C are banana republics (say B is bananas and C is coffee, while A is food), then $(W_A^B + W_A^C)$ in (9.23) would be expected to exceed unity.

7. Recall that $W_A^A + W_B^A = 1$ and $W_B^B + W_A^B = 1$.

8. It is doubtful that in an N country world (where N is large) one could make a case for

overshooting based on reasonable parameter values. Pending future research, this statement is to be regarded as tentative.

9. The model would be internally inconsistent if this were in fact not the case, since one can rename country B as C and country C as B.

10. This can be seen by evaluating $\Delta(dQ^B/d\bar{M}^A)$ by using (9.4).

11. That adjustment occurs according to a third-order differential equation system can be seen by noting that the model incorporates three different sources of dynamics, that is, equations (9.16) through (9.18). These equations can be reduced to a simple homogenous system

$$(\dot{p}^A, \dot{p}^B, \dot{p}^C)' = K(p^A - \bar{p}^A, p^B - \bar{p}^B, p^C - \bar{p}^C)',$$

where K is a 3×3 matrix of coefficients and the prime denotes a column vector. It should also be noted that there is no possibility of perfect foresight expectations along this adjustment path. The reason for this is that actual exchange rates also follow a third-order process, while expected exchange rates follow first-order processes as postulated in (9.11) and (9.12).

REFERENCES

Arndt, S. 1976. "On Exchange Rate Dynamics." Discussion Paper. Mimeographed. Washington, D.C.: U.S. Treasury.

Bhandari, J. "Exchange Rate Overshooting Revisited." *Manchester School*, in press.

_____. 1981. "A Simple Transnational Model of Large Open Economies." *Southern Economic Journal* (April): in press.

Bhandari, J., and D. Hanson. 1980. "The International Transmission of Anticipated Economic Disturbances." Mimeographed, Carbondale, IL: Southern Illinois University.

Bhandari, J., and S. Turnovsky. 1980. "Alternative Monetary Policies in an Inflationary Equilibrium Model of the Open Economy." Mimeographed. Carbondale, IL.

Bilson, J. 1979. "The Vicious Circle Hypothesis." *IMF Staff Papers* 26 (March): 1–37.

Branson, W. 1976. "Asset Markets and Relative Prices in Exchange Rate Determination." Seminar paper no. 66. I.I.E.S., Sweden.

Dornbusch, R. 1979. "Monetary Stabilization, Intervention and Real Appreciation." Mimeographed. Rio de Janeiro, Brazil.

_____. 1976. "Expectations and Exchange Rate Dynamics." *Journal of Political Economy* 84 (December): 1161–76.

Dornbusch, R., and S. Fischer. 1978. "Exchange Rates and the Current Account." Mimeographed. Cambridge, MA: MIT.

Frankel, J. 1979. "On the Mark—A Theory of Floating Exchange Rates Based on Real Interest Differentials." *American Economic Review* 69 (September): 610–22.

Frenkel, J., and C. A. Rodriguez. 1980. "Anatomy of the Exchange Rate Overshooting Hypothesis." Mimeographed. Chicago.

Gray, M., and S. Turnovsky. 1979. "The Stability of Exchange Rate Dynamics under Perfect Myopic Foresight." *International Economic Review* 20 (October): 643–60.

Niehans, J. 1977. "Exchange Rate Dynamics with Stock/Flow Interaction." *Journal of Political Economy* 85 (December): 1245–57.

Turnovsky, S. "The Asset Market Approach to Exchange Rate Determination." *Journal of Macroeconomics.* in press.

Wilson, C. 1979. "Anticipated Shocks and Exchange Rate Dynamics." *Journal of Political Economy* 87 (June): 639–47.

Witte, W. Forthcoming. "Policy Interdependence under Flexible Exchange Rates: A Dynamic Analysis of Price Interactions." In *Economic Interdependence and Flexible Exchange Rates*, edited by J. Bhandari and B. Putnam. Cambridge: MIT Press.

_____. 1979. "Dynamic Adjustment in an Open Economy with Flexible Exchange Rates." *Southern Economic Journal* 45 (April): 1072–90.

10

A DYNAMIC MODEL OF
ENTREPÔT TRADE

INTRODUCTION

It is now widely recognized that most, if not all, of the world's economies were substantially affected by supply shocks in the 1970s. In particular the worldwide recession of 1974/75 is generally attributed in large part to the quadrupling of crude oil prices that occurred between late 1973 and early 1974. Similarly, the recessions that afflicted many economies in 1980 are also blamed on the oil price increase in 1979. Yet despite the enormous public attention focused on the oil crisis, economic modeling of this phenomenon is still at a fairly early stage, and a number of important questions remain to be addressed.

The literature contains a number of static models with imported inputs of which Cordon (1977), Findlay and Rodriguez (1977), and Benavie (1978) are examples. Schmid (1976) analyzes a static fixed exchange rate two-country model with intermediate imports, and Bruno and Sachs (1979) and Dornbusch (1980) emphasize the real aspects of adjustment of real wages and employment in imported input-dependent economies. Nontechnical surveys are provided by Cordon and Oppenheimer (1975) and Dunn (1980).

There seem, however, to be relatively few dynamic macromodels that incorporate imported inputs—papers by Buiter (1978), Rodriguez (1980), Krugman (forthcoming), and Obstfeld (1980) fall in this category. Obstfeld assumes that prices and wages always adjust to hold the economy at full employment and focuses on the implications of an input price increase for asset accumulation through accumulated current account imbalances, while Rodriguez utilizes a currency-substitution framework. Krugman, on the other

---

David Burton of Michigan State University collaborated on this chapter.

hand, looks at both the capital and current accounts of the balance of payments in a three-country framework in which oil is not explicitly used in production in the two oil-importing countries. The production input nature of oil is also suppressed in Purvis and Buiter (forthcoming).

This chapter represents an attempt to construct a macrodynamic model with an imported factor of production in which the supply side of the economy is explicitly modeled and wages are sticky and respond slowly to excess demand for labor. In particular the production technology of the economy is designed so that the demand for the imported input is price inelastic. The model also has a reasonably well-developed financial sector and contains two assets: domestic money and a traded bond. This framework may be regarded as an elaboration of the simple but elegant framework of Dornbusch (1976) to include a detailed specification of the supply side of the economy. Inevitably, the treatment of the supply side is achieved only at a cost; to keep the model manageable it proved necessary to overlook the role of wealth accumulation through the current account of the balance of payments and also to make the familiar small-country assumption.

The model is used to address a number of questions. The static and dynamic efects of an increase in the price of the imported input on key macroeconomic variables such as output, the exchange rate, and prices are examined. The effects of an increase in the money supply are also analyzed. For most of the chapter it is assumed that the input price is denominated in foreign currency, but the implications of the input price being denominated in domestic currency are also discussed.

As in Dornbusch (1976), exchange rate expectations play an important role in the model, and its properties are analyzed both in the case where expectations are formed according to a general regressive scheme and where agents have perfect foresight. Although in this model perfect foresight is just a special case of regressive expectations, perfect foresight is nonetheless imposed directly, since this allows the nature of perfect foresight paths to be examined and the effects of anticipated input price and monetary shocks to be analyzed.

Perhaps the most important conclusions to emerge from this chapter are that certain conventionally received notions, such as depreciation of domestic currency, following an imported input price increase, are subject to considerable qualification and are contingent upon specific parameter magnitudes. Thus, it is empirical analysis alone that can definitively settle some of these issues.

The chapter is organized as follows. The model is set out in detail in the second section. The following section considers the long- and short-run effects of input price and monetary shocks when expectations are formed regressively and the input price is denominated in foreign currency. In the fourth section the implications of pricing the imported input in domestic currency are considered. Perfect foresight is directly imposed in the fifth section, and the effects of anticipated and unanticipated shocks to the system are examined. Finally, a summary of the main results and some concluding comments are presented in the last section.

THE ANALYTICAL FRAMEWORK

Consider a small open economy operating under a regime of floating exchange rates. Domestic aggregate demand is divided between a domestically produced commodity and the output of a large foreign country.[1] Domestic residents have free access to a worldwide capital market dealing in homogeneous, riskless, one-period government securities. Because of the assumption of the absence of transactions costs and risk premiums, domestic speculators regard securities denominated in either domestic or foreign currency as perfectly substitutable, given a proper premium or discount to offset anticipated depreciation or appreciation of domestic currency. Domestic final output is produced via a diminishing-returns-to-scale Constant Elasticity of Substitution production function that depends on labor and an imported input (oil). For the purposes of this chapter it does not matter whether the intermediate input is imported from the large foreign economy (which also supplies a final commodity to the home country) or from a third country, although the latter scenario is clearly more realistic. Consequently, the reader may interpret this framework as applying to a three-country world—a small domestic economy, a large foreign economy that supplies a final commodity and securities to the home economy, and a third country that supplies only the input. Given the further assumption that in the short run employment is demand determined and that the world supply of the input (oil) is perfectly elastic at the prevailing foreign currency price, the actual intensity levels of utilization of both domestic labor and the input are determined entirely by domestic demand conditions. Continuous domestic monetary stock equilibrium prevails, and there is no currency substitution. Domestic price level flexibility ensures continual commodity market equilibrium, while nominal wages adjust slowly according to a measure of excess demand in the domestic labor market. There are other assumptions, and these are introduced as the analysis is presented.

Aggregate supply of domestic output is governed by a diminishing-returns-to-scale CES production technology. In terms of natural units of the relevant variables this is described by

$$Y^s = A[\alpha L^{-\rho} + (1 - \alpha)N^{-\rho}]^{-\mu/\rho}, \qquad 0 < \alpha < 1, 0 < \mu < 1, \rho > 0,$$

$$(10.1')$$

where Y^s is the level of output, L and N are the labor and oil inputs, respectively, and μ is a returns-to-scale parameter.[2] ρ is a parameter that is related to the elasticity of substitution between inputs via $\sigma = 1/(1 + \rho)$. The stated assumption on ρ implies that the elasticity of substitution is less than unity. Our choice of the CES production function is dictated by the consideration that this is the simplest production technology that is capable of generating inelastic input demands (resulting from limited short-run technical substitutability possibilities). Given the essential nature of oil and the fact that empirical estimates of the short-run elasticity of demand for oil are universally far below unity, it seems that an important aspect of any framework incorporating imported oil would be to presume this feature. It is easily verified that the Cobb-Douglas production function (embodying a unitary elasticity of substitution) is capable of generating inelastic input demand functions.

Since the rest of the model is most conveniently specified in logarithmic terms, it is necessary to log-linearize (10.1'). As shown in the Appendix to Chapter 10, the log-linear approximation to (10.1') is

$$y^s = \mu z l + \mu(1 - z)n, \tag{10.1}$$

where lowercase letters denote logarithmic values and z is an arbitrary linearization point defined by

$$z \equiv \frac{(\alpha L^{-\rho})^0}{(\alpha L^{-\rho})^0 + [(1 - \alpha)N^{-\rho}]^0} < 1.$$

For future use we also express (10.1) alternatively as

$$y^s = \alpha' l + \beta' n, \qquad 0 < \alpha', \beta' < 1, (\alpha' + \beta') < 1, \tag{10.1''}$$

where α' and β' are to be interpreted as the relevant supply elasticities, respectively, and are related to μ and z via $\alpha' \equiv \mu z$ and $\beta' \equiv \mu(1 - z)$. Domestic profit maximization implies that the actual input intensity levels are given by the input demand functions

$$l^d = -a_1(w - p) - a_2(p_n - p), \qquad a_1, a_2 > 0 \tag{10.2a}$$

and

$$n^d = -b_1(p_n - p) - b_2(w - p), \qquad b_1, b_2 > 0, \tag{10.2b}$$

where $(w - p)$ is the logarithm of the domestic real wage, and $(p_n - p)$ is the logarithm of the real domestic price of the intermediate input. The parameters a_i and b_j are related to the technological parameters of the economy by

$$a_1 \equiv \frac{(1 - \mu) + z(\mu + \rho)}{(1 + \rho)(1 - \mu)} \; ; \; a_2 \equiv \frac{(\mu + \rho)(1 - z)}{(1 + \rho)(1 - \mu)}$$

$$b_1 \equiv \frac{(1 - \mu z) + \rho(1 - z)}{(1 + \rho)(1 - \mu)} \; ; \; b_2 \equiv \frac{(\mu + \rho)z}{(1 + \rho)(1 - \mu)}$$

It is clear that $a_1 > b_2$ and $b_1 > a_2$, so that

$$(a_1 b_1 - a_2 b_2) > 0. \tag{10.3}$$

In what follows use will be made of (10.3). We also note that an inelastic demand for the oil input (that is, $b_1 < 1$) requires that $(\mu/z) < (\mu + \rho)/(1 + \rho)$, and we assume that the arbitrary linearization point z is chosen in such a way that this condition is satisfied. Finally, in view of (10.2), the aggregate supply function (10.1″) may be expressed in terms of input prices as

$$y^s = -a'(w - p) - b'(p_n - p), \tag{10.4}$$

where $a' \equiv (\alpha' a_1 + \beta' b_2)$ and $b' \equiv (\alpha' a_2 + \beta' b_1)$ are the relevant supply elasticities with respect to input prices.

Aggregate demand for domestic final output is assumed to depend upon net (value-added) income and the real exchange rate and is given by the following logarithmic semireduced form:

$$y^d = \gamma'_1 v + \delta'_1(e + p^* - p) + \sigma'_1 x, \qquad \gamma_1, \delta'_1, \sigma'_1 > 0, \quad (10.5)$$

where v is the logarithm of value-added income (defined below), and $(e + p^* - p)$ is the logarithm of the real exchange rate between domestic and foreign final goods. The domestic nominal exchange rate is defined according to the indirect quotation—that is, the number of units of domestic currency per unit foreign currency. x is a domestic fiscal variable that we subsequently ignore, and the parameters γ'_1 and δ'_1 are to be interpreted as the relevant elasticities.[3] Defining the level of domestic value-added income in natural units as

$$V = Y - N \cdot R$$

$$R \equiv \frac{P_N}{P},$$

the logarithmic approximation to V is (as discussed in the Appendix to Chapter 10)

$$v = \frac{y}{1-s} - \frac{s}{1-s}(1-b_1)(p_n - p) + \frac{sb_2}{1-s}(w-p), \quad (10.6)$$

where s is the share of the intermediate input (oil) in gross domestic output (that is, $s \equiv (N \cdot R)/Y$). Substituting (10.6) into (10.5) and noting that the elasticity γ'_1 is related to the derivative $\gamma_1 = (\partial Y^d/\partial V)$ via $\gamma'_1 = \gamma_1(1-s)$, we can express the aggregate demand function in terms of its fundamental determinants as

$$y^d = -\delta_0(p_n - p) + \delta_1(e + p^* - p) + \delta_2(w-p), \quad (10.7)$$
$$\delta_0, \delta_1, \delta_2 > 0,$$

where

$$\delta_0 \equiv \frac{\gamma_1^s(1-b_1)}{(1-\gamma_1)}, \quad \delta_1 \equiv \frac{\delta'_1}{(1-\gamma_1)}, \quad \text{and } \delta_2 \equiv \frac{\gamma_1 s b_2}{(1-\gamma_1)}.$$

The term involving the real price of the oil input is not intended to capture substitution possibilities between domestic final output and oil, for we explicitly assume that oil is a pure intermediate good.[4] Rather, this term captures the reduced-form effect of a change in the price of the input on domestic value-added income and hence an aggregate demand. A similar interpretation holds for the term involving the real wage rate. As seen by (10.6), an increase in the real price of oil reduces value-added income for given gross output (since $b_1 < 1$) and subsequently lowers aggregate demand for domestic final output. An increase in the real wage rate has the opposite implication. The share of oil in domestic output, s, is seen to be involved in both δ_0 and δ_2, and a ceteris paribus increase in this share leads to increases in both coefficients. Thus the more dependent the domestic economy upon imported oil, the greater the demand-deflationary impact of an increase in the real price of the imported input.

The next equation of the model is the condition of continuous monetary equilibrium. Specifically, the logarithm of money demand is assumed to be linear in the nominal interest rate and the logarithm of value-added income. Substituting for the latter from (10.6), the reduced-form representation of the money market condition is

$$m - q = -\lambda i - \pi_1(w-p) - \pi_2(p_n - p), \quad (10.8)$$

where

$$\pi_1 \equiv \frac{\phi}{1-s} [\alpha' a_2 + b_2(\beta' - s)] \gtrless 0$$

and

$$\pi_2 \equiv \frac{\phi}{1-s} [\alpha' a_2 + \beta' b_1 + s(1 - b_1)] > 0.$$

λ is the interest rate semielasticity of real money demand (the interest rate being measured in terms of natural units), and ϕ is the elasticity of money demand with respect to net output, which is set equal to unity in what follows. The price index q is given by a geometric average of domestic and foreign final output prices, that is,

$$q = gp + (1 - g)(e + p^*), \qquad 0 < g < 1, \tag{10.9}$$

where the parameter g indicates the degree of openness of the domestic economy.

The next three equations of the model refer to the determination of the domestic currency price of the intermediate input and to the assumption of perfect international capital mobility between the domestic and foreign economies:

$$p_n = p_n^* + e \tag{10.10}$$

$$i = i^* + \dot{e}^E \tag{10.11}$$

$$\dot{e}^E = -\theta(e - \bar{e}), \qquad \theta > 0. \tag{10.12}$$ [5]

According to (10.10), the oil input price is denominated in terms of foreign currency (say, dollars) and its domestic equivalent given by a simple purchasing power parity relationship (in the absence of transportation costs and tariffs). Equation (10.11) asserts that the domestic interest rate is equal to the foreign interest rate plus the expected rate of depreciation of domestic currency vis-à-vis foreign currency. The latter is given by the simple regressive scheme postulated in (10.12). It will be shown below that this scheme is consistent with perfect foresight of exchange rates for a particular value of the expectational parameter θ. $\bar{e}$ is the logarithm of the steady-state exchange rate, assumed known to domestic agents. [6]

The final equation of the model concerns dynamic adjustment. Specifically, we assume that nominal wages adjust slowly, according to a measure of unemployment in the labor market. It is assumed that while in the long run labor supply is fixed, in the short run employment is determined by the demand for labor, which in turn is determined by both the real wage rate and the real price of oil (see equation [10.2a]). Thus,

$$\dot{w} = -h[a_1(w - p) + a_2(p_n - p)], \qquad h > 0, \qquad (10.13)$$

where h measures the speed with which wage contracts are renegotiated and the fixed equilibrium labor supply is suppressed. It is possible to extend (10.13) to incorporate inflationary expectations; but no essential change is introduced by this modification, and we retain, therefore, the simplest possible adjustment rule hypothesized in (10.13). In the steady state the natural rate of unemployment prevails and wage adjustment ceases. Corresponding to this, the steady-state real wage rate must stand in a particular relation with the steady-state real oil price. The specification of the model is completed by noting that continuous commodity market equilibrium prevails, that is, $y^d = y^s$.

IMPLICATIONS OF AN UNEXPECTED INCREASE IN THE WORLD PRICE OF THE IMPORTED INPUT

Long-Run Effects

Consider first the steady-state implications of an unanticipated increase in the world price of the intermediate input (p^*_n). We assume for the purposes of this analysis that the foreign price level p^* and the world interest rate i^* are unaffected by this disturbance—the justification for this being the further assumption that the foreign economy is sufficiently large so as to be independent of economic events occurring either in the small domestic economy or in the oil-exporting nation.[7] The steady-state of this model is described by $i = i^*$ and $\dot{w} = 0$ with the implication that $(\bar{w} - \bar{p}) = -(a_2/a_1)(\bar{e} + p^*_n - \bar{p})$, where overbars denote steady-state values. Using the steady-state analogues in the previous equations and the implication noted above, the effects of such a disturbance upon the steady-state exchange rate and price level are obtained by the matrix equation

$$
\begin{bmatrix}
(\delta_1 - A) & -(\delta_1 - A) \\
\\
(1 - g - B) & (g + B)
\end{bmatrix}
\begin{bmatrix}
\dfrac{d\bar{e}}{dp_n{}^*} \\
\\
\dfrac{d\bar{p}}{dp_n{}^*}
\end{bmatrix}
=
\begin{bmatrix}
A \\
\\
B
\end{bmatrix},
$$

$$(10.14)$$

where we have introduced the definitional notation

$$
A \equiv \left[\frac{\gamma^{s(1-Z)}}{1 - \gamma_1} - Z\beta' \right] \gtrless 0,
\tag{10.15}
$$

$$
B \equiv \frac{s}{1 - s}(1 - Z) + \frac{Z\beta'}{1 - s} > 0,
$$

and

$$
Z \equiv \left(b_1 - \frac{a_2 b_2}{a_1} \right) > 0 \text{ but} < 1.
$$

The matrix of coefficients is given by

$$
\Delta = (\delta_1 - A).
\tag{10.16}
$$

Note first that (10.16) can also be rewritten more explicitly (by substituting the definitions of A and Z) as

$$
\Delta = \frac{1}{1 - \gamma_1} [\delta'_1 + \beta'(1 - \gamma_1)(b_1 - \frac{a_2 b_2}{a_1}) - \gamma_1 s(1 - b_1 + a_2 b_2)],
$$

$$(10.16')$$

which would appear to be ambiguous without further restrictions. Since the signs of all steady-state results depend upon the sign of the coefficient matrix, it follows that the first point of interest is that none of the steady-state results can be taken for granted. Consequently, the conventionally accepted notion that an increase in oil prices leads inevitably to a weakening of the importing nation's currency (in the long run) is to be viewed with some caution. Rather, this conclusion is contingent upon certain specific (and perhaps plausible) parameter magnitudes, as will be seen presently.

We assume that $\Delta > 0$. As (10.16') indicates, this is consistent with a wide variety of assumptions concerning parameter magnitudes. For example, the lower the share of the input in total output (s) or the greater the elasticity of output with respect to oil (β'), the more likely that $\delta > 0$. One sufficient condition that ensures that $\Delta > 0$ is $\delta'_1 > 1$, and in what follows below this condition will be assumed to hold.[8] The interpretation of this condition is that the demand for domestic output is elastic with respect to the final commodity terms of trade. The parameter δ'_1 is related to the degree of substitutability between domestic and foreign (final) commodities, the case of $\delta'_1 \to \infty$ corresponding to purchasing power parity. Hence, our subsequent analysis can be interpreted as applying to a relatively open economy. This case will also be seen to be the one that corresponds to a decline in steady-state gross output following the increase in p_n^*.

Using (10.14), the steady-state effect upon the exchange rate is given by

$$\frac{d\bar{e}}{dp_n^*} = Ag + \frac{B\delta'_1}{1 - \gamma_1} \, ,$$

which from (10.15) can be written as

$$\Delta \frac{d\bar{e}}{dp_n^*} = \left(\frac{s}{1 - \gamma_1} \right) \left(1 - b_1 + \frac{b_2 a_2}{a_1} \right) \left(\frac{\delta'_1}{1 - s} + g\gamma_1 \right)$$

$$+ \left(b_1 - \frac{b_2 a_2}{a_1} \right) \beta' \left(\frac{\delta'_1}{(1 - \gamma_1)(1 - s)} - g \right) > 0.$$

$$(10.17)$$

Provided that $\delta'_1 > 1$, as assumed earlier, the steady-state exchange rate is seen to depreciate unambiguously following the input price increase (recall that γ_1, s, and g are all fractions). It is possible to assess the contribution of each parameter to the steady-state multiplier, but this will be left to the interested reader. Two results are of interest. Since equation (10.17) is increasing in s while Δ is decreasing in the latter, it follows that the long-run exchange rate multiplier is unambiguously increasing in s—i.e., the more dependent the domestic economy upon the imported input, the more severe the steady-state exchange depreciation that is induced by an increase in input prices. However, the effect of g (the degree of substitutability between final commodities) upon the long-run exchange rate is given by the term A (since Δ is independent of g); and as seen from (10.15), the latter cannot be unambiguously signed. Thus, there is no necessary presumption that increased openness as measured by g enhances the susceptibility of the domestic economy to external influences. Finally, for very small s and small δ'_1 it is conceivable that both $\Delta > 0$ and $d\bar{e}/dp_n^* < 0$. This possibility exists because with small s an increase in p_n^* changes disposable income little in relation to gross output, and long-run goods market equilibrium requires an appreciation of the real exchange rate (see equation [10.19]). But if δ'_1 is also small, the equilibrium real appreciation will be large and a fall (appreciation) in the nominal exchange rate may be required. In our subsequent analysis in the third and fourth sections we emphasize the results corresponding to larger values of δ_1' since this configuration better characterizes a relatively open economy (from the point of view of both final commodities and imported inputs).

The effect of the oil price increase upon the steady-state price level is given by

$$\Delta \frac{d\bar{p}}{dp_n^*} = \frac{\delta_1'}{1 - \gamma_1} B - A(1 - g)$$

or more explicitly by

$$\Delta \frac{d\bar{p}}{dp_n^*} = \left(\frac{s}{1 - \gamma_1} \right) \left(1 - b_1 + \frac{b_2 a_2}{a_1} \right) \left(\frac{\delta_1'}{1 - s} - (1 - g)\gamma_1 \right)$$

$$\text{(10.18)}$$

$$+ \beta' \left(b_1 - \frac{b_2 a_2}{a_1} \right) \left(\frac{\delta_1'}{(1 - s)(1 - \gamma_1)} + (1 - g) \right) > 0.$$

Hence, the long-run price level also increases following the input price disturbance. Furthermore, the magnitude of the price movement is increasing in s confirming again our earlier result that increased dependence upon foreign oil imports implies that further increases in the world oil price are likely to affect the domestic economy more severely. It may also be verified that the effect of the degree-of-openness parameter upon the long-run price multiplier is, as earlier, ambiguous without further assumptions.

Given the above results, it is straightforward to evaluate the impact upon the real domestic price of oil and the real exchange rate between final commodities, i.e.,

$$\Delta \frac{d(\bar{e} + p^* - \bar{p})}{dp_n^*} = \left(\frac{\gamma_1 s}{1 - \gamma_1} \right) \left(1 - b_1 + \frac{b_2 a_2}{a_1} \right)$$

$$\text{(10.19)}$$

$$- \left(b_1 - \frac{b_2 a_2}{a_1} \right) \beta' \equiv A$$

and

$$\Delta\frac{d(\bar{e} + p_n^* - \bar{p})}{dp_n^*} = \frac{\delta_1'}{1 - \gamma_1} > 0. \tag{10.20}$$

The real domestic price of oil increases with the increase in the world price of the input, and this effect is increasing in the parameter s. The movement in the long-run real exchange rate may be in either direction, the possibility of an increase being related positively to share of oil s. For example, as $s \to 0$, the long-run real exchange rate appreciates (improves). Moreover, in view of (10.20) and the steady-state analogue of (10.13) it follows that the long-run real wage rate $(\bar{w} - \bar{p})$ unambiguously declines in the steady state, as does the level of gross output that is,

$$\Delta\frac{d\bar{y}}{dp_n^*} = -\left(b_1 - \frac{b_2 a_2}{a_1}\right)\beta'\left(\frac{\delta_1'}{1 - \gamma_1}\right) < 0.[9] \tag{10.21}$$

Whether the nominal wage rate increases of decreases in the steady state is determined by the condition

$$\Delta\frac{d\bar{w}}{dp_n^*} = \left(\frac{\delta_1'}{1 - \gamma_1}\right)\left(B - \frac{a_2}{a_1}\right) - A(1 - g) \gtrless 0. \tag{10.22}$$

Interestingly, the long-run nominal wage rate may increase or decrease following the oil price increase. To gain further insight into the likely determinants of the ultimate movement in the long-run nominal wage rate, substitute for the definitional parameters A, B, and Z in (10.22). After some algebra it can be shown that $(d\bar{w}/dp_n^*)$ is positive if

$$a_1 s(1 - b_1) + (a_1 b_1 - a_2 b_2)$$
$$\times \left\{\beta' + \frac{(1 - g)(1 - s)[\gamma_1 s + \beta'(1 - \gamma_1)]}{\delta_1'}\right\}$$
$$- a_2 + a_2 s(1 + b_2) - \frac{(1 - g)(1 - s)a_1\gamma_1 s}{\delta_1'} > 0.$$

If δ_1' is sufficiently large in relation to the other parameters of the economy (which are all fractions), then a sufficient condition for the nominal wage to increase is

$$a_1 s(1 - b_1) + (a_1 b_1 - a_2 b_2)\beta' - a_2 + a_2 s(1 + b_2) > 0. \tag{10.23}$$

From (10.23) it is clear that the likelihood of an increase in the nominal wage rate is positively related to the value of the oil share s. By substituting the definitions of a_i and b_j, it can further be shown that if s is close to zero or if ρ is very high, implying a very low elasticity of substitution between factors, the long-run nominal wage rate declines.[10] Consequently, a country that is heavily dependent upon imported oil is likely to witness an increase in the long-run aggregate wage level following an increase in the world oil price along with an increase in both the long-run price and exchange rate levels. By contrast an economy that uses relatively little imported oil in its domestic production process experiences long-run price inflation and exchange depreciation coupled with wage deflation. Moreover, the price and exchange rate adjustments are of a smaller order of magnitude than in the more oil-dependent economy.

Dynamics and Stability

Having characterized the long-run effects of an increase in the world input price, we now turn our attention to a discussion of the dynamic behavior of the economy and an investigation of impact (short-run) effects. The dynamics of the economy under consideration are governed by a single differential equation (equation [10.13]), which can alternatively be expressed in deviational form as

$$\dot{w} = -ha_1(w - \bar{w}) + h(a_1 + a_2)(p - \bar{p}) - ha_2(e - \bar{e}). \quad (10.24)$$

Equation (10.24) can be reduced to its final homogeneous form as follows. Using the commodity and money market clearing conditions in deviational form, it is possible to obtain two equations in the three states $(p - \bar{p})$, $(w - \bar{w})$, and $(e - \bar{e})$. Solving the resulting equations simultaneously for $(p - \bar{p})$ and $(e - \bar{e})$, it can be shown that the solutions are

$$(p - \bar{p}) = Q(w - \bar{w}) \quad (10.25a)$$

and

$$(e - \bar{e}) = M(w - \bar{w}), \quad (10.25b)$$

where

$$Q \equiv \frac{(\delta_1 - \delta_0 + b')\pi_1 + (\delta_2 + a')(1 + \lambda\theta - g - \pi_2)}{(\delta_1 - \delta_0 + b')(1 + \lambda\theta + \pi_1) + (\delta_2 + a')(1 + \lambda\theta - g - \pi_2)}$$

and

$$M \equiv \frac{(\delta_1 - \delta_0 + b')Q - (\delta_2 + a')(1 - Q)}{(\delta_1 - \delta_0 + b')}.$$

Using (10.25), (10.24) can be reduced to

$$\dot{w} = -h[a_1 - (a_1 + a_2)Q + a_2 M](w - \bar{w}). \tag{10.26}$$

The solution to (10.26) is given by

$$w_t = \bar{w} + (w_0 - \bar{w})\exp^{-hNt},$$

where

$$N \equiv a_1 - (a_1 + a_2)Q + a_2 M.$$

Stability requires that N be positive, which in turn can be shown to require that the denominator of Q be positive. Tedious calculations demonstrate that for values of θ (the expectational parameter) close to the perfect foresight value, $N > 0$, and the model is unambiguously stable. Furthermore, even for θ values substantially different from the perfect foresight value, it is quite possible that the model is stable.[11] The stability of the domestic economy under perfect foresight is discussed and demonstrated in the fifth section.

Impact Effects

The short-run or impact effects of the oil price disturbance upon the domestic economy may be characterized by reference to (10.25). Since the denominator of Q is positive (given stability), it is clear from the definition of the latter that Q is contained in the interval $(0, 1)$. Utilizing (10.25a),

$$\frac{d(p_0 - \bar{p})}{dp_n^*} = -Q \frac{d\bar{w}}{dp_n^*} \tag{10.27}$$

from which it follows that if the long-run wage level increases, then the short-run price level undershoots its steady-state value, and conversely for a decline in $\bar{w}$. Further, since $(d\bar{p}/dp_n^*) > (d\bar{w}/dp_n^*)$ (recall that the steady-state real wage level declines), it follows that the short-run price level (p_0) increases upon impact. During adjustment the price level may increase or decline to its long-run value, but if the nominal wage level increases in the steady state, nominal wage and price levels increase through the adjustment process. In the opposite case both the wage and price levels decline during adjustment.

The effect upon the instantaneous exchange rate is somewhat more difficult to characterize precisely. From (10.25b) it can be seen that

$$\frac{d(e_0 - \bar{e})}{dp_n^*} = -M \frac{d\bar{w}}{dp_n^*}.$$

It is straightforward to show that $|M| < 1$; however, its sign is determined by :

$$\text{Sign } M = \text{sign}[(\delta_1 - \delta_0 + b')\pi_1 - (\delta_2 + a')(g + \pi_2)], \quad (10.28)$$

which is indeterminate without further restrictions. The likelihood of $M > 0$ can be shown to be negatively related to the oil share s, but for small values of s it can be shown that $M > 0$.[12] In the same circumstances, it will be recalled, the long-run nominal wage level declines following the oil price increase, so that the spot exchange rate (e_0) depreciates in excess of the steady-state exchange rate. In a highly oil-dependent economy it is possible that $M < 0$ while $(d\bar{w}/dp_n^*) > 0$, as shown earlier. Consequently, spot depreciation and exchange rate overshooting also occur in an economy that is heavily dependent on oil imports. For intermediate values of s there is the likelihood that M and $(d\bar{w}/dp_n^*)$ are of the same sign, implying exchange rate undershooting.[13] For either very low or high values of s, then, exchange rate adjustment takes the form of declining nominal exchange rates. The dynamic behavior of the real exchange rate is also easily characterized in the case of a highly oil-dependent economy (i.e., large s). In this case, as shown earlier, the price level increases over time so that the real exchange rate declines continuously (having undergone overshooting). Further, the real domestic price of oil ($e + p_n^* - p$) also declines during adjustment in the same circumstances. Since the long-run real oil price is unambiguously increased following an increase in the world price of oil, it follows that the short-run increase in the real domestic price of oil exceeds the corresponding long-run increase for a highly oil-dependent economy. For low values of s some of these conclusions are reversed.

Finally, consider the effect of the oil price shock upon the short-run level of gross output, y. Writing (10.4) in deviational form and using equations (10.25), it follows that

$$(y_0 - \bar{y}) = (1 - Q)\left[-a' + \frac{b'(\delta_2 + a')}{\delta_1 - \delta_0 + b'}\right](w_0 - \bar{w}). \quad (10.29)$$

Substituting the definitions of a' and b' on the right-hand side of (10.29), it follows that the sign of $(y_0 - \bar{y})$ in relation to $w_0 - \bar{w}$ is determined by

$$-(\alpha'a_1 + \beta'b_2)[\delta'_1 - \gamma_1 s(1 - b_1)] + \gamma_1 s b_2(\alpha'a_2 + \beta'b_1),$$

which can easily be reduced to

$$-(\alpha'a_1 + \beta'b_2)(\delta'_1 - \gamma_1 s) - \alpha'\gamma_1 s(a_1 b_1 - a_2 b_2) < 0. \qquad (10.30)$$

Thus, we may write

$$(y_0 - \bar{y}) = -H(w_0 - \bar{w}), \qquad (10.31)$$

where

$$H > 0.$$

If the oil-share s is large, as is the case in an oil-dependent economy, then, as seen before, the long-run nominal wage increases, current output declines less than long-run or steady-state output $\bar{y}$, and adjustment is characterized by a declining level of gross output.[14] Opposite results obtain for an economy that is relatively independent of oil imports for its domestic production.

At this point it is convenient to summarize our results for an economy that is heavily dependent upon imported oil (in the sense of a high value of the parameter s). An exogenous, unanticipated increase in the world price of imported oil is seen to lead to steady-state stagflation coupled with long-run depreciation. Long-run price and wage levels increase, while steady-state gross output declines. Moreover, the real domestic price of oil and the real exchange rate between final commodities also increase in the long run, although the real wage rate declines. In the short run the price level also increases and the spot exchange rate depreciates. However, the price level undershoots and the exchange rate overshoots its steady-state response, so that adjustment is characterized by increasing wage-price levels and a declining nominal exchange rate. Consequently, the real domestic price of oil and the real exchange rate also decline during adjustment, having undergone overshooting of their ultimate responses. In the most likely case the short-run level of gross output also declines, but this decline falls short (in an absolute sense) of the ultimate steady-state decline in the latter. Some (although not all) of these results are reversed for low values of the oil share s.

In conclusion of this section we note two other specific issues. First, we consider briefly the perfect foresight solution to the expectational parameter θ; second, we discuss the implications of an unanticipated nominal monetary expansion in our framework. The stable solution to the perfect foresight value of θ will be seen to be the same as the value of the stable root of the dynamic solution discussed in the fifth section. Time differentiating (10.25b) yields

$$\dot{e} = M\dot{w}.$$

Substituting for $\dot{w}$ from (10.26),

$$\dot{e} = -MhN(w - \bar{w}).$$

And utilizing equations (10.25) again,

$$\dot{e} = -hN(e - \bar{e}). \tag{10.32}$$

The perfect foresight value of θ obtained by ensuring that the actual depreciation given by (10.32) coincides with the expected depreciation as specified in (10.12). This involves the solution to

$$hN(\theta, \ldots) = \theta. \tag{10.33}$$

Equation (10.33) can be shown to be a quadratic in θ, with one negative root and the other positive. The positive root is (as expected) identical to the stable root of the dynamic solution discussed in the fifth section. This section dispenses with the expectational scheme and imposes perfect foresight directly.

The effects of monetary expansion can be dealt with briefly. In the absence of any underlying source of money illusion all of the nominal wage level, the exchange rate, and the price level increase equiproportionately with the money supply in the long run. From equations (10.25) it can be seen that

$$\frac{dp_0}{dm} = (1 - Q) > 0,$$

while

$$\frac{de_0}{dm} = (1 - M) > 0.$$

Thus, the short-run price level increases, although less than proportionately. Meanwhile, the spot exchange rate depreciates, the extent of the depreciation being determined by (10.28), as earlier. In a highly oil-dependent economy the oil share s is large, so that M may be negative. In this case exchange rate overshooting occurs. Finally, the real exchange can be shown to depreciate unambiguously irrespective of whether the short-run exchange rate response is overproportional or underproportional :

$$\frac{d(e_0 + p^* - p_0)}{dm} = (Q - M) > 0.[15]$$

It is possible to assess the sensitivity of these short-run multipliers with respect to the structural parameters of the economy, but this is left to the interested reader.

OIL PRICE DENOMINATED IN DOMESTIC CURRENCY

In this section we investigate the steady-state consequences of an unanticipated increase in the price of the oil input if the latter is denominated not in terms of foreign currency, as has been hitherto assumed, but in terms of domestic currency. The issue of the currency denomination of imported oil is of obvious interest, given OPEC's stated intention of denominating their oil exports in future years in terms of a basket of currencies rather than in terms of the dollar alone.

The case where more than one currency is involved in the oil price denomination can clearly be interpreted as one that is intermediate to the two polar cases we have examined in this chapter (i.e., pure foreign currency and pure domestic currency pricing). To analyze the long-run consequences of an oil price increase when the latter is denominated in terms of domestic currency, it is convenient to introduce some new definitional notation. Let

$$X \equiv \left(\delta_1 - a' \frac{a_2}{a_1} + b' - \delta_0 - \delta_2 \frac{a_2}{a_1} \right) \equiv (\delta_1 - A)$$

and

$$C \equiv \left(g + \pi_2 - \pi_1 \frac{a_2}{a_1} \right) \equiv (g + B),$$

where A and B are as defined in (10.15). In terms of this notation the matrix of coefficients under foreign currency pricing in (10.14) is

$$\Delta = XC + X(1 - C) \equiv X. \tag{10.34}$$

The only substantive change with domestic currency pricing is that (10.14′), which is an alternative expression of (10.14) and applicable to foreign currency pricing—

$$
\begin{bmatrix} X & -X \\ 1 - C & C \end{bmatrix}
\begin{bmatrix} \dfrac{d\bar{e}}{dp_n^*} \\ \dfrac{d\bar{p}}{dp_n^*} \end{bmatrix}
=
\begin{bmatrix} (-X + \delta_1) \\ (C - g) \end{bmatrix}
\tag{10.14'}
$$

—is now replaced by

$$
\begin{bmatrix} X - U & -X \\ 1 - C + \pi_2 - \dfrac{\pi_1 a_2}{a_1} & C \end{bmatrix}
\begin{bmatrix} \dfrac{d\bar{e}}{dp_n} \\ \dfrac{d\bar{p}}{dp_n} \end{bmatrix}
=
\begin{bmatrix} (-X + \delta_1) \\ (C - g) \end{bmatrix},
\tag{10.14*}
$$

where $\bar{p}_n$ is now the exogenous variable and U is defined by

$$
U \equiv b' - \delta_0 - \delta_2 \frac{a_2}{a_1} - a' \frac{a_2}{a_1} .
$$

The determinant of the coefficient matrix under domestic currency pricing is defined by

$$
\Delta^* = XC + X(1 - C) + X\left(\pi_2 - \pi_1 \frac{a_2}{a_1} \right) - CU.
\tag{10.35}
$$

We now show that $\Delta^* > \Delta$. For this to be true it is neccessary that

$$
X\left(\pi_2 - \pi_1 \frac{a_2}{a_1} \right) - U\left(g + \pi_2 - \pi_1 \frac{a_2}{a_1} \right) > 0
$$

or

$$
(X - U)\left(\pi_2 - \pi_1 \frac{a_2}{a_1} \right) - Ug > 0.
$$

By substituting the definitions of X, U, π_1, and π_2 in the above expression, it can be shown that $\Delta^* > \Delta$ if

$$\left(b_1 - \frac{a_2 b_2}{a_1} \right) \left[\frac{\delta_1}{1-s}(\beta' - s) - g \left(\beta' + \frac{\gamma_1 s}{1 - \gamma_1} \right) \right]$$

$$+ \frac{\delta_1 s}{1-s} + \frac{g \gamma_1 s}{1 - \gamma_1} > 0. \tag{10.36}$$

Equation (10.36) is clearly positive if the second expression in square brackets is positive. Writing this expression in full, we obtain

$$\frac{(1-\gamma_1)Z\beta'[\delta_1 - g(1-s)] + \delta_1 s(1-\gamma_1)(1-Z) + g\gamma_1 s(1-s)(1-Z)}{(1-s)(1-\gamma_1)},$$

which is unambiguously positive under our earlier assumptions. Hence, it follows that all long-run multipliers are reduced in absolute size under domestic currency pricing as compared with foreign currency pricing.

The policy implications of this section are surprisingly straightforward. A move by, say, OPEC to denominate their oil exports in terms of the dollar and the franc (or the franc alone) would clearly be welcomed by France, for future increases in the price of imported oil will affect the French economy less severely than if dollar pricing were continued. The invoicing of imported oil in terms of domestic currency is thus seen to imply better insulation of the domestic economy against future oil price increases. it is also possible to show that short-run effects of the oil price shock are somewhat less severe under domestic currency pricing if certain plausible conditions hold. To economize on space we do not present these results here.

PERFECT FORESIGHT

In this section we dispense with the regressive expectations scheme (10.12) that has hitherto been used and impose perfect foresight directly. This approach allows us to characterize the entire class of perfect foresight paths as well as permitting an analysis of anticipated (or preannounced) changes in the input price. It will be shown that the perfect foresight equilibrium is not necessarily a unique saddle point; however, the condition that ensures saddle-point stability is one that was utilized in the third section to sign the steady-state results.[16]

Perfect foresight requires that the regressive expectations equation (10.12) be replaced by the requirement

$$\dot{e}^E = \dot{e}. \tag{10.12'}$$

Eliminating y from equations (10.4) and (10.7), the resulting equation for p together with equations (10.8) through (10.11), (10.12'), and (10.13) can be used to express the dynamics of the system as

$$\begin{bmatrix} \dot{e} \\ \dot{w} \end{bmatrix} = \begin{bmatrix} c_1 & c_2 \\ d_1 & d_2 \end{bmatrix} \begin{bmatrix} e \\ w \end{bmatrix} + \begin{bmatrix} c_3 & c_4 \\ d_3 & d_4 \end{bmatrix} \begin{bmatrix} p_n^* \\ m \end{bmatrix}, \tag{10.37}$$

where all lowercase variables are now redefined as deviations from their respective initial steady-state values. Since the price of foreign-produced goods and the foreign interest rate are assumed constant, both variables have been dropped from the analysis. The coefficients in (10.37) are defined as follows:

$$c_1 = \frac{a' + b' + \delta_1 + \delta_2 - \delta_0 + \pi_1(b' + \delta_1 - \delta_0) - (a' + \delta_2)(g + \pi_2)}{\lambda(a' + b' + \delta_1 + \delta_2 - \delta_0)}$$

$$c_2 = \frac{(a' + \delta_2)(g + \pi_2) - \pi_1(b' + \delta_1 - \delta_0)}{\lambda(a' + b' + \delta_1 + \delta_2 - \delta_0)}$$

$$c_3 = \frac{(b' - \delta_0)(\pi_1 + g) - \pi_2(a' + \delta_1 + \delta_2)}{\lambda(a' + b' + \delta_1 + \delta_2 - \delta_0)}$$

$$c_4 = \frac{1}{\lambda}$$

$$d_1 = \frac{ha_1(b' + \delta_1 - \delta_0) - ha_2(a' + \delta_2)}{a' + b' + \delta_1 + \delta_2 - \delta_0}$$

$$d_2 = -d_1$$

$$d_3 = \frac{ha_1(b' - \delta_0) - ha_2(a' + \delta_1 + \delta_2)}{a' + b' + \delta_1 + \delta_2 - \delta_0}$$

$$d_4 = 0.$$

Before we can examine the effects of oil price and other shocks on the system, we must first address the question of the stability of the economy under perfect foresight. The roots of the characteristic equation for (10.37) are

$$r_{1,2} = \frac{(c_1 + d_2) \pm [(c_1 + d_2)^2 - 4(c_1 d_2 - c_2 d_1)]^{1/2}}{2}, \quad (10.38)$$

and the product of the roots is given by

$$r_1 \cdot r_2 = c_1 d_2 - c_2 d_1 = \frac{ha_2(a' + \delta_2) - ha_1(b' + \delta_1 - \delta_0)}{\lambda(a' + b' + \delta_1 + \delta_2 - \delta_0)} = -\frac{d_1}{\lambda}.$$

$$(10.39)$$

It is a straightforward matter to show both that $(a' + b' + \delta_1 + \delta_2 - \delta_0) > 0$ and that $[ha_2(a' + \delta_2) - ha_1(b' + \delta_1 - \delta_0)] = -a_1 \Delta$. It follows that when $\Delta > 0$, the product of the roots of the characteristic equation is negative and the system is characterized by saddle-point-type instability, which is a common property of perfect foresight models. As in the previous sections it will be assumed throughout this section that $\Delta > 0$. It is perhaps worth emphasizing, though, that if $\Delta < 0$, it appears that the system may have either two positive or two negative roots. In the former case the economy is completely unstable, whereas in the latter case, if the exchange rate is free to jump when the economy is subjected to an unexpected shock, as will be assumed below, the perfect foresight path is not unique.

The problem of instability when $\Delta > 0$ and the economy has a saddle point can be resolved by what is now a standard procedure in perfect foresight models. Following Gray and Turnovsky (1979), perfect foresight is suspended at the instant an unanticipated shock occurs, and the exchange rate (and the price level) is allowed to jump so that the economy jumps to the stable arm of the saddle.[17] The size of the exchange rate jump is determined by imposing the terminal condition that steady-state real balances are finite. This condition is not as arbitrary as it may seem and can be justified on the grounds that it corresponds to the transversality conditions that some optimizing models involving money and perfect foresight must satisfy.[18] The complete solutions for e and w are given by

$$e_t = \frac{(d_1 + r_1)}{d_1}$$

$$\times \exp^{r_1 t} \left(A_1 + B_1 \int_0^t p_{n\tau}^* \exp^{-r_1 \tau} d\tau + D_1 \int_0^t m_\tau \exp^{-r_1 \tau} d\tau \right)$$

$$+ \frac{(d_1 + r_2)}{d_1}$$

$$+ \exp^{r_2 t}\left(A_2 + B_2 \int_0^t p_{nt}^* \exp^{-r_2 \tau} dt + D_2 \int_0^t m_\tau \exp^{-r_2 \tau} d\tau\right) \tag{10.40}$$

and

$$w_t = \exp^{r_1 \tau}\left(A_1 + B_1 \int_0^t p_{nt}^* \exp^{-r_1 \tau} d\tau + D_1 \int_0^t m_\tau \exp^{-r_2 \tau} d\tau\right)$$

$$+ \exp^{r_2 t}\left(A_2 + B_2 \int_0^t p_{nt}^* \exp^{-r_2 \tau} d\tau + D_2 \int_0^t m_\tau \exp^{-r_2 \tau} d\tau\right), \tag{10.41}$$

where B_1, B_2 and C_1, C_2 are given by (10.42) and (10.43), respectively :

$$\begin{bmatrix} B_1 \\ B_2 \end{bmatrix} = \begin{bmatrix} \dfrac{d_1 + r_1}{d_1} & \dfrac{d_1 + r_2}{d_1} \\ 1 & 1 \end{bmatrix}^{-1} \begin{bmatrix} c_3 \\ d_3 \end{bmatrix} \tag{10.42}$$

and

$$\begin{bmatrix} D_1 \\ D_2 \end{bmatrix} = \begin{bmatrix} \dfrac{d_1 + r_1}{d_1} & \dfrac{d_2 + r_2}{d_2} \\ 1 & 1 \end{bmatrix}^{-1} \begin{bmatrix} c_4 \\ d_4 \end{bmatrix} . \tag{10.43}$$

The arbitrary constraints A_1 and A_2 are given by the initial condition

$$A_1 + A_2 = w_0 \tag{10.44}$$

as well as by the terminal condition that steady-state real balances are finite. If m_t and P_{nt}^* are bounded as $t \to \infty$, a sufficient condition for real balances to remain finite, if r_1 is the positive root, is

$$A_1 + B_1 \int_0^\infty p_{nt}^* \exp^{-r_1 \tau} d\tau + D_1 \int_0^\infty m_\tau \exp^{-r_1 \tau} d\tau = 0.[19] \tag{10.45}$$

We are now is a position to analyze the effects of both unanticipated and anticipated shocks to the input price and the money supply in the perfect foresight case. The long-run effects are, of course, the same as those set out in the third section, but it is worth noting again that long-run appreciation of the exchange rate in response to an oil price increase is possible if both s and δ_1' are small.[20]

The major concern of this section, however, is with impact effects. Consider first an unanticipated increase in the oil price, when the money supply is held constant, that is, $m = 0$. Solving for A_1, A_2 and B_1, B_2 from (10.42), (10.44), and (10.45), substituting those solutions in (10.40), setting $t = 0$, and differentiating with respect to p_n^* yields

$$\frac{de_0}{dp_n^*} = -\frac{(b' - \delta_0)(\pi_1 + g) - \pi_2(a' + \delta_1 + \delta_2)}{\lambda}$$

$$-\frac{[ha_1(b' - \delta_0) - ha_2(a' + \delta_1 + \delta_2)][(d_1 + r_2)/d_1]}{r_1(a' + b' + \delta_1\delta_2 - \delta_0)} \qquad (10.46)$$

which gives the jump in e required to place the system on the stable arm of the saddle when an unexpected increase in p_n^* occurs.

While it proved difficult to draw precise conclusions from (10.46) algebraically, it was possible to show numerically that it is consistent with a wide range of possible outcomes. In agreement with the results derived in the third section—for parameter values such that the long-run exchange rate depreciates (which may be the case for both relatively small and large values of s)—(10.46) may imply either overshooting or undershooting of the exchange rate. Furthermore, it is possible that de_0/dp_n^* may be negative for cases where the exchange rate appreciates in the long run.

From equations (10.7) and (10.4) the impact multiplier for the price of the home good is

$$\frac{dp_0}{dp_n^*} = \frac{(b' + \delta_1 - \delta_0)(de_0/dp_n^*) + b' - \delta_0}{a' + b' + \delta_1 + \delta_2 - \delta_0}. \qquad (10.47)$$

Substituting (10.46) for de_0/dp_n^* in (10.47) yields an expression that like (10.46) itself is not amenable to direct interpretation. Nonetheless, it is possible to show numerically that the price level may over- or undershoot on impact.

We turn now to the question of the effect of an unanticipated increase in the price of oil on output. The impact multiplier from equation (10.4) is

$$\frac{dy_0}{dp_n^*} = (a' + b') \frac{dp_0}{dp_n^*} - b' \frac{de_0}{dp_n^*} - b', \tag{10.48}$$

where dp_0/dp_n^* and de_0/dp_n^* are given by equations (10.47) and (10.46), respectively. It can be shown that (10.48) is consistent with both over- and undershooting of output with respect to its long-run level, which it will be recalled from (10.21) is unambiguously les than its initial value. Furthermore, for large values of s an increase in output or impact is possible, as also noted previously. If s is large, an increase in p_n^* causes a large fall in disposable income relative to gross output, which via the demand for money causes a large increase in the price of the home good. The effect of the latter on the real wage and the real oil price may outweigh the effect of the depreciation of the exchange rate (necessary to stimulate aggregate demand) on the real oil price and cause output to increase.

It is also interesting to note that the case of small s and small δ_1' (where the exchange rate may appreciate in both the long and short run, as discussed above) is consistent with a decline in output on impact as well as in the long run. This outcome seems to be broadly consistent with the experience of the United Kingdom following the 1979 oil price increase.[21]

We next consider briefly the implications of an anticipated oil price increase for our economy. Consider an OPEC announcement at $t = 0$ of a permanent oil price increase at some future date $t = T > 0$.[22] It is assumed that this announcement has no effect on the oil price until $t = T$.[23] Under these conditions the exchange rate (and the price of the doemstic good) jumps at the instant the announcement is made, and the size of the jump in the spot exchange rate is given by equation (10.46) multiplied by $\exp^{-r_1 T}$. Then the jump in the exchange rate is of the same sign but smaller in magnitude than in response to an unanticipated increase. The effect on the price of the domestic good is

$$\frac{dp_0}{dp_{nT}^{*e}} = \frac{(b' + \delta_1 - \delta_0)(de_0/dp_{nT}^{*e})}{a' + b' + \delta_1 + \delta_2 - \delta_0}, \tag{10.49}$$

which is of the same sign as de_0/dp_{nT}^*, since $(b' + \delta_1 - \delta_0) > 0$ is a necessary condition for $\Delta > 0$, but smaller in magnitude. The impact effect on output is

$$\frac{dy_0}{dp_{nT}^{*e}} = (a' + b') \frac{dp_0}{dp_{nT}^{*e}} - b' \frac{de_0}{dp_{nT}^{*e}}, \tag{10.50}$$

which is ambiguous in sign.

Finally, the effects of both anticipated and unanticipated increase in the money supply are examined. The long-run multipliers are, of course, the familiar ones shown in the third Section. The impact effect of an unanticipated increase in the money supply from (10.40), (10.44), and (10.45) is

$$\frac{de_0}{dm} = \frac{1}{\lambda r_1} \, , \tag{10.51}$$

which is positive but may be greater or less than 1. Hence, over- and undershooting of the exchange rate are both possible, as also seen earlier. The short-run effect of the price of domestic goods, from (10.7) and (10.4), is

$$\frac{dp_0}{dm} = \frac{(b' + \delta_1 - \delta_0)(de_0/dm)}{a' + b' + \delta_1 + \delta_2 - \delta_0} > 0, \tag{10.52}$$

which is positive but smaller in magnitude than de_0/dm. The impact on output of an increase in money supply, from equation (10.4), is given by

$$\frac{dy_0}{dm} = (a' + b') \frac{dp_0}{dm} - \frac{b' de_0}{dm} . \tag{10.53}$$

Substituting for dp_0/dm and de_0/dm from (10.51) and (10.52) and further substituting for a' and b' from the values given for equation (10.4), it is straightforward to show that $dy_0/dm > 0$ provided $\delta'_1 > \gamma_1 s$, which is a sufficient condition for the system to have a saddle point. Lastly, in the case of a permanent increase in the money supply at $t = T$ anticipated at $t = 0$, the impact effects on e, p, and y are given by equations (10.51), (10.52), and (10.53), respectively, each multiplied by $\exp^{-r_1 T}$. The multipliers for anticipated monetary disturbances are thus of the same sign but smaller in magnitude than their unanticipated counterparts.

CONCLUSION

This chapter has extended a typical macrodynamic model of the open economy under floating exchange rates to explicitly incorporate the supply side of the economy. A specific innovative feature of our framework is the introduction of an imported intermediate input into the analysis. We have investigated the static, steady-state, and dynamic implications of unanticipated as well as anticipated increases in the price of the imported input. An issue of some relevance here is the currency denomination of the imported input. Perhaps the central message of our investigation is that certain conventionally accepted notions (such as the association between the weakness of a nation's currency and its dependence on imported oil) need to be carefully qualified and are contingent upon certain specific parameter magnitudes. Our principal conclusions may be summarized as follows.

First, if the domestic economy under consideration is such that its demand for the imported input is inelastic, if domestic and foreign final output is somewhat substitutable (which will be the case for economies that are relatively open with respect to final goods), and if the share of the imported input in total gross output is not negligible, then an unanticipated increase in the foreign currency price of the imported input leads to steady-state depreciation coupled with wage-price inflation and a decline in gross output in the steady state. Moreover, the real domestic price of oil and the real exchange rate between final commodities also increase in the steady state, although the real wage rate declines. Qualitatively similar results would emerge if the input were denominated in terms of domestic currency; however, all of the steady-state multipliers are reduced (in an absolute sense) in the latter case. Some of these results are reversed in the case of a less open and less oil-dependent economy. The responsiveness of these multipliers to various structural parameters was investigated. For example, it was shown that the higher the share of the input in total gross output, the more severely the domestic economy is affected by the external disturbance.

Second, the impact effects of the input price disturbance are somewhat less clear in the absence of further assumptions on parameter magnitudes. The instantaneous price level increases following the disturbance; and if the share of imported oil in total output is large, the latter increase falls short of the eventual steady-state increase in the price level. Hence, the adjustment process is characterized by the increasing wage and price levels. Whether the exchange rate and output levels rise or fall during adjustment is also dependent upon the oil share. For both low and high values of the latter nominal exchange rates decline during adjustment. It is even possible that the spot exchange rate appreciates on impact and then increases to ultimately attain its depreciated steady-state value.

And third, the perfect foresight equilibrium of the model is not necessarily a saddle point. Specifically, there is the possibility of nonuniqueness. However, the condition that guarantees saddle point stability is the same as the one that follows from the prior assumptions made in the first conclusion. The effects of an anticipated disturbance are qualitatively similar to those resulting from the corresponding unanticipated shock but of a less severe nature than in the latter case.

The analysis of this chapter can clearly be extended in several directions. One possibility is to consider wealth adjustment that results from accumulated current account imbalances. Such a framework might be relevant if a longer time frame were considered. Another extension is to relax the assumption of a passive policy regime and to explicitly incorporate activist monetary policy. A natural question in this setting relates to the nature of the optimal monetary policy, when the optimum is defined in terms of the perceived loss from the oil price increase. Finally, our framework is also limited by the small-country assumption. Important questions regarding policy interdependence and coordination cannot be addressed unless an explicit multicountry model is developed. It is hoped that future research will address itself to some of these issues.

APPENDIX TO CHAPTER 10

The log-linear approximation to the CES production function is based on the following considerations. Given equation (10.1') in the text and assuming that $A = 1$ for convenience, this equation may also be expressed as

$$Y^{-\rho/\mu} = \alpha L^{-\rho} + (1 - \alpha)N^{-\rho}, \tag{10.1A}$$

where uppercase letters denote natural variables, and lowercase letters denote the corresponding logarithmic values. Applying the logarithmic operation to (10.1A), we may write

$$\frac{-\rho}{\mu^{y}}y = \ln\left[\alpha \exp^{\ln L^{-\rho}} + (1 - \alpha)\exp^{\ln N^{-\rho}}\right]. \tag{10.2A}$$

Expanding the right-hand side of (10.2A) by a first-order Taylor series, obtain

$$\frac{-\rho}{\mu^{y}}y = \ln K^{\circ} + \frac{\alpha L^{-\rho^{\circ}}}{K^{\circ}}(\ln L^{-\rho} - \ln L^{-\rho^{\circ}})$$

$$+ \frac{(1 - \alpha)N^{-\rho^{\circ}}}{K^{\circ}}(\ln N^{-\rho} - \ln N^{-\rho^{\circ}}), \tag{10.3A}$$

where $K^{\circ} \equiv [\alpha L^{-\rho^{\circ}} + (1 - \alpha)N^{-\rho^{\circ}}]$. Multiply (10.3A) by $-\mu/\rho$ and collect all constant terms, whence

$$y = K' + \mu z l + (1 - z)\mu n, \tag{10.4A}$$

where

$$z \equiv \frac{\alpha L^{-\rho^{\circ}}}{\alpha L^{-\rho^{\circ}} + (1 - \alpha)N^{-\rho^{\circ}}}.$$

If the constant term in (10.4A) is ignored, the latter is identical to equation (10.1) in the text.

The log-linear approximation to value added that is reported in equation (10.6) in the text is derived as follows. Recall that V (in natural terms) is defined by

$$V = Y - RN,$$

which may be rewritten as

$$V = \exp^{\ln Y} - \exp^{\ln (RN)} \tag{10.5A}$$

whence

$$\ln V \equiv v = \ln [\exp^{\ln Y} - \exp^{\ln (RN)}]. \tag{10.6A}$$

Expanding (10.6A) by a first-order Taylor series, obtain

$$V = \ln V^o + \frac{Y^o}{V^o} (\ln Y - \ln Y^o)$$

$$- \frac{(RN)^o}{V^o} [\ln (RN) - \ln (RN^o)], \tag{10.7A}$$

or collecting constants and using logarithmic notation,

$$V = \ln V' + \frac{Y^o}{V^o} y - \frac{(RN)^o}{V^o} [(p_n - p) + n]. \tag{10.8A}$$

Note that

$$\frac{Y^o}{V^o} \simeq \frac{1}{1 - s}$$

and

$$\frac{(RN)^o}{V^o} \simeq \frac{1}{1 - s}$$

where s is defined as in the text. Hence, suppressing the constant in (10.3A), we may write

$$V = \frac{y}{1-s} - \frac{s}{1-s} [(p_n - p) + n]. \qquad (10.9A)$$

Next, recall that n is given (from [10.26]) as

$$n = -b_1(p_n - p) - b_2(w - p).$$

Substituting (10.26) into (10.9A) yields

$$V = \frac{y}{1-s} - \frac{s}{1-s} (1 - b_1)(p_n - p) + \frac{sb_2}{1-s} (w - p),$$

$$(10.10A)$$

which is identical to equation (10.6) in the text.

NOTES

1. The foreign economy is large insofar as it is independent of economic events occurring in the domestic economy.

2. The fixed short-run level of capital stock is suppressed in (10.1').

3. In the interest of analytical simplicity we have excluded the real interest rate as a determinant of domestic aggregate demand. The inclusion of the latter in the aggregate demand function is usually justified on the basis of the investment component of aggregate demand. To validate this argument, it is further necessary to assume that the commodities in question are nonperishable and storable. We have not made this assumption.

4. We have also assumed that there is no domestic production of oil. Such an assumption is quite realistic for a number of OECD countries.

5. This assumption would imply that our framework is only applicable to, say, a developed West European economy trading with the United States and completely dependent upon OPEC for oil imports. The lack of organized capital markets in developing nations would make our model inappropriate for the latter.

6. The prediction of the steady-state exchange rate is not necessarily a trivial matter. To avoid further complexities we do not address this issue here; see Bhandari (in press) for a discussion of this subject.

7. If the domestic economy were, say, France and the large foreign economy the United States, in view of the fact that the United States imports less than half of its oil requirement, it can be argued that the U.S. price level is much less sensitive to OPEC price increases than the French price level.

8. Notice that the last (negative) term in (10.16') is composed of the product of three fractions and is less than unity. Therefore, $\delta_1' > 1$ ensures that $\Delta > 0$. Actually, a milder

condition, $\delta'_1 > \gamma_1 s$, is also sufficient. Use will be made of the milder requirement in the fifth section.

9. Clearly,

$$\frac{d \mid d\bar{y}/dp_n^* \mid}{ds} > 0,$$

implying that the gross output movement in absolute terms is also increasing in s. Also note that if it is assumed that $\Delta < 0$, long-run gross output increases following the oil price increase. We regard this as an unlikely outcome, and this is another reason for out assumption that $\Delta > 0$.

10. In terms of production function parameters, it can be shown that (10.23) holds if

$$\frac{z(\mu + \rho)}{(1 + \rho)} + \left[1 + \frac{z(\mu + \rho)}{1 - \mu} \right] - \mu s - \rho(1 - z) + (\mu + \rho)(1 - z)s$$

$$+ \frac{z(\mu + \rho)s}{(1 - \mu)} \left[\frac{(\mu + \rho)(1 + z)}{1 + \rho} - \mu \right] > 0.$$

If $s = 0$, this condition cannot hold.

11. Even if $\theta \approx 0$ (which is definitely not the perfect foresight value of the expectational parameter), stability can be shown to require that

$$(\alpha'a_1 + \beta'b_2)[(1 - \gamma_1)(1 - \gamma_1)(1 - s) - s + sb_1(1 - \gamma_1) + \delta'_1]$$
$$+ [1 - s(1 + b_2)][\delta'_1 + (1 - \gamma_1)(\alpha'a_2 + (1 - \gamma_1)\beta'b_1)] + \gamma_1 sb_2(1 - g)(1 - s)$$
$$+ \alpha'\gamma_1 s(a_1b_1 - a_2b_2) - \gamma_1 s(1 - s)(1 - b_1) > 0.$$

If

$$s < \frac{1}{1 + b_2},$$

this condition is almost certainly satisfied. Any positive value of θ contributes further to stability, as can be seen by inspection of the denominator of Q.

12. If $s = 0$, it can be shown that $M = a'[\delta_1 - g(1 - \gamma_1)]/(1 - \gamma_1) > 0$.

13. Under these circumstances it is also conceivable (although perhaps implausible) that the spot exchange rate appreciates. It can be easily shown that

$$\frac{de}{dp_n^*} < 0$$

requires that

$$\left[1 - M \left(\frac{d\bar{w}/dp_n^*}{d\bar{e}/dp_n^*} \right) \right] < 0.$$

If both M and $d\bar{w}/dp_n^*$ are positive or of different signs, then spot appreciation is not possible (recall that both M and $[(d\bar{w}/dp_n^*)/(d\bar{e}/dp_n^*)]$ are < 1). Only if both are negative and large in absolute terms is there a possibility of spot appreciation. It is left to the reader to evaluate the likelihood of this event in terms of the structural parameter of the economy.

14. For values of s in the neighborhood of unity a perverse outcome characterized by an increase in the short-run level of gross output is possible. During adjustment, output falls, as in the "normal" case, to its lowered steady-state value.

15. Note that $(Q - M) = \dfrac{(\delta_2 + a')(1 - Q)}{(\delta_1 - \delta_0 + b')} > 0$.

16. We assume that oil is denominated in terms of foreign currency.

17. Perfect foresight must also be suspended if an unanticipated announcement of a future shock is made.

18. See, for example, Brock (1974).

19. This is a sufficient condition that w_t is bounded as $t \to \infty$ (see Gray and Turnovsky [1979]) and also ensures that real balances remain finite.

20. This will violate the assumption that $\delta_1' > 1$ made in the third section but can still be consistent with the saddle point case—i.e., $\Delta > 0$.

21. To properly consider the U.K. case, it would be necessary to take into account domestic production of the imported input.

22. The oil price increase need not be announced; all that is required is for information to become available, which causes an expectation of an increase at $t = T$.

23. An immediate rise in oil prices will not occur if producers are prevented from cutting back production because of supply contracts and if consumers have no storage capacity.

REFERENCES

Benavie, A. 1978 "Foreign Prices and Income in a Macromodel with Two Domestic Sectors." *International Economic Review* 19 (October) 611–31.

Bhandari, J. In press. "Expectations, Exchange Rate Volatility and Non-Neutral Disturbances." *International Economic Review*.

Brock, W. 1974 "Money and Growth: The Case of Long Run Perfect Foresight." *International Economic Review* 15 (October): 750–77.

Bruno, M., and J. Sachs. 1979 "Macroeconomic Adjustment with Import Price Shocks: Real and Monetary Aspects." Seminar Paper no. 118, University of Stockholm, Sweden.

Buiter, W. 1978 "Short Run and Long Run Effects of External Disturbances under a Floating Exchange Rate." *Economica* 45 (August): 251–72.

Corden, W. M. 1977 *Inflation, Exchange Rates and the World Economy*. edited by T. Rybezynski. Chicago: University of Chicago Press.

Corden, W. M., and P. Oppenheimer. 1975 "Economic Issues for the Oil-Importing Countries." In *The Economics of the Oil Crisis*, edited by T. Rybezynski. New York: Holmes and Meier.

Dornbusch, R. 1980 "Relative Prices, Employment and the Trade Balance in a Model with Intermediate Goods." Mimeographed. Cambridge: MIT.

———. 1976 "Expectations and Exchange Rate Dynamics." *Journal of Political Economy* 84 (December): 1161–76.

Dunn, R. 1980 "Exchange Rates, Payments Adjustment and OPEC: Why Deficits Persist." *Princeton Essays i: International Finance*, no. 137 (December).

Findlay, R., and C. Rodriguez. 1977 "Intermediate Imports and Macroeconomic Policy under Flexible Exchange Rates." *Canadian Journal of Economics* 10 (May): 208–17.

Gray, M., and S. Turnovsky. 1979 "The Stability of Exchange Rate Dynamics under Perfect Myopic Foresight." *International Economic Review* 20 (October):643–66.

Krugman, P. Forthcoming. "Oil and the Dollar." In *Economic Interdependence and Flexible Exchange Rates*, edited by J. Bhandari and B. Putnam. Cambridge; MIT Press.

Obstfeld, M. 1980 "Intermediate Imports, the Terms of Trade and the Dynamics of the Exchange Rate and Current Account." *Journal of International Economics* 10 (November): 461–80.

Purvis, D., and W. Buitero. Forthcoming. "Oil, Disinflation and Export Competitiveness." In *Economic Interdependence and Flexible Exchange Rates,* edited by J. Bhandari and B. Putnam. Cambridge: M.I.T. Press.

Rodriguez, C. 1980. "Flexible Exchange Rates and Imported Inputs: A Dynamic Analysis of the Interactions between the Monetary and Real Sectors for a Small Open Economy." In *The Functioning of Flexible Exchange Rates*, edited by D. Bigman and T. Taya. Cambridge: Ballinger.

Schmid, M. 1976 "A Model of Trade in Money, Goods and Factors." *Journal of International Economics* 6 (November): 347–61.

11

INTERMEDIATE IMPORTS, THE CURRENT ACCOUNT, AND FLEXIBLE EXCHANGE RATES: A DYNAMIC GENERAL EQUILIBRIUM MODEL

This chapter deviates from the previous chapters by assigning a more explicit role to the process of asset accumulation and hence to the balance of payments in exchange rate determination. A key difference between the present chapter and the earlier ones is that the domestic and foreign security markets are brought to the fore via a portfolio balance-type approach rather than the approach hitherto followed, which essentially suppresses the bond sector by the use of the arbitrage relation. Another distinguishing feature of the model developed in this chapter (which can be viewed to be an extension of Obstfeld [1979]) is the source of dynamic adjustment. In previous chapters the dynamics resulted from price stickiness and/or demand adjustment, while in Chapter 10 we assumed that prices were flexible but that nominal wages adjusted over time. In this chapter we make the polar assumption that all nominal variables adjust instantaneously. The dynamic path of the economy is then governed by foreign asset accumulation (as well as by expectational adjustment). To give some substance to our analysis we examine the static and dynamic consequences of an increase in the real price of an intermediate input. In this way the results of this chapter may be compared and contrasted with those emerging from the previous chapter where a similar issue is considered.

The point of departure of the model developed here from other well-known portfolio balance models such as Branson (1976) and Turnovsky (in press) is that unlike the latter, the real sector of the model is given considerable attention rather than disposed of via an instantaneous purchasing power parity relationship. Thus, the resulting analysis involves considerable interplay between the real and monetary sectors of the economy and may be more properly referred to as a general equilibrium model. The dynamic nature of the model results from the accumulation of assets and the evolution of exchange market expectations. The approach utilizes the assumption of perfect foresight, thus permitting an analysis of both unanticipated and anticipated shocks. Although the framework can clearly be used to analyze several disturbances, the discussion is limited to the static and dynamic effects of an increase in the real price of the intermediate import. Static Keynesian-type models to analyze this issue are provided by Izzo and Spaventa (1974), Findlay and Rodriguez (1977), Findlay (1979), and Dornbusch (1979), while the real aspects of the problem are emphasized in Bruno and Sachs (1978). This chapter may also be viewed as an extension to these approaches by including a full menu of assets as well as by incorporating exchange rate expectations and imperfect international capital mobility.

The first section lays out the analytical framework, while the impact effects of the shock are discussed in the second section. In the third section the assumption of perfect foresight of exchange rates is invoked, leading to a discussion of the transitional dynamics and stationary state of the model. The fourth section concludes this chapter and notes that conventional beliefs concerning the impact of the oil price disturbance on the exchange rate and current account need to be carefully qualified. The Appendix to Chapter 11 provides the basis for some of the expressions used in the text.

THE ANALYTICAL FRAMEWORK

The analysis focuses on a small economy and is based on a number of simplifying assumptions. The domestic economy produces a single traded good, the production of which requires domestic labor and the intermediate input (oil). Home consumption is divided between the home good and an imported (final) good, and these goods are regarded by domestic agents as being imperfectly substitutable. The domestic economy is assumed to be small enough in import markets so that the supply of the imported commodities is perfectly elastic at the existing foreign currency prices. On the other hand, the demand curve for domestic exports is of the usual downward shape, reflecting the fact that foreign residents also view the two final goods as imperfect substitutes. All goods (including the intermediate good) are perishable, and domestic agents allocate their wealth among the available financial assets, which are assumed to be gross substitutes. These are domestic money, domestic (nontraded), bonds and foreign bonds.[1] There is no currency substitution, so that domestic portfolios do not include foreign currency. In addition, foreign residents do not hold either domestic money or the domestically issued bond. There is no distinction between base money and bank credit, and all considerations of physical capital accumulation are suppressed. Domestic nominal wages are flexible, so that full employment prevails. This assumption is in direct contrast to the unemployment scenario considered in the previous chapter. Finally, the price of domestic goods adjusts so that the home goods market clears continuously. For convenience it is assumed that the domestic country's net foreign asset position is always positive.

The following notation is employed:

y: real domestic output,
s: intensity level of intermediate input in domestic production,
$\bar{L}$: domestic employment,
P: domestic currency price of the home good,
P^*: foreign currency price of the imported final good,
e: domestic exchange rate (domestic price of foreign exchange),
M: domestic nominal money supply,
B: nominal stock of domestic bonds (denominated in domestic currency),
F: nominal stock of foreign bonds (denominated in foreign currency) held by domestic residents,
A: domestic nominal wealth,
L: fraction of domestic wealth allocated to holdings of domestic money,
H: fraction of domestic wealth allocated to holdings of domestic bonds,
G: fraction of domestic wealth allocated to holdings of foreign bonds,
α: real price of the intermediate input,
v: domestic real value added,
r: yield on domestic bonds,
r^*: yield on foreign bonds assumed to be exogenously fixed,
ε: rate of expected depreciation of domestic currency,
c: real domestic consumption expenditure,
X: real domestic exports,
I: real domestic imports, and
T: domestic terms of trade.

Dots denote time derivatives, and overbars denote steady-state values. Partial derivatives are indicated by subscripts.

Production of the domestic good is described by a well-behaved constant returns to scale (CRS) production function:

$$y = y(s, \bar{L}), \qquad y_1, y_2 > 0, \tag{11.1}$$

where $\bar{L}$ is the full-employment labor input. Profit maximization implies the intermediate input demand function

$$s = J(\alpha), \; J_1 < 0. \tag{11.2}$$

Consequently, domestic value added, v, is given by

$$v = y[J(\alpha), \bar{L}] - \alpha J(\alpha) \tag{11.3}$$

The asset sector of the model is quite deliberately in the spirit of earlier work on the portfolio balance approach to flexible exchange rates (see, for example, Branson [1976]; Turnovsky [in press]) and is described by the following equilibrium relationships:

$$M = L(v, r, r^* + \varepsilon) \cdot A, \; L_1 > 0, \; L_2 < 0, \; L_3 < 0, \tag{11.4}$$

$$B = H(v, r, r^* + \varepsilon) \cdot A, \; H_1 < 0, \; H_2 > 0, \; H_3 < 0, \tag{11.5}$$

$$eF = G(v, r, r^* + \varepsilon) \cdot A, \; G_1 < 0, \; G_2 < 0, \; G_3 > 0, \tag{11.6}$$

$$A = M + B + eF. \tag{11.7}$$

The signs of the partial derivatives follow from the assumption of gross substitutability. Clearly the fractions of wealth—L, H, and G—add up to unity and only two of equations (11.4) through (11.6) are independent. In what follows, the analysis will be conducted with (11.4) and (11.5). Thus, the demand functions for financial assets depend upon net income v (or value added)[2] and the relevant yields and are homogeneous of degree one in domestic wealth. At any point in time the stocks of M, B, and F are fixed, although domestic monetary authorities may of course conduct open market operations in either the domestic bond market or the foreign exchange market. In the absence of such policy actions the stock of domestically held foreign assets changes with the status of the current account. This will be detailed below.

The real sector of the model is described by the home goods market equilibrium condition

$$y[J(\alpha), \bar{L}] = c\left(v, \frac{A}{P}\right) + X(T) - \frac{1}{T} I(T, c), \tag{11.8}$$

where $c_1, c_2 > 0$; $X_1 < 0$; $I_1, I_2 > 0$; $c_1 < 1$; and $I_2 < 1$. Total demand for the home good is given by the sum of domestic consumption and exports less imports or by the sum of domestic absorption and the real trade balance. Real domestic consumption is assumed to be determined by net income and real wealth, while domestic exports depend upon the terms of trade. Imports, on the other hand, are determined by both the terms of trade and the level of total domestic consumption expenditure. The signs of the partial derivatives above are entirely conventional.

Given the level of expected depreciation ε, the asset market relations (11.4) and (11.5) along with (11.7) determine the domestic interest rate and exchange rate, so that the existing asset stocks are willingly held. Then, given the exchange rate, the domestic price level is determined from (11.8) to be compatible with goods market equilibrium. The solutions for the interest rate, exchange rate, and domestic price level correspond to a short-run or instantaneous equilibrium. The transition from the latter to a steady-state equilibrium is governed by the evolution of exchange rate expectations and the accumulation of foreign assets. In the steady state all accumulation has ceased (and expectational phenomena have been eliminated), so that the current and capital accounts are each zero. The transitional dynamics and steady-state properties of the model are examined in detail in the third section. Meanwhile, we turn to the impact effects of an unannounced increase in the real price of the intermediate input, α.

IMPACT EFFECTS OF AN INCREASE IN THE INPUT PRICE

Effects on Asset Prices

Consider first the effect of an increase in α upon domestic value added, v. Thus, from (11.3)

$$\frac{\partial v}{\partial \alpha} = y_1 J_1 - J - \alpha J_1.$$
(11.9)

Defining $-J_1 \frac{\alpha}{J} \equiv \eta$ as the elasticity of demand of the intermediate input, $y_1 \frac{s}{y} \equiv \beta$ as the elasticity of output supply with respect to the intensity level s, and θ_s as the share $\frac{\alpha s}{y}$, equation (11.9) can be seen to be negative when

$$\eta \left(1 - \frac{\beta}{\theta_s} \right) < 1.$$
(11.10)

Equation (11.10) confirms the widely held view that with a low elasticity of demand of the intermediate input the materials price increase leads to a decline in domestic net real income. Alternatively, with a supply elasticity greater than the share θ_s, (11.10) is also necessarily satisfied.

Consider next the effects of the increase in α upon the domestic interest rate and exchange rate. Taking total differential of (11.4) and (11.5) and using (11.7), the impact on the domestic interest rate is

$$\frac{dr}{d\alpha} = \frac{\dfrac{L_1}{L} - \dfrac{H_1}{H}}{\dfrac{H_2}{H} - \dfrac{L_2}{L}} \cdot \left(\frac{\partial v}{\partial \alpha} \right), \tag{11.11}$$

which is of the same sign as $\partial v / \partial \alpha$, that is, the effect on net income. Further, the semielasticity of the exchange rate with respect to α is obtained as

$$\frac{de}{d\alpha} \frac{1}{e} = \frac{1}{G} \left(\frac{H_1 L_2 - H_2 L_1}{L H_2 - H L_2} \right) \cdot \left(\frac{\partial v}{\partial \alpha} \right).^3 \tag{11.12}$$

Several aspects of (11.12) should be noted. First as G, the fraction of domestic wealth allocated to foreign bonds, decreases to zero, the exchange rate response increases (in absolute terms) without limit. Next, there are two sources of ambiguity in (11.12). One is the effect on domestic value added, while the other stems from the term $(H_1 L_2 - H_2 L_1)$. Assuming that (11.10) is satisfied—$\partial v / \partial \alpha < 0$—the spot exchange rate is seen to depreciate if

$$\left| \frac{H_1}{H_2} \right| < \left| \frac{L_1}{L_2} \right| \tag{11.13}$$

and appreciate if the reverse inequality holds. Equation (11.13) relates spot depreciation to the relative semielasticity ratios between income and the domestic interest yield for domestic bonds as compared with money. This is thus another example of the importance of asset substitutability emphasized by Tobin (1969). A special case, however, removes the second source of ambiguity in (11.12). If domestic and foreign bonds are perfectly substitutable, $H_2 \rightarrow \infty$ and $H_3 \rightarrow -\infty$. This clearly implies that provided net income declines, the spot exchange rate always depreciates. The same point can be seen from (11.13).

This discussion makes it clear that the conventional explanation that links weakness of certain currencies to unanticipated input price increases needs to be qualified. This conclusion is in conformity with results obtained in the pure currency-substitution framework of Obstfeld (1979). For example, the combination of a low input demand elasticity (resulting from poor technical substitution possibilities) with limited substitutability between domestic and foreign (world) securities is seen to imply that the spot exchange rate appreciates following the materials price shock. Finally, the fraction of domestic wealth allocated to foreign securities plays an important role, and the direction of exchange rate change notwithstanding, the lower the fraction, the greater the absolute magnitude of the exchange rate change.

Effect on Domestic Price

Given the behavior of the exchange rate, the impact on the domestic price level is obtained by solving for the market clearing level of prices $P = P[e(\alpha), \alpha]$. Hence,

$$\frac{dP}{d\alpha} = \frac{\partial P}{\partial e} \frac{de}{d\alpha} + \frac{\partial P}{\partial \alpha} . \tag{11.14}$$

It is easy to show that for goods market equilibrium the elasticity of the price level with respect to the exchange rate is positive but less than 1. Thus, the semielasticity of the price level with respect to α can be obtained as

$$\frac{dP}{d\alpha} \frac{1}{P} = \eta_{P.e} \left(\frac{de}{d\alpha} \frac{1}{e} \right) + \frac{\partial P}{\partial \alpha} \frac{1}{P} , \tag{11.15}$$

where $\eta_{P.e}$ is the elasticity of the price level with respect to the exchange rate for goods market equilibrium, and the last term measures the semielasticity of the price level with respect to α, given the exchange rate.[4] Denoting by Q the Marshall-Lerner expression $(X_1 - I_1 + I)$ and assuming initially balanced trade and a unity value for the initial terms of trade,

$$\frac{dP}{d\alpha} \frac{1}{P} = \eta_{P.e} \left(\frac{de}{d\alpha} \frac{1}{e} \right) + \frac{y_1 J_1 - c_1(1 - I_2)\dfrac{\partial \iota}{\partial \alpha}}{Q - c_2(1 - I_2)\dfrac{A}{P}} , \tag{11.16}$$

where

$$\eta_{P.e} = \frac{Q - c_2(1 - I_2)\dfrac{eF}{P}}{Q - c_2(1 - I_2)\dfrac{A}{P}} > 0 \text{ but } < 1$$

if the Marshall-Lerner stability criterion is satisfied, that is, $Q < 0$. Inspection of (11.16) reveals several sources of ambiguity. Even if the materials price shock leads to a decline in value-added income and to spot depreciation,

(11.16) is ambiguous because of the second term. The latter measures the effect on the goods market of an increase in α for a given exchange rate. It can be seen that the input price increase leads to a decline in gross output y and, to the extent that net output declines, to a decline in consumption as well as import demand. The net change in excess demand for given prices and exchange rates is given by the term $[y_1 J_1 - c_1(1 - I_2)\partial v/\partial \alpha]$. In addition to this direct effect exchange depreciation also impinges upon excess commodity demand by enhancing the terms of trade and increasing domestic nominal wealth. The latter exchange/depreciation-induced effect is captured by the first term in (11.16).

Although other conditions can be found, a strongly sufficient condition for domestic prices to increase in the face of a decline in net value-added income (i.e., $\partial v/\partial \alpha < 0$) and spot depreciation is that

$$y_1 J_1 - c_1(1 - I_2) \frac{\partial v}{\partial \alpha} < 0. \tag{11.17}$$

Defining $k \equiv c_1(1 - I_2) < 1$, (11.17) can be reduced to

$$\eta \left[1 + \left(\frac{1 - k}{k} \right) \frac{\beta}{\theta_s} \right] > 1 \tag{11.18}$$

Reference to (11.10) and (11.18) indicates that these two conditions place upper and lower bounds upon admissible finite values of η, the input demand elasticity if the input price rise is to lead to decreased net output, spot depreciation, as well as increased domestic prices, that is,

$$\left(1 - \frac{\beta}{\theta_s} \right) < \frac{1}{\eta} < \left[1 + \left(\frac{1 - k}{k} \right) \frac{\beta}{\theta_s} \right]. \tag{11.19}$$

Clearly, (11.19) will not be satisfied by very low input demand elasticities, although it is compatible with high supply elasticities, that is, β. These investigations thus reveal that it is the elasticity of supply of output with respect to the intermediate input that may play a more crucial role in determining the short-run response of the economy than the input demand elasticity.

As pointed out earlier, conditions can easily be found such that the spot exchange rate appreciates following the materials price increase. In particular suppose that substitutability between domestic and foreign assets is so poor that (11.13) does not hold and the spot rate appreciates. Then a sufficient condition for domestic prices to decline as well is

$$\eta \left[1 + \left(\frac{1 - k}{k} \right) \frac{\beta}{\theta_s} \right] < 1, \tag{11.20}$$

which is clearly satisfied for low values of the input demand elasticity (as is [11.10]). In general, therefore, the conditions that ensure that prices and exchange rates move in the same direction following the input price shock are different depending upon whether there is initial spot depreciation or appreciation. In the former case high supply elasticities are called for and in the latter, a low input demand elasticity.

As a final exercise consider the effects of the increase upon the terms of trade P/e.[5] Thus,

$$\frac{dT}{d\alpha} \frac{1}{T} = \frac{de}{d\alpha} \frac{1}{e} (\eta_{P.e} - 1) + \frac{\partial P}{d\alpha} \frac{1}{P}. \tag{11.21}$$

If there is initial spot depreciation and $\partial P/\partial\alpha \ 1/P < 0$, the terms of trade worsen following the input price increase.[6] It is left to the interested reader to work out other cases.

TRANSITIONAL DYNAMICS AND THE STEADY STATE

The dynamics of the model are governed by two relations. One relationship is the condition that with a freely floating exchange rate the balance of payments is in equilibrium, implying that the current account surplus equals the net inflow of foreign assets in the absence of government intervention. The second relationship results from the evolution of exchange rate expectations. As indicated earlier, the approach adopted in this chapter assumes perfect foresight with respect to exchange rate movements. We turn first to the latter source of dynamic evolution.

From (11.4) and (11.5) one can solve for the exchange rate (and domestic interest rate) as a function of α, F, and ε. Thus,

$$e = e(\alpha, F, \varepsilon), \ e_1?, \ e_2 < 0, \ e_3 > 0, \tag{11.22}$$

where e_1 is the exchange rate response to an increase in α for a given value of foreign assets and rate of expected depreciation and has been previously derived as (11.12) in the second section. It is easy to verify that the elasticity of the exchange rate with respect to F is -1—hence, the sign of e_2. Finally, an increase in ε also increases the current exchange rate.[7] Next, inverting (11.22) and imposing the perfect foresight requirement $\dot{e}/e = \varepsilon$, we obtain

$$\frac{\dot{e}}{e} = \varepsilon(\alpha, F, e), \; \varepsilon_1?, \; \varepsilon_2 > 0, \; \varepsilon_3 > 0, \tag{11.23}$$

where $\varepsilon_1 = -e_1/e_3$, $\varepsilon_2 = -e_2/e_3$, and $\varepsilon_3 = 1/e_3$. The balance of payments equilibrium condition yields

$$\dot{F} = [TX(T) - I(T, c) - J(\alpha) \cdot \alpha T] + r^*F, \tag{11.24}$$

where the first term is the trade balance, and the second is the service account, both being measured in terms of foreign currency. Equation (11.24) can be reduced to a function similar in form to (11.23), i.e.,

$$\dot{F} = \dot{F}(\alpha, F, e), \; \dot{F}_1?, \; \dot{F}_2 < 0, \; \dot{F}_3 > 0, \tag{11.25}$$

where

$$\dot{F}_1 = -\eta \frac{\beta}{\theta_s} (1 - c_1) \left(1 - \frac{\theta_s y}{Q} \right) + \frac{c_1 I_2 \beta y}{Q}$$

$$- (1 - \eta) \left\{ 1 - c_1 \left[1 - \frac{\theta_s y}{Q} (1 - I_2) \right] \right\}$$

$$- c_2 \left[1 - \frac{\theta_s y}{Q} (1 - I_2) \right] \frac{A}{P} (G - \eta_{P,e})$$

$$\times \left[\frac{L_2 H_1 - L_1 H_2}{(LH_2 - HL_2)G} \right] J \left[\eta \left(1 - \frac{\beta}{\theta_s} \right) - 1 \right] \underset{<}{\overset{>}{=}} 0,$$

$$\dot{F}_2 = -c_2 \left(\frac{A}{P \cdot F} \right) \eta_{P,e} \left[1 - \frac{J \cdot \alpha(1 - I_2)}{Q} \right] + r^*$$

which is negative if the system is stable, and

$$\dot{F}_3 = -c_2 \frac{A}{P} (G - \eta_{P,e}) \left[1 - \frac{J\alpha(1 - I_2)}{Q} \right],$$

which is positive.[8] The system represented by (11.23) and (11.25) is shown in Figure 11.1. The slopes of the $\dot{e}/e = 0$ and $\dot{F} = 0$ curves follow from the signs of the partials noted above. K is the point of long-run equilibrium, and the dotted line shows the saddle point adjustment path. Consider now the

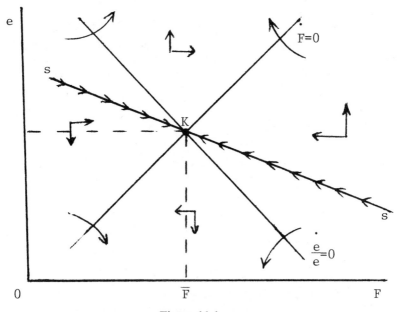

Figure 11.1

long-run effects of an unannounced input price increase. The $\dot{e}/e = 0$ locus is seen to shift horizontally by the amount

$$\left. \frac{dF}{d\alpha} \right|_{\frac{\dot{e}}{e} = 0} = -\frac{\varepsilon_1}{\varepsilon_2}, \tag{11.26}$$

while the $\dot{F} = 0$ locus undergoes the horizontal shift

$$\left. \frac{dF}{d\alpha} \right|_{\dot{F} = 0} = -\frac{\dot{F}_1}{\dot{F}_2}. \tag{11.27}$$

The signs of both expressions are ambiguous, depending upon the signs of ε_1 and $\dot{F}_1$. Note, however, that if the spot rate depreciates ($e_1 > 0$), it is clear that $\varepsilon_1 < 0$, and hence the $\dot{e}/e = 0$ locus shifts to the right. The direction of shift of the $\dot{F} = 0$ locus is of the same sign as the sign of $\dot{F}_1$ and is quite ambiguous without further restrictions. To gain further insight into the likely outcome, we analyze various special cases corresponding to specific parameter magnitudes. In particular we evaluate the likelihood of the conventional result associating exchange depreciation and a current deficit with a low input demand elasticity.

Assume for simplicity that $|Q| \to \infty$. No essential difference is made if this assumption were not invoked. However, it does simplify some of the analytical expressions considerably. Then the signs of $\dot{F}_2$ and $\dot{F}_3$ are not altered, but $\dot{F}_1$ is now given by

$$\dot{F}_1 \Big/_{|Q| \to \infty} = -\eta \frac{\beta}{\theta_s} (1 - c_1) - (1 - \eta)(1 - c_1)$$

$$- c_2 \frac{A}{P} (G - \eta_{P,e}) \left[\frac{L_2 H_1 - L_1 H_2}{(LH_2 - HL_2)G} \right]$$

$$\times J \left[\eta \left(1 - \frac{\beta}{\theta_s} \right) - 1 \right], \qquad (11.28)$$

which is still sign indeterminate without knowledge of the degree of asset substitutability. Assume for expositional purposes that this key parameter is such that $(L_2 H_1 - H_1 L_2) > 0$—that is, poor asset substitutability prevails— and that $\theta_s < \beta$. It follows that $\dot{F}_1 < 0$ for all values of $\eta \leq 1$ including $\eta = 0$. From (11.27) this implies that the $\dot{F} = 0$ locus shifts to the left. Further, under the same assumptions $e_1 < 0$, implying that $\varepsilon_1 > 0$ or that the $\dot{e}/e = 0$ locus also undergoes a leftward shift. This outcome is illustrated in Figure 11.2. Depending upon the relative shifts in the two curves, there may be equilibrium depreciation or appreciation. The diagram illustrates the case of equilibrium appreciation. The ambiguity in the effect on the equilibrium exchange rate notwithstanding, it is clear that the spot rate appreciates unambiguously from K to L and thereafter depreciates over time to the new stationary equilibrium at K'. Thus, exchange rate overshooting has occurred, and the spot rate appreciates to a greater proportional extent than the steady-state exchange rate. Furthermore, had the relative shifts in the two curves been such that equilibrium depreciation occurred, the spot exchange rate movement would have mispredicted even the direction of the ultimate change in the exchange rate. Finally, it can be seen that the current account moves unambiguously into deficit, not surplus, under these circumstances, and the steady-state level of foreign assets decumulates from $\bar{F}$ to $\bar{F}'$[9]. Thus, the combinations of low asset substitutability, low input demand elasticity, and high substitutability leads inevitably to spot appreciation coupled with a current account deficit.[10]

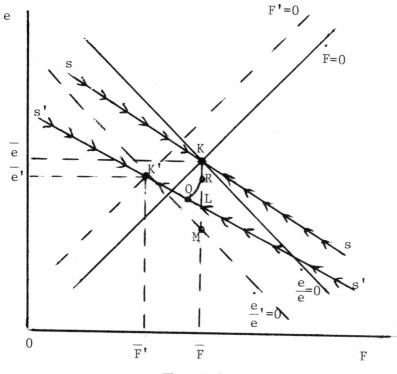

Figure 11.2

To see the role of the degree of asset substitutability further, consider the case where η is again close to zero but where financial assets are highly substitutable. In this case the $e/e = 0$ locus clearly shifts to the right, while the $F = 0$ locus may shift either to the right or left, depending upon the magnitude of c_1 in relation to c_2. If the $F = 0$ locus shifts to the right, the situation is the opposite to that discussed above, and correspondingly the spot exchange rate must depreciate, while the current account goes into surplus. Further, the greater the value of the input demand elasticity η, the greater the current surplus. Next consider the case wherein the $F = 0$ locus shifts to the left, while the $e/e = 0$ locus moves to the right by virtue of the assumption of high substitutability between domestic and foreign assets. The higher the value of $|Q|$ and the lower the value of c_2 (the wealth effect upon consumption demand), the more likely that the $F = 0$ locus shifts to the left (assuming that $\eta \simeq 0$).[11] Figure 11.3 represents one such possibility. Upon impact the spot exchange rate depreciates discretely to L and thereafter

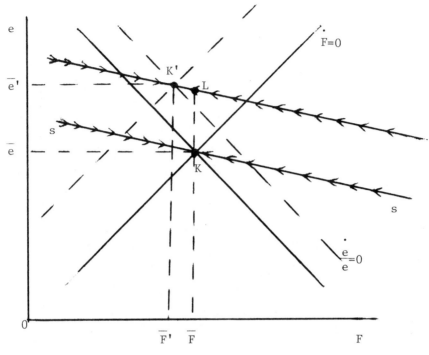

Figure 11.3

depreciates further to its stationary equilibrium at K'. The adjustment path is characterized by a declining level of foreign assets in view of the current account deficit that emerges. Hence, the conventionally expected outcome (i.e., exchange depreciation coupled with a current deficit) can be associated with the circumstances that are popularly believed to lead to this outcome (low or zero input demand elasticity).

Consider finally the effects of an anticipated increase in the input price α. For expositional purposes assume that both the input demand elasticity and the degree of asset substitutability are low enough for Figure 11.2 to be relevant. At the instant the input price increase is announced, the exchange rate depreciates discretely to point R. R lies above the short-run equilibrium point L that is applicable to an unanticipated price shock. At R there is anticipation of further appreciation, and the economy moves to Q with an appreciating exchange rate and foreign asset decumulation. At Q the announcement goes into effect, and the exchange rate depreciates along the stable arm of the saddle to the new stationary state at K'. Thus, the anticipation of the future shock reduces the extent of exchange rate overshooting. An important lesson of this exercise is, however, that the conventional association of a current surplus with an appreciating exchange rate is true of an unanticipated disturbance but not of an anticipated shock. This point has been also noted in a somewhat different context by Dornbusch and Fischer (1980).

CONCLUSION

This chapter has examined the short- and long-run effects of an increase in the real price of an imported input under a system of freely floating exchange rates. The analysis indicates that the conventional association of such a shock with exchange depreciation and a current account deficit is subject to considerable qualification. Specifically, neither spot depreciation nor steady-state depreciation is the inevitable consequence; nor is it true that a current account deficit will always result. The likelihood of these occurrences can in fact be related to a few critical parameters of the economy, such as the input demand elasticity, output supply elasticity, degree of substitutability between domestic and foreign bonds, and the fraction of domestic portfolios allocated to foreign assets. It is possible to associate exchange depreciation coupled with a current deficit with an inelastic demand for the input. For this to be the case it is necessary that domestic and foreign assets be highly substitutable. If the latter were poor substitutes, the same circumstances would lead instead to spot appreciation accompanied by a current deficit rather than a current surplus. The adjustment path of the economy was examined under the assumption of perfect foresight of exchange rates, both in response to an unanticipated and an anticipated input price shock. An implication of the dynamic analysis is that the association between a current surplus and an appreciating exchange rate will not hold in the face of an anticipated disturbance.

APPENDIX TO CHAPTER 11

The purpose of this appendix is to demonstrate the derivations of certain expressions utilized in the text. The elasticity of the price level with respect to the exchange rate $\eta_{P,e}$ for goods market equilibrium is obtained as follows.

Differentiating the goods market condition

$$y = c\left(y, \frac{A}{P}\right) + X(T) - \frac{1}{T} i(T, c)$$

and denoting by $Q(< 0)$ the Marshall-Lerner expression $(X_1 - I_1 + I)$ and assuming that $T = 1$ initially, we have

$$\frac{\partial T}{\partial e} = \frac{-c_2(1 - I_2)}{Q} \frac{\partial(A/P)}{\partial e} \quad, \tag{11.1A}$$

since $\partial y/\partial e = 0$. Next,

$$\frac{\partial(A/P)}{\partial e} = \frac{eF}{P}(1 - \eta_{P,e}) - \left(\frac{M + B}{P}\right)\eta_{P,e},$$

while

$$\frac{\partial T}{\partial e} = \frac{1}{e}(\eta_{P,e} - 1)$$

by definition. Therefore,

$$(\eta_{P,e} - 1) = \frac{-c_2(1 - I_2)}{Q} \frac{eF}{P}(1 - \eta_{P,e}) - \left(\frac{M + B}{P}\right)\eta_{P,e}.$$

Collecting terms,

$$\eta_{P,e} = \frac{Q - c_2(1 - I_2)\dfrac{eF}{P}}{Q - c_2(1 - I_2)\dfrac{A}{P}} \quad, \tag{11.2A}$$

which can easily be seen to be positive but less than 1. Next consider the derivation of the derivatives $\dot{F}_1, \dot{F}_2,$ and $\dot{F}_3$. From the adjustment equation

$$\dot{F} = [TX(T) - I(T, c) - J(\alpha) \cdot \alpha T] + r^*F$$

and

$$\dot{F}_3 = \frac{\partial\dot{F}}{\partial e} = Q\frac{\partial T}{\partial e} - I_2\frac{\partial c}{\partial e} - J \cdot \alpha\frac{\partial T}{\partial e} \quad.$$

Recalling the solution for $\partial T/\partial e$ from (11.1A) and that $\partial c/\partial e = c_2[\partial(A/P)/\partial e]$,

$$\dot{F}_3 = -c_2\frac{\partial(A/P)}{\partial e}\left[1 - \frac{J\alpha}{Q}\left(1 - I_2\right)\right].$$

Since

$$\frac{\partial A/P}{\partial e} \, e = \frac{eF}{P}(1 - \eta_{P,e}) - \left(\frac{M+B}{P}\right)\eta_{P,e},$$

we obtain

$$\frac{\partial A/P}{\partial e} \, e \, \frac{P}{A} = G(1 - \eta_{P,e}) - (1 - G)\eta_{P,e} = G - \eta_{P,e}.$$

Consequently,

$$\dot{F}_3 = -c_2 \frac{A}{P \cdot e}(G - \eta_{P,e})\left[1 - \frac{J\alpha(1 - I_2)}{Q}\right].$$

Substituting for the definitions of G and for $\eta_{P,e}$ from (11.2A), it is easily shown that $\dot{F}_3 > 0$.

Similarly, it is shown that

$$\dot{F}_2 = \frac{\partial \dot{F}}{\partial F} = Q\frac{\partial T}{\partial F} + r^* - I_2\frac{\partial c}{\partial F} - J\alpha\frac{\partial T}{\partial F},$$

and

$$\frac{\partial T}{\partial F} = \frac{-c_2(1 - I_2)}{Q} \frac{\partial(A/P)}{\partial F},$$

and that

$$\frac{\partial c}{\partial F} = c_2\left[\frac{\partial(A/P)}{\partial F}\right],$$

so that

$$\dot{F}_2 = -c_2\frac{\partial(A/P)}{\partial F}\left[1 - \frac{J\alpha}{Q}(1 - I_2)\right] + r^*.$$

The expressions in the text can be obtained by evaluating $\partial(A/P)/\partial F$ and recalling that $\eta_{e,F} = -1$.

Finally,

$$\dot{F}_1 = \frac{\partial \dot{F}}{\partial \alpha} = Q\frac{\partial T}{\partial \alpha} - I_2\frac{\partial c}{\partial \alpha} - J\alpha\frac{\partial T}{\partial \alpha} - (\alpha J_1 + J).$$

From the goods market we obtain

$$\frac{\partial T}{\partial \alpha} = \frac{y_1 J_1}{Q}[1 - c_1(1 - I_2)] + \frac{c_1}{Q}(1 - I_2)(J + \alpha J_1)$$

$$- \frac{c_2(1 - I_2)}{Q}\frac{\partial (A/P)}{\partial \alpha}, \tag{11.3A}$$

while

$$\frac{\partial c}{\partial \alpha} = c_1(y_1 J_1 - J - \alpha J_1) + c_2\frac{\partial (A/P)}{\partial \alpha}, \tag{11.4A}$$

whence

$$\dot{F}_1 = y_1 J_1(1 - c_1)\left(1 - \frac{J\alpha}{Q}\right) - y_1 J_1\frac{J\alpha}{Q}c_1 I_2 + c_1(\alpha J_1 + J)$$

$$\times \left[1 - \frac{J\alpha}{Q}(1 - I_2)\right] - (\alpha J_1 + J) - c_2\frac{\partial (A/P)}{\partial \alpha}$$

$$\times \left[1 - \frac{J\alpha}{Q}(1 - I_2)\right]. \tag{11.5A}$$

Recall the definition of η and that

$$\frac{\partial (A/P)}{\partial \alpha} = \frac{\partial (A/P)}{\partial e} \cdot \frac{\partial e}{\partial \alpha} = \frac{\partial e}{\partial \alpha}\frac{A}{P}(G - \eta_{P,e}).$$

Also note that one can write $\partial v/\partial \alpha = J[\eta(1 - \beta/\theta_s) - 1]$ and recall further the definitions of β and θ_s from which it is clear that $y_1/\alpha = \beta/\theta_s$. Putting all the pieces together, (11.5A) can be transformed to yield equation (11.25) in the text.

NOTES

1. For convenience it is assumed that these bonds are risk-free fixed-price variable-yield securities. Consequently, we can abstract from capital gains and losses caused by interest rate variations.

2. Strictly speaking, the income variable should include real net interest income, ei^*F/P, received from abroad. We have ignored this complication in the interest of analytical simplicity.

3. The semielasticity rather than the derivative or elasticity is computed to bring the role of G to the fore.

4. Identical results are obtained by directly differentiating the goods market equilibrium condition (11.8).

5. The foreign price level P^* is assumed to be fixed at unity for convenience.

6. Recall that

$$\frac{\partial P}{\partial \alpha} \frac{1}{P} = \frac{y_1 J_1 - c_1(1 - I_2)\dfrac{\partial v}{\partial \alpha}}{Q - c_2(1 - I_2)\dfrac{A}{P}} + \eta_{p,e}\left(\frac{de}{d\alpha} \cdot \frac{1}{e}\right)$$

7. $\dfrac{e_3}{e} = \dfrac{(L_2 H_3 - L_3 H_2)}{G(L H_2 - H L_2)} > 0.$

8. The derivation of these expressions is discussed in the Appendix to Chapter 11.

9. The effect on the current account is given by $dF/d\alpha = \dot{F}_3(de/d\alpha + \dot{F}_1$, which is clearly negative in this case. It can be shown that $d\bar{e}/d\alpha = -\dot{F}_2 \varepsilon_1 + \varepsilon_2 \dot{F}_1/\dot{F}_2 \varepsilon_3 - \varepsilon_2 \dot{F}_3$, which is indeterminate in general. More interestingly, $\partial(d\bar{e}/d)/\partial\eta > 0$, indicating that higher values of η are likely to lead to less appreciation or more depreciation in the steady state.

10. It is also possible to compare the adjustment path of the economy under perfect foresight with that under static expectations. Consider Figure 11.2, for example. Under static expectations the impact equilibrium occurs at M on the new $\dot{e}/e = 0$ locus. Thereafter, the exchange rate declines to K'. Consequently, static expectations are associated with a sharper exchange rate appreciation that rational expectations (or perfect foresight).

11. In the limit when $|Q| \rightarrow \infty$ and $c_2 = 0$,

$$\dot{F}_1 \bigg|_{\eta \,=\, 0} = -(1 - c_1),$$

that is, the $\dot{F}_1 = 0$ locus unambiguously shifts leftward. This locus can also shift to the left for a finite value of $|Q|$, provided that $c_2 \simeq 0$.

REFERENCES

Branson, W. 1976. "Asset Markets and Relative Prices in Exchange Rate Determination." Seminar Paper no. 66, I.I.E.S., Sweden.

Bruno, M., and J. Sachs. 1978. "Macroeconomic Adjustment with Import Price Shocks: Real and Monetary Aspects," Seminar Paper no. 118, I.I.E.S., Sweden.

Dornbusch, R. 1979. "Relative Prices, Employment and the Trade Balance in a Model with Intermediate Goods." Mimeographed. Rio de Janeiro, Brazil.

Dornbusch, R., and S. Fischer. 1980. "Exchange Rates and the Current Account." *American Economic Review* 70 (December): 1960–71.

Findlay, R. 1979. "Oil Supplies and Employment Levels: A Simple Macro Model." Mimeographed. New York.

Findlay, R., and C. Rodriguez. 1977. "Intermediate Imports and Macroeconomic Policy under Flexible Exchange Rates." *Canadian Journal of Economics* (May): 208–17.

Izzo, L., and L. Spaventa. 1974. "Some Internal and External Effects of the Rise in the Price of Oil." *Banca Nazionale del Lavoro Quarterly Review* (March): 12–27.

Obstfeld, M. 1979. "Intermediate Imports and the Dynamics of the Current Account." Mimeographed. New York.

Tobin, J. 1969. "A General Equilibrium Approach to Monetary Theory." *Journal of Money, Credit and Banking* (February): 266–81.

Turnovsky. S. In press. "The Asset Market Approach to Exchange Rate Determination." *Journal of Macroeconomics*.

12

EXCHANGE RATE AND PRICE LEVEL DYNAMICS IN A SIMPLE MONETARY MODEL

Michael Mussa

This chapter explores the properties and implications of a simple monetary model of the dynamic behavior of the exchange rate and the general price level of a small open economy. Three features of the present analysis distinguish it from other recent analyses of exchange rate and price level dynamics in simple monetary models.[1] First, even in a model that abstracts from changes in real economic conditions requiring adjustments of relative prices and assumes purchasing power parity as a condition of equilibrium, the equilibrium exchange rate and domestic price level do not depend simply on the ratio of the domestic nominal money supply to real demand to hold domestic money (determined by domestic real income and other exogenous factors).[2] Rather, because expectations of future exchange rates and price levels influence the conditions for current economic equilibrium, and because these expectations are endogenously determined through the requirement of consistency with the structure of the economic system, the current equilibrium exchange rate and domestic price level depend on expectations concerning money supplies and exogenous factors affecting money demands in all future periods. Second, the analysis of exchange rate and price level dynamics is not, as in many models, primarily an analysis of the process of convergence of the exchange rate and price level toward fixed long-run levels or growth paths.[3] Rather, the analysis of equilibrium dynamics incorporates both a determination of expected changes in the equilibrium exchange rate and price level due to expected changes in the money supplies and the exogenous factors influencing money demands; and a determination of unexpected changes in the equilibrium exchange rate and price level due to new information that alters expectations concerning future money supplies and exogenous determinants of money demands. In addition the analysis of disequilibrium dynamics, under the assumption of a sticky domestic price level, encompasses both an analysis of the process of convergence of the exchange rate and the price level toward their respective equilibrium paths, given an intitial state of disequilibrium; and an analysis of how disequilibrium is generated by unexpected changes in the equilibrium path of the domestic price level. Third, the analysis of disequilibrium dynamics does not rely on an adjustment rule that allows the domestic price level to respond only to the existing state of disequilibrium, thereby leading to anomalies whenever the equilibrium price level is expected to be changing.[4] Rather, because the price level adjusts to expected changes in its own equilibrium value, as well as to the existing state of disequilibrium, the economic system always converges in a sensible fashion toward its expected equilibrium path; only unexpected events associated with new information about future money supplies or determinants of money demands lead to the creation of new disequilibrium.

The chapter is organized in the following manner. The basic model of the determination of the equilibrium exchange rate and domestic price level is presented in the first section. The implications of this model for the dynamic behavior of the equilibrium exchange rate and price level are investigated in the second section. In the third section this dynamic analysis is extended to the disequilibrium case where the domestic price level is sticky and where its adjustment is controlled by an economically appropriate form of price adjustment rule. In the fourth section the general analysis of disequilibrium dynamics is illustrated for the special case of a permanent increase in the level of the domestic money supply, starting at some specific future date. The fifth section discusses the implications of the present analysis for six important issues in recent discussions of exchange rate dynamics: the meaning of the idea that an exchange rate is an asset price; the appropriate concept of "the equilibrium exchange rate" when changing conditions are expected to alter the economically appropriate exchange rate over time; the several distinct meanings of the concept of "rational expectations," as applied in analyses of exchange rate behavior; the theoretical reason why exchange rate changes should incorporate a random component that, as an empirical matter, appears to dominate actual exchange rate changes; the appropriate form of price adjustment rule to deal with the phenomenon of disequilibrium associated with a sticky-price level; and the nature of exchange rate overshooting in a model that assumes a sticky-price level.

It should be emphasized that the formal model that underlies the discussion of these general issues embodies a number of highly restrictive, simplifying assumptions. The model focuses exclusively on monetary factors influencing the evolution of the price level and exchange rate of a small open economy. It abstracts from changes in real economic conditions that affect relative prices and current account imbalances as factors influencing the evolution of the price level and the exchange rate. It assumes that the domestic money supply and all factors affecting the demand to hold domestic money, other than the domestic price level and the domestic nominal interest rate, are determined exogenously. It ignores, specifically, endogenous determination of the level of domestic income, portfolio balance effects of changes in asset stocks, currency-substitution effects on the demand to hold domestic money, risk premiums in the foreign exchange market, and any response of monetary policy to events in either the domestic economy or the foreign exchange market. The point is that, despite these restrictive assumptions, we obtain from a simple monetary model a much richer analysis of exchange rate and price level dynamics than has been suggested by many other treatments of such a simple model. This increased richness arises primarily from explicit treatment of situations in which economic conditions affecting the price level and the exchange rate are expected to be changing over time, and in which these expectations are subject to continual revision in the light of newly accruing information. The implicit assertion is that the general qualitative features of the present analysis, based on a simple monetary model, carry over to more elaborate and realistic models of price level and exchange rate behavior.[5]

THE EQUILIBRIUM EXCHANGE RATE AND PRICE LEVEL

To develop the main points of this chapter, it is convenient to use a simple monetary model of the determination of prices and the exchange rate for a small open economy. Domestic money is assumed to be held only by domestic residents, and the requirement for equilibrium in the domestic money market is expressed by the condition

$$p + k + \eta \cdot i = m, \quad \eta > 0, \tag{12.1}$$

where p is the logarithm of the domestic price level, k is a shift parameter (representing the effect of changes in income and other exogenous factors affecting money demand), i is the nominal interest rate on securities denominated in domestic money, and m is the logarithm of the domestic money supply. International mobility of financial capital requires that the interest rate on securities denominated in domestic money satisfy the interest arbitrage condition

$$i = i^* + f, \tag{12.2}$$

where i^* is the (exogenously given) interest rate on securities denominated in world money, and f is the forward discount on domestic money in the foreign exchange market. Ignoring the possible effect of risk premiums in the forward foreign exchange market, it is assumed that

$$f(t) = E\{[e(t + 1) - e(t)]; t\}, \tag{12.3}$$

where e is the logarithm of the spot exchange rate (defined as the price of a unit of world money in terms of domestic money), and $E[X(s); t]$ denotes the expectation of $X(s)$ based on information available at time t.

In full equilibrium domestic goods are viewed as perfect substitutes for goods available in world markets. This implies that the full equilibrium values of the domestic price level and the exchange rate must be consistent with the requirement of purchasing power parity:

$$\bar{p} = \bar{e} + p^*, \tag{12.4}$$

where a bar superscript denotes the full equilibrium value of a variable. Combining this requirement with the money market equilibrium condition and the interest arbitrage condition, it follows that

$$\bar{e} = m - k - p^* + \eta \cdot i^* + \eta \cdot \bar{f}. \tag{12.5}$$

The appearance of the equilibrium forward discount, $\bar{f}$, as one of the determinants of the equilibrium exchange rate is of critical importance because it provides the key dynamic link through which the current equilibrium exchange rate is connected with events that are expected to influence the equilibrium exchange rate in future periods.[6]

To complete the analysis of the determination of the equilibrium exchange rate and the equilibrium domestic price level, it is necessary to specify how the expectations of future exchange rates that influence $\bar{f}$ are formed. It is assumed that these expectations are rational, in the sense that they are consistent with equation (12.5) in all future periods. This assumption implies that the expected path of the equilibrium exchange rate, based on information available at time t, must satisfy the following, forward-looking difference equation:

$$E[\bar{e}(s + 1); t] = (1/\eta) \cdot (E[\bar{e}(s); t]$$
$$- E\{[m(s) - k(s) - p^*(s) + \eta \cdot i^*(s)]; t\}). \tag{12.6}$$

The economically relevant solution of this difference equation can be written in the form

$$E[\bar{e}(s); t] = E[F(s); t] - E[p^*(s); t],^7 \tag{12.7}$$

where $F(s)$ is an exponentially weighted average of the exogenous factors affecting the equilibrium exchange rate and price level in period s and beyond:

$$F(s) = (1/1 + \eta) \cdot \sum_{j=0}^{\infty} (\eta/1 + \eta)^j \cdot E[w(s + j); t]. \tag{12.8}$$

The exogenous factors that determine $F(s)$, the w's, measure the excess of the domestic nominal money supply over the exogenous components of the demand for domestic money:

$$w(u) = m(u) - k(u) + \eta \cdot r^*(u), \tag{12.9}$$

where r^* is the real interest rate in the rest of the world, that is,

$$r^*(u) = i^*(u) - E\{[p^*(u + 1) - p^*(u)]; u\}. \tag{12.10}$$

Further, assuming that expectations are consistent with (12.4), it follows from (12.7) that the expected equilibrium path of the domestic price level is determined by

$$E[\bar{p}(s); t] = E[F(s); t]. \tag{12.11}$$

The result (12.11) is familiar from rational expectations models of inflationary dynamics in a closed economy.[8] In such models the equilibrium price level expected for any future period is an exponentially weighted average of expected differences between money supply and the exogenous component of money demand further in the future. This is because the equilibrium price level at any moment must equate money demand and money supply at that moment, and money demand depends on the expected inflation rate, which, in turn, depends on the exogenous factors that will affect the equilibrium price level in the future. The only modification of this closed-economy result in the present open-economy model is the appearance of the world real interest rate r^* as one of the factors determining the exogenous component of the demand to hold domestic money. It is the real interest rate r^* rather than the nominal interest rate i^* that influences domestic money demand because, in full equilibrium, the exchange rate adjusts to maintain purchasing power parity and thus severs any link between the domestic nominal interest rate (which influences the demand to hold domestic money) and the purely inflationary component of the world nominal interest rate.

An important feature of the results (12.7) and (12.11), which describe the expected equilibrium paths of the exchange rate and the domestic price level, is that they are valid for any assumption about expectations concerning the behavior of the w's. For example, suppose that k, i^*, and p^* have known constant values, k_0, i_0^* and p_0^*, respectively. if it is also assumed that m is expected to equal its current value, $m(t)$, in all future periods, the critical determinant of both $E(\bar{e}(s); t)$ and $E(\bar{p}(s); t)$ is given by

$$E[F(s); t] = m(t) - k_0 + \eta \cdot i_0^* \text{ for all } s \geq t. \tag{12.12}$$

Thus, in this special case we have the result that is assumed in some discussions of exchange rate dynamics where the equilibrium domestic price level and the equilibrium exchange rate are expected to be constant and are proportional to the current domestic money supply. However, for alternative assumptions about the expected path of m it will not generally be true that the expected equilibrium domestic price level and exchange rate will either be constant or proportional to the current domestic money supply. In particular consider the case where m is expected to be constant at its current level $m(t)$ until period $T - 1 \geq t$ and then increase to a higher constant level m_T for all $s \geq T$. In this case we have

$$E[F(s); t] = m_T - k_0 + \eta \cdot i_0^* \text{ for } s \geq T \tag{12.13}$$

and

$$E[F(s); t] = m(t) + [m_T - m(t)] \cdot (\eta(1 + \eta)^{s-T} - k_0 + \eta \cdot i_0^*$$
$$\text{for } s < T. \tag{12.14}$$

Thus, the increase in the money supply that is expected to occur at time T influences the expected equilibrium path of the exchange rate and the domestic price level before time T. This example illustrates the general and important point that the equilibrium exchange rate and domestic price level at any date should reflect not only the contemporaneous domestic money supply and exogenous elements in money demand but also expectations concerning the future behavior of these basic determinants of the exchange rate and the price level.

THE DYNAMICS OF EQUILIBRIUM

From the results (12.7) and (12.11) we may determine the causes of changes in the full equilibrium exchange rate and domestic price level. The change in each consists of two basic components: the expected change based on information available at time t and the unexpected change induced by new information received between t and $t+1$. These two components may be determined by applying the expected change operator—$D^e[X(t)] = E\{[X(t+1) - X(t)]; t\}$—and the unexpected change operator—$D^u[X(t)] = E[X(t+1); t+1] - E[X(t+1); t]$—to (12.7) and (12.11). For the expected change in the equilibrium domestic price level we have

$$D^e[\bar{p}(t)] = D^e\{E[F(t); t]\}$$

$$= (1/1 + \eta) \cdot \sum_{j=0}^{\infty} (\eta/1 + \eta)^j$$

$$\times E\{[w(t+j+1) - w(t+j)]; t\}. \tag{12.15}$$

Thus, the expected equilibrium inflation rate is an exponentially weighted average of expected future changes in the w's. In accord with purchasing power parity the expected change in the equilibrium exchange rate is equal to the excess of the expected equilibrium domestic inflation rate over the expected inflation rate in the rest of the world:

$$D^e[\bar{e}(t)] = D^e\{E[F(t); t]\} - D^e[p^*(t)]. \tag{12.16}$$

The unexpected component of the change in the equilibrium domestic price level is an exponentially weighted average of changes in expectations of future w's;

$$D^u[\bar{p}(t)] = D^u\{E[F(t); t]\}$$

$$= (1/1 + \eta) \cdot \sum_{j=0}^{\infty} (\eta/1 + \eta)^j$$

$$\times \{E[w(t+j+1); t+1] - E[w(t+j+1); t]\}. \tag{12.17}$$

Purchasing power parity dictates that the unexpected change in the equilibrium exchange rate must equal the excess of the unexpected component of the domestic equilibrium inflation rate over the unexpected component of the inflation rate in the rest of the world:

$$D^u[\bar{e}(t)] = D^u[F(t)] - D^u[p^*(t)]. \tag{12.18}$$

Two features of these results for the determinants of changes in the equilibrium price level and equilibrium exchange rate deserve special notice. First, any systematic and predictable element in the change in the equilibrium price level or equilibrium exchange rate ought to be incorporated in the expected change components given in (12.12) and (12.13). In contrast the unexpected change components ought to be completely random and unpredictable since they reflect the impact of new information that, by definition, ought to be unpredictable. Second, the unexpected components of the change in the equilibrium price level and the equilibrium exchange rate could be quite large, even if the expected components of change were small. This is so because there is no necessary relationship between the magnitude of expected changes in the w's or in p^*'s, based on information at time t, and the change in expectations about the future w's or about $p^*(t + 1)$ that results from new information received between t and $t + 1$.[9]

To obtain more specific results concerning changes in the equilibrium price level and exchange rate, it is necessary to make specific assumptions about expectations concerning changes in the w's and in p^* based on information available at time t and about how these expectations change in the light of new information received between t and $t + 1$. One approach is simply to make some arbitrary assumption about expectations formation and revision that is useful for the purpose of some theoretical exercise. Another more general and more revealing approach is to assume that expectations are formed and revised in a rational manner, that is, in a manner consistent with the information that economic agents possess concerning the processes that actually generate the exogenous factors that drive the behavior of the equilibrium price level and equilibrium exchange rate.

This assumption of rational expectations is different from the assumption of rational expectations employed in the first section. In the first section it was assumed that economic agents used their expectations about future w's and p^*'s in a manner consistent with the structure of the economic system to deduce expected future paths for the equilibrium domestic price level and equilibrium exchange rate. The new assumption is that economic agents form and revise their expectations about future w's and p^*'s in a manner that optimally exploits the information available about the processes generating these variables. This assumption of rationality in expectation formation and revision is analytically separable from the assumption that these expectations are used in a rational manner.

To illustrate the assumption of rationality in the formation and revision of expectations, suppose that k, i^*, and p^* are known to be constant (at k_0, i_0^* and p_0^*, respectively) and that m is an observable variable that is known to follow a random walk, that is,

$$m(s) = m(s - 1) + x(s), \tag{12.19}$$

where $x(s)$ is a serially independent random variable with zero mean and finite variance. In this case

$$D^e[\bar{p}(t)] = D^e[\bar{e}(t)] = 0 \qquad (12.20)$$

and

$$D^u[\bar{p}(t)] = D^u[\bar{e}(t)] = m(t + 1) - m(t). \qquad (12.21)$$

These results reflect the fact that when m is known to follow a random walk, the rational prediction of any future m is always the current m, and the rational revision of the prediction of any future m is always equal to the observed change in m.

Alternatively, suppose that k, i^*, and p^* are known to be constant and that m has a fixed mean m_0 plus a serially independent error. In this case

$$D^e[\bar{p}(t)] = D^e[\bar{e}(t)] = - (1/1 + \eta) \cdot [m(t) - m_0] \qquad (12.22)$$

and

$$D^u[\bar{p}(t)] = D^u[\bar{e}(t)] = + (1/1 + \eta) \cdot [m(t) - m_0]. \qquad (12.23)$$

These results reflect the fact that any current deviation of $m(t)$ from m_0 is expected to persist only one period, and that any new deviation of $m(t + 1)$ from m_0 is entirely a surprise and is also expected to persist from only one period.

Finally, consider the case where k, i^*, and p^* are known to be constant and the change in m is described by a random walk plus noise, that is,

$$m(s) = m(s - 1) + v(s) + x(s), \qquad (12.24)$$

where $x(s)$ is a serially independent random variable with zero mean and finite variance, and v follows a random walk

$$v(s) = v(s - 1) + z(s), \qquad (12.25)$$

where $z(s)$ is a serially independent random variable with zero mean, finite variance, and zero covariance with $x(s)$. In this case expected changes in the equilibrium price level and exchange rate reflect current beliefs concerning the long-run rate of monetary expansion, which are summarized by current expectations concerning the level of the random walk component of the change in m, that is,

$$D^e[\bar{p}(t)] = D^e[\bar{e}(t)] = \hat{v}(t) \equiv E[v(t); t]. \qquad (12.26)$$

Unexpected changes in both $\bar{p}$ and $\bar{e}$ reflect both the unexpected change in m, $D^u[m(t)] = m(t + 1) - m(t) - \hat{v}(t)$, and the (unexpected) change in expectations concerning the long-run rate of monetary expansion:

$$D^u[\bar{p}(t)] = D^u[\bar{e}(t)] = m(t + 1) - m(t) - \hat{v}(t)$$
$$+ \eta \cdot [\hat{v}(t + 1) - \hat{v}(t)]. \qquad (12.27)$$

The change in expectations concerning v depends on the information that economic agents possess concerning the decomposition of the observed change in the money supply between its random walk and noise components. If the decomposition is known,

$$\hat{v}(t + 1) - \hat{v}(t) = v(t + 1) - v(t). \qquad (12.28)$$

However, if only the total change in m and the variances of its components are known, it is rational to employ an adaptive expectations mechanism in revising expectations concerning v; specifically,

$$\hat{v}(t + 1) - \hat{v}(t) = A \cdot \{[m(t + 1) - m(t)] - \hat{v}(t)\}.^{10} \qquad (12.29)$$

According to this mechanism, a fraction A of the difference between the observed change in the money supply, $m(t + 1) - m(t)$, and previously expected change, $\hat{v}(t) = E\{[m(t + 1) - m(t)]; t\}$, is attributed to a change in v. The fraction A reflects the relative likelihood that an unexpected change in m is due to a random change in v rather than to pure noise. Combining (12.29) and (12.27), it follows that when economic agents do not know the decomposition of the change in m between its random walk and noise components, the equilibrium price level and exchange rate respond more than proportionately to an unexpected increase in the money supply:

$$D^u[\bar{p}(t)] = D^u[\bar{e}(t)] = (1 + \eta) \cdot [m(t + 1) - m(t) - \hat{v}(t)]. \qquad (12.30)$$

These three examples illustrate the general principle that when expectations about the future behavior of the exogenous variables m, k, i^*, and p^* are formed in a rational manner, the expected and unexpected components of changes in the equilibrium price level and exchange rate depend on the nature of the stochastic processes generating these exogenous variables. In particular even in the case where all exogenous variables other than the domestic money supply are constant, there need not be a proportional response of the equilibrium price level and exchange rate to changes in the domestic money supply.

STICKY PRICES AND DISEQUILIBRIUM DYNAMICS

In analyzing equilibrium dynamics the domestic price level was assumed to adjust immediately to maintain purchasing power parity. Different results are obtained if it is assumed that the domestic price level is sticky and responds slowly to disequilibrium. A simple price adjustment rule that captures this idea is

$$D[p(t) = \beta \cdot [e(t) + p^*(t) - p(t)], \quad \beta > 0, \qquad (12.31)$$

where $D[p(t)] = p(t + 1) - p(t)$ and where the extent of disequilibrium is assumed to be measured by the divergence from purchasing power parity. Unfortunately this rule is inadequate when the equilibrium domestic price level is expected to be changing over time. For example, this rule cannot produce persistent price inflation as an equilibrium response to persistent monetary expansion in excess of the growth of real money demand. To correct this deficiency, it is necessary to add an acceleration term to (12.31), which adjusts the domestic price level to expected changes in its equilibrium value, and to write the price adjustment rule as

$$D[p(t)] = \beta \cdot [e(t) + p^*(t) - p(t)] + D^e[e(t) + p^*(t)]. \quad (12.32)$$

Rationality of expectations, in the sense of consistency with the structure of the economic system, requires that expectations concerning the future time paths of the domestic price level and the exchange rate take account of the price adjustment rule (12.32) and of the requirements of momentary equilibrium other than purchasing power parity, as expressed by equations (12.1), (12.2), and (12.3). The implications of equations (12.1) through (12.3) are summarized by the forward-looking difference equation that characterizes the expected change in the exchange rate:

$$D^e[e(t)] = (1/\eta) \cdot [p(t) - m(t) + k(t)] - i^*(t). \qquad (12.33)$$

The expected future paths of the domestic price level and the exchange rate must form a solution to the system of simultaneous difference equations (12.32) and (12.33), applied to expectations of future price levels and exchange rates, based on information available at time t, and must be consistent with the initial condition associated with the predetermined value of $p(t)$.[11]

The economically relevant solution of this system is given by

$$E[p(s); t] = E[\bar{p}(s); t] + [p(t) - \bar{p}(t)] \cdot (1 - \beta)^{s-t} \qquad (12.34)$$

and

$$E[e(s); t] = E[\bar{e}(s); t] + [e(t) - \bar{e}(t)] \cdot (1 - \beta)^{s-t}, \qquad (12.35)$$

where $E[\bar{p}(s); t]$ and $E[\bar{e}(s); t]$ are the expected equilibrium values of p and e for time s, based on information available at time t, as determined by (12.7) and (12.11). From (12.34) and (12.35) it is apparent that the expected divergence between the actual and the equilibrium price level and between the actual and the equilibrium exchange rate at any future date s are proportional to the divergences existing at time s, and that these divergences are expected to decay exponentially with the factor $(1 - \beta)^{s-t}$. This convergence toward equilibrium is expected to occur regardless of the complexity of expected future movements in the equilibrium price level and equilibrium exchange rate. This strong convergence property reflects the operation of the price adjustment rule (12.32), which corrects the domestic price level for existing disequilibrium and for future expected changes in the equilibrium price level.

The existing state of disequilibrium at time t is determined by the divergence between the predetermined domestic price level and the exponentially weighted average of expected future exogenous factors that determines the current full equilibrium domestic price level; specificially,

$$\bar{p}(t) - p(t) = E[F(t); t] - p(t) \equiv Q(t). \qquad (12.36)$$

The divergence of the current exchange rate from its full equilibrium value is a reflection of the divergence between $p(t)$ and $\bar{p}(t)$:

$$e(t) - \bar{e}(t) = - (1/\beta\eta) \cdot [p(t) - \bar{p}(t)] = (1/\beta\eta) \cdot Q(t). \quad (12.37)$$

The explanation of (12.37) is essentially the same as in Dornbusch's (1976) model of exchange rate dynamics.[12] When the domestic price level is below its full equilibrium value, maintenance of money market equilibrium (described by equation [12.1]) requires that the domestic nominal interest rate exceed its full equilibrium value by an amount

$$i(t) - \bar{i}(t) = (1/\eta) \cdot [\bar{p}(t) - p(t)], \qquad (12.38)$$

where

$$\bar{i}(t) = i^*(t) + D^e[\bar{e}(t)] = r^*(t) + D^e[\bar{p}(t)]. \qquad (12.39)$$

To maintain interest parity (equation [12.2]) with a higher-than-equilibrium domestic nominal interest rate, the actual forward premium on foreign exchange $f(t) = D^f[e(t)]$ must exceed the full equilibrium forward premium $\bar{f}(t) = D^f[\bar{e}(t)]$ by the amount

$$f(t) - \bar{f}(t) = i(t) - \bar{i}(t). \tag{12.40}$$

From (12.35) it follows that the actual exchange rate must be below the full equilibrium exchange rate by an amount sufficient to justify the required excess of $f(t)$ over $\bar{f}(t)$, which also must equal

$$D^e[e(t) - \bar{e}(t)] = -\beta \cdot [e(t) - \bar{e}(t)]. \tag{12.41}$$

For equations (12.38), (12.40), and (12.41) to be simultaneously satisfied, the divergence of the exchange rate from its full equilibrium value must be inversely related to the divergence of the domestic price level from its full equilibrium value in the manner indicated by (12.37).

When the domestic price level is sticky and its adjustment is governed by (12.32), the analysis of price level and exchange rate dynamics needs to be modified from that given in the second section to take account of the evolution of disequilibrium. Specifically, from (12.34) and (12.36) it follows that the expected change in the domestic price level between t and $t + 1$, based on information available at time t, is given by

$$D^e[p(t)] = D^e[\bar{p}(t)] + D^e[Q(t)], \tag{12.42}$$

where $D^e[\bar{p}(t)]$ is the expected change in the full equilibrium price level as determined by equation (12.15) in the second section, and

$$D^e[Q(t)] = -\beta \cdot Q(t) = -\beta \cdot [\bar{p}(t) - p(t)] \tag{12.43}$$

reflects the expected change in the state of disequilibrium existing at time t through the operation of the price adjustment rule. The expected change in the exchange rate also has an equilibrium component and a disequilibrium component:

$$D^e[e(t)] = D^e[\bar{e}(t)] - (1/\eta\beta) \cdot D^e[Q(t)], \tag{12.44}$$

where $D^e[\bar{e}(t)]$ is given by (12.16), and where the disequilibrium component in $D^f[e(t)]$ reflects the result (12.37).

Since the change in the domestic price level between t and $t + 1$ is determined at time t by the price adjustment rule (12.32), the unexpected change in the domestic price level is necessarily zero; that is,

$$D^u[p(t)] = 0. \tag{12.45}$$

It follows that since unexpected changes in the equilibrium domestic price level cannot immediately affect the actual price level, they contribute instead to the existing state of disequilibrium as reflected in the fact that

$$D^u[Q(t)] = D^u[\bar{p}(t)] = D^u\{E[F(t); t]\}. \tag{12.46}$$

In contrast to the domestic price level, the exchange rate at time $t + 1$ is free to adjust to unexpected changes in its own full equilibrium value and to the spillover effect the disequilibrium created by unexpected changes in the full equilibrium price level:

$$D^u[e(t)] = D^u[\bar{e}(t)] + (1/\eta\beta) \cdot D^u[Q(t)]. \tag{12.47}$$

Further, making use of (12.18) and (12.46), it follows that

$$D^u[e(t)] = (1 + 1/\eta\beta) \cdot D^u\{E[F(t); t]\} - D^u[p^*(t)]. \tag{12.48}$$

Thus, because of the spillover of disequilibrium, the exchange rate responds more than proportionately to new information that induces an unexpected change in the weighted average of future exogenous factors that determine both the equilibrium exchange rate and the equilibrium price level. This more-than-proportionate response of the exchange rate is a generalization of Dornbusch's overshooting effect, which will be discussed more thoroughly in the next section.

THE RESPONSE TO AN EXPECTED FUTURE INCREASE IN THE MONEY SUPPLY

To illustrate the preceding analysis of disequilibrium dynamics, it is useful to consider an example where all exogenous variables other than the money supply are constant and expected to remain so, where prior to time t the domestic money supply is constant at m_0 and expected to remain so, and where there is no disequilibrium prior to time t. At time t information is received that at some future date $T \geq t$ the money supply will rise to a new level $m_T > m_0$ and then remain there. After time t there are no further changes in any exogenous variables or in expectations concerning these variables.

Under these assumptions the actual and expected paths of the exchange rate, the equilibrium exchange rate, the price level, the equilibrium price level, and the state of disequilibrium—measured by $Q(u) = \bar{p}(u) - p(u)$—are as described in Figure 12.1. Based on information available at any date $s < t$, the exchange rate and the equilibrium exchange rate, and the price

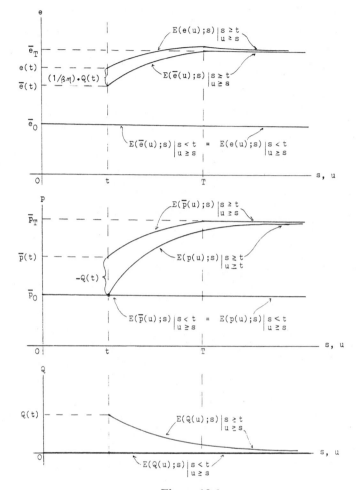

Figure 12.1

level and equilibrium price level expected for any time $u \geq s$ are constant at the values given by

$$E[e(u); s] = E[\bar{e}(u); s] = \bar{e}_0 \equiv m_0 - k_0 + \eta \cdot i_0^* - p_0^* \quad (12.49)$$

and

$$E[p(u); s] = E[\bar{p}(u); s] = \bar{p}_0 \equiv m_0 - k_0 + \eta \cdot i_0^*; \quad (12.50)$$

and the expected state of disequilibrium at any future time, $E[Q(u); s]$, is zero. Based on information available at any date $s \geq t$, the expected equilibrium exchange rate and equilibrium price level for any time $u \geq T$ rise by the amount of the increase in m at T to the constant levels given by

$$E[\bar{e}(u); s] = \bar{e}_T = m_T - k_0 + \eta \cdot i_0^* - p_0^* \qquad (12.51)$$

and

$$E[\bar{p}(u); s] = \bar{p}_T = m_T - k_0 + \eta \cdot i_0^*; \qquad (12.52)$$

for any time u between t and T they rise to the values given by

$$E[\bar{e}(u); s] = \bar{e}_0 + (m_T - m_0) \cdot (\eta/1\eta)^{T-u} \qquad (12.53)$$
$$= \bar{e}_T - (m_T - m_0) \cdot [1 - (\eta/1 + \eta)^{T-u}]$$

and

$$E[\bar{p}(u); s] = \bar{p}_0 + (m_T - m_0) \cdot (\eta/1 + \eta)^{T-u}$$
$$= \bar{p}_T - (m_T - m_0) \cdot [1 - (\eta/1 + \eta)^{T-u}]. \qquad (12.54)$$

As explained at the end of the first section, the increase in the expected equilibrium exchange rate and price level during the interval between t and T reflects the dependence of the equilibrium exchange rate and price level on expectations concerning a weighted-average future difference between the domestic nominal money supply and the exogenous component of the real demand to hold domestic money.

The increase in the equilibrium domestic price level at time t is entirely unexpected and therefore creates an amount of disequilibrium that is measured by

$$Q(t) = \bar{p}(t) - \bar{p}_0 = (m_T - m_0) \cdot [\eta/(1 + \eta)]^{T-t}. \qquad (12.55)$$

The operation of the price adjustment rule and the rationality of expectations ensure that the actual level of disequilibrium at any time $u \geq t$ and the expected level of disequilibrium at this time, based on information at any date $s \geq t$, are only a fraction of the disequilibrium created at time t; specifically, for $s \geq t$ and $u \geq s$

$$E[Q(u); s] = Q(u) = (1 - \delta)^{u-t} \cdot Q(t). \qquad (12.56)$$

In particular the level of disequilibrium at time T when the increase in the money supply actually takes place is given by

$$Q(T) = (m_T - m_0) \cdot [(1 - \delta) \cdot (\eta/1 + \eta)]^{T-t}. \qquad (12.57)$$

These results for the path of disequilibrium illustrate three important implications of the price adjustment rule (12.32), which allows the domestic price level to adjust to anticipated changes in its own equilibrium value as well as to the existing level of disequilibrium. First, the event that creates disequilibrium is not the change in an exogenous variable, specifically the increase in m at time T, but rather the receipt of information that alters expectations concerning the paths of the exogenous variables. Second, the further in advance that information is received concerning a future change in an exogenous variable, the smaller is the disequilibrium that the receipt of this information generates when it is received. Third, the further in advance that information is received concerning a future change in an exogenous variable, the smaller is the fraction of the initial disequilibrium created by the receipt of this information that remains when the change in the exogenous variable actually occurs.

In the limit, when the increase in the money supply is anticipated far in advance, it creates only a small amount of disequilibrium when it is first anticipated, and only a small fraction of this small amount of disequilibrium remains when the increase in the money supply actually occurs. This would not be true if the price level adjusted only in response to existing disequilibrium and not to anticipated changes in its own equilibrium value. In particular, if the price adjustment rule (12.31) were used in place of (12.32), the increase in the money supply at time T would always create a finite amount of disequilibrium at time T, regardless of how far in advance information about this money supply increase was received.[13]

The existence of disequilibrium after time t implies that the actual price level and actual exchange rate diverge from their respective expected equilibrium time paths, based on information for any date $s \geq t$. Since the domestic price level is sticky, its level at t, $p(t) = \bar{p}_0$, is below its equilibrium level, given by (12.54) with $s = t$ and $u = t$, by the amount of disequilibrium created by the unexpected increase in the equilibrium price level at time t. The domestic price level remains below its equilibrium path after t and converges exponentially toward its equilibrium path in accord with

$$p(u) - E[\bar{p}(u); s] = - Q(u) = - (1 - \delta)^{u-t} \cdot Q(t) \text{ for } u \geq s \geq t.$$

$$(12.58)$$

The spillover effect of disequilibrium causes the exchange rate to lie above its equilibrium path; and it, too, converges exponentially to its equilibrium path as disequilibrium is eliminated:

$$e(u) - E[\bar{e}(u); s] = (1/\eta\beta) \cdot Q(u) \quad \text{for } u \geq s \geq t. \qquad (12.59)$$

In particular the initial response of the exchange rate (which is not sticky) is to rise above its previous level $\bar{e}_0$ by more than the increase in the equilibrium exchange rate:

$$e(t) - e_0 = (1 + 1/\eta\beta) \cdot (m_T - m_0) \cdot (\eta/1 + \eta)^{T-t}. \quad (12.60)$$

If the increase in the money supply occurs at or near time t (that is, if T is equal to or close to t), $e(t)$ will exceed its new steady-state level $\bar{e}_T$. However, if the increase in the money supply is to occur farther in the future, then, as illustrated in Figure 12.1, $e(t)$ will rise above its old level $\bar{e}_0$ and above its current equilibrium level $E[\bar{e}(t); t]$ but not above its new steady-state level $\bar{e}_T$.

These results for the path of the exchange rate illustrate and generalize Dornbusch's overshooting effect. As in Dornbusch's (1976) model, if there is an unexpected, permanent increase in the domestic money supply at time t, the spillover effect of disequilibrium created by the sticky domestic price level causes the current exchange rate $e(t)$ to rise by more (proportionately) than the increase in the money supply by more than the increase in its own steady-state value. For this result it is critical that the increase in the money supply be permanent and that it be unexpected before it actually occurs. If the increase in the money supply were not a permanent, constant increase in the expected level of m for all future periods, the effect on the equilibrium path of the exchange rate would not be a constant upward shift for all dates subsequent to the money supply increase.[14] If the increase in the money supply were anticipated in advance (i.e., if $T > t$), the current exchange rate might not rise by more (proportionately) than the future increase in the money supply and in its own steady-state level. The further in advance the increase in the money supply is anticipated, the smaller will be the initial response of the exchange rate, and the smaller will be the divergence of the exchange rate from its new steady-state value when the increase in the money supply actually occurs. The general manifestation of the overshooting effect of the exchange rate induced by a sticky price level, therefore, is not a more-than-proportionate response of the exchange rate to money supply changes. It is instead the fact that the actual exchange rate $e(t)$ always responds more than the current equilibrium exchange rate $E[\bar{e}(t); t]$ to new information about present and future levels of the domestic money supply.

IMPLICATIONS AND CONCLUSIONS

The results of the preceding analysis may be used to illuminate a number of issues concerning the behavior of exchange rates. First, the present analysis assists in clarifying the idea expressed in many recent papers that exchange rates are asset prices that are determined primarily by the willingness of wealth holders to hold existing stocks of various assets, especially national monies. In the present analysis it is clear that conditions of asset market equilibrium—specifically, the money market equilibrium condition and the interest parity condition—play a vital role in determining the dynamic behavior of the exchange rate in both the equilibrium and the disequilibrium models of exchange rate dynamics. Moreover, in both of these models the exchange rate has the critical property of all asset prices that its current value depends not only on current economic conditions but also on expectations of future conditions, and that unexpected changes in the exchange rate reflect new information that alters expectations about future economic conditions.[15] In the equilibrium model, however, the flow market equilibrium condition embodied in the requirement of purchasing power parity is of coordinate importance with the asset market equilibrium conditions in determining the behavior of the exchange rate; and the exchange rate is not fundamentally different from the domestic price level in terms of its dependence on expectations of future economic conditions. The distinction between the exchange rate, which is an asset price that responds immediately to new information about future economic conditions, and the domestic price level, which shows no such response, is present only in the disequilibrium model where purchasing power parity is not imposed as one of the requirements of momentary equilibrium. Even in this disequilibrium model, however, the flow market equilibrium condition is relevant for determining the dynamic behavior of the exchange rate since this condition influences the way in which changes in the expectations of future events induce equilibrium and disequilibrium changes in the exchange rate.

Second, the present analysis establishes an economically meaningful concept of the equilibrium exchange rate without special assumptions about the time paths of the exogenous variables that determine the equilibrium exchange rate. In many other analyses of exchange rate behavior it is assumed that the domestic money supply and other relevant determinants of the equilibrium exchange rate have constant long-run level or rate of growth. This definition of *equilibrium* is appropriate, given the assumption concerning the exogenous variables determining the equilibrium exchange rate; but it is not a general definition, and, more important, it tends to confuse the idea of a constant long-run level or rate of change of the exchange rate with the more fundamental idea of an exchange rate that is consistent with all of the requirements of economic equilibrium. In contrast, in the present analysis the equilibrium path of the exchange rate is defined in terms of the relevant conditions of economic equilibrium and is valid for any assumption about the paths of the exogenous variables that determine the equilibrium path of the exchange rate.

Third, the present analysis indicates several distinct meanings of the concept of "rational expectation," as applied in simple models of exchange rate dynamics. Many such models focus on the process of convergence of the exchange rate to a fixed long-run equilibrium value when there is some temporary source of disequilibrium such as a sticky domestic price level or a divergence of asset stocks from long-run desired levels.[16] In such models, *rationality of expectations* means that expectations concerning exchange rate changes (and changes in other endogenous variables) along the path of convergence to long-run equilibrium must be consistent with the convergence process. In the present analysis this is one of the meanings of *rational expectations*. Specifically, in the third section expectations concerning the process of convergence toward the economy's equilibrium path are assumed to be consistent with the price adjustment rule that governs this adjustment process. In addition, here rationality of expectations means that expectations concerning the future equilibrium paths of the price level and the exchange rate must depend on expectations concerning the future paths of the exogenous variables (the domestic money supply, the shift factor in domestic money demand, the world interest rate, and the world price level) in a manner that reflects the structure of the economic system. Specifically, this implies the dependence of the current equilibrium price level and exchange rate on an exponentially weighted average of expected future ratios of the domestic money supply to the exogenous component of the real demand to hold domestic money.[17]

Finally, the concept of rational expectations can be applied to the formation and revision of expectations concerning the exogenous factors that drive the behavior of the price level and the exchange rate. This means assuming that these expectations are formed and revised in a manner that is consistent with the knowledge of economic agents concerning the processes that generate these exogenous variables. This assumption is distinct from the other assumptions of rational expectations that are employed in the present analysis.[18]

Fourth, this analysis reveals the fundamental reason why exchange rate changes should include a random component, which, as an empirical matter, appears to dominate actual changes in exchange rates. In both the equilibrium and disequilibrium analyses of exchange rate dynamics, the expression for the change in the exchange rate includes an unexpected change component that measures the response of the exchange rate to new information that alters expectations concerning the present and future behavior of exogenous variables relevant for determining the exchange rate. Since, by definition, *new information* ought to be unpredictable, this unexpected component of the change in the exchange rate ought to be random. In constrast, it should be noted that the expected component of the change in the exchange rate, including the expected movement of the exchange rate toward its equilibrium value, should be systematic rather than random. For this reason models of exchange rate dynamics that focus on the process of convergence toward a fixed long-run equilibrium are inherently incapable of rationalizing the random movements that appear to dominate actual exchange rate changes.

Fifth, this analysis incorporates a price adjustment rule that is capable of dealing with the general situation where the domestic price level is sticky and responds slowly to disequilibrium but where the equilibrium price level is not necessarily expected to remain constant. The critical ingredient in this price adjustment rule is the acceleration term, which adjusts the domestic price level to expected changes in its equilibrium value as well as to the existing state of disequilibrium. With this acceleration term the economy converges toward its expected equilibrium path at an exponential rate, regardless of the complexity of this expected equilibrium path; and new disequilibrium is created only when new information alters expectations concerning the equilibrium path of the domestic price level. Without the acceleration term in the price adjustment rule, all sorts of peculiarities can arise in the analysis of disequilibrium dynamics. For instance, persistent price inflation and exchange rate depreciation cannot exist as an equilibrium phenomenon, even if there is persistent domestic monetary expansion in excess of the growth of the real demand to hold domestic money. Also, in the absence of the acceleration term in the price adjustment rule, changes in exogenous variables always create disequilibrium even if they are anticipated very far in advance because the price level does not appropriately adjust to the expected effects of these changes on the equilibrium price level. In particular, if the money supply is expected to remain constant up to some time T and then increase by a finite amount to a new contant level, the change in the money supply at T will create a finite addition to disequilibrium at T even if this change is anticipated infinitely far in advance.

Finally, the analysis helps to clarify Dornbusch's concept of exchange rate overshooting. When the domestic price level is sticky, receipt of information that alters expectations concerning the exogenous monetary factors that determine the expected equilibrium paths of the price level and the exchange rate creates disequilibrium in the domestic goods market that spills over to affect the exchange rate. As a consequence the current exchange rate, which is not sticky, responds to this new information more strongly than the current equilibrium exchange rate. In particular, the exchange rate responds more than proportionately to an unexpected, permanent increase in the level of the domestic money supply.[19] New information about a future permanent increase in the money supply need not, however, induce a more-than-proportionate response of the current exchange rate, only a response that is greater than the change in the current equilibrium exchange rate.

NOTES

1. A number of recent papers treat models that are very similar to the model analyzed in this chapter. See, for instance, Dornbusch (1976), Barro (1978), Bilson (1978), and Mussa (1976). The results obtained in these papers, however, are less general than the results discussed here, either because they make restrictive assumptions about the nature of the process generating the behavior of the domestic money supply or because they do not deal adequately (or at all) with sticky prices and disequilibrium dynamics.

2. A number of monetary models of exchange rate determination, such as those analyzed by Frenkel and Clements (1980) and Hodrick (1978), view the exchange rate between two countries as determined by the ratio of their nominal money supplies divided by the ratio of the real demands to hold their national monies (as affected by income levels, interest rates, etc.). This procedure is perfectly acceptable for some purposes, but it unfortunately tends to conceal the essential dynamic linkage between the current exchange rate and expectations concerning money supplies and factors affecting money demands in future periods.

3. For example, Dornbusch's (1976) well-known analysis of exchange rate dynamics focuses on the process of convergence of the exchange rate to its new long-run equilibrium level subsequent to a permanent increase in the domestic money supply. There is, however, no analysis of what determines the expected equilibrium path of the exchange rate or changes in this expected equilibrium path, except in the special case of constant domestic money supply that is subject to a once-and-for-all change. A similar remark applies to many other analyses of exchange rate dynamics: they treat dynamics as the analysis of the process of convergence of the exchange rate toward its long-run equilibrium level, not as the analysis of what determines expected and unexpected changes in the equilibrium exchange rate. In particular, any dynamic analysis that is conducted in terms of a phase diagram is almost inevitably limited to an analysis of the process of convergence of the exchange rate toward some fixed long-run equilibrium or steady-state growth path.

4. The price adjustment rule used by Dornbusch (1976) deals adequately with the specific case of an unexpected, permanent increase in the domestic money supply, which is analyzed in his paper. It does not deal adequately, however, with an expected future increase in the money supply, such as that analyzed in Wilson (1979). For further discussion of the deficiencies of the simple "price responds to excess demand" form of adjustment rule, see Mussa (1978).

5. It can be shown that the introduction of real disturbances requiring adjustments in relative prices does not affect the main conclusions of this chapter; see Mussa (1980). Other changes in theoretical structure may, of course, lead to more profound modifications of the results.

6. The general importance of such a linkage between the current exchange rate and expected future exchange rates is emphasized especially in Frenkel and Mussa (1980).

7. The general form of the forward-looking solution to (12.6) has an additional term of the form $C \cdot [(1 + \eta)/\eta]^{s-t}$, where C is an arbitrary constant. This constant is set equal to zero in order to obtain an economically sensible solution to (12.6). As is well known, this assumption is controversial in some quarters.

8. See, for example, Sargent and Wallace (1973) and Mussa (1975).

9. The general importance of "news" is explaining movements in exchange rates is emphasized in Dornbusch (1980), Frenkel (Forthcoming), Frenkel and Mussa (1980), and Mussa (1977, 1979).

10. This result is derived in Muth (1960). It is applied to the specific case of a monetary model of exchange rate dynamics in Mussa (1976).

11. The deficiencies of the price adjustment rule (12.31) in a closed-economy, rational

expectations model of inflation, with sticky prices, are examined in Mussa (1978). In that paper it is shown that a two-part price adjustment rule of the general form of (12.32) is essential to correct these deficiencies. The arguments and analysis in that paper carry over to the present open-economy model.

Different assumptions about the measure of disequilibrium to which the domestic price level responds will lead to slightly different versions of (12.31) and, correspondingly, of (12.32). For example, it might be assumed that the domestic price level responds to excess demand in the domestic goods market, which is a function both of the divergence of the domestic price level from purchasing power parity and of the divergence of the domestic real interest rate from its equilibrium value. This alternative specification of the measure of disequilibrium would imply a slightly different version of (12.32) and a slightly different analysis of disequilibrium dynamics. All of the important qualitative features of the present analysis, however, would be preserved.

12. Dornbusch (1976; 1980, chap. 11) postulates a more complex definition of the measure of excess demand to which the domestic price level responds. This leads to a somewhat more complex story of how disequilibrium spreads from the domestic goods market to affect the exchange rate, the forward premium, the domestic interest rate, and so on. In all essential respects, however, Dornbusch's analysis of the spillover effects of disequilibrium in the domestic goods market is the same as that given here.

13. Wilson (1979) analyzes the effect of a future anticipated change in the level of the money supply in the context of Dornbusch's (1976) model with Dornbusch's price adjustment rule. Because the price adjustment rule in Wilson's model excludes an acceleration term that adjusts the domestic price level for expected changes in its own equilibrium level, the increase in the money supply at time T always creates a finite increment to disequilibrium, even if it is anticipated very far in advance. Moreover, in Wilson's model a perfectly foreseen constant rate of increase of the money supply would lead to a steady-state disequilibrium in which the domestic price level would be pushed up only by a constant excess of the equilibrium price level over the actual price level. In contrast, in the present model, where the price adjustment rule includes an appropriate acceleration term, steady state will occur as an equilibrium phenomenon in the presence of a steady rate of monetary expansion in excess of the growth of the real demand to hold domestic money.

14. As illustrated by the examples discussed at the end of the second section, the equilibrium exchange rate and domestic price level may respond less than proportionately, exactly proportionately, or more than proportionately to an observed increase in the money supply, depending on the nature of the stochastic process that is believed to generate the behavior of the money supply. For this reason overshooting of the exchange rate, in the sense of actual movements that exceed equilibrium movements, should not be identified with exchange rate changes that are more than proportional to changes in the money supply.

15. This point is emphasized especially in Frenkel and Mussa (1980).

16. In the model presented in Dornbusch (1976; 1980, chap. 11) the source of disequilibrium is a sticky domestic price level. Rationality of expectations in this model means that economic agents understand the economic system sufficiently well to use the correct estimate of the speed of convergence of the economy toward its long-run equilibrium in forming expectations about the rate of change of the exchange rate. In other models, such as those of Kouri (1976), Calvo and Rodriguez (1977), Dornbusch and Fischer (1980), and Dornbusch (1980, chap. 13), the source of disequilibrium is a level of distribution of asset stocks that is inconsistent with current account balance. The dynamic process in such models is driven by the redistribution of asset stocks associated with current account imbalances, and long-run equilibrium is achieved when the level or distribution of asset stocks is consistent with current account balance in all countries. Rationality of expectations in such models means that

economic agents take account of the process driving the economy toward long-run equilibrium in forming expectations about changes in exchange rates, prices, and other variables relevant to their behavior.

17. Since m is defined as the logarithm of the money supply and k is defined as the logarithm of the exogenous component of real money demand, the formal expressions for $\bar{p}$ and $\bar{e}$ involve exponentially weighted averages of differences between m and k.

18. If the behavior of the money supply is determined endogenously by a reaction function describing the behavior of the central bank, then rationality of expectations, in the sense of consistency with the structure of the economic system, includes the requirement that expectations should take appropriate account of the form of this reaction function. For analysis of a model with this feature, in a closed-economy context, see Sargent and Wallace (1973).

19. As emphasized by Obstfeld (1979), if the demand for money responds to unexpected increases in the money supply, because of their effect on the level of income, an unexpected monetary expansion may not lead to a more-than-proportionate response of the current exchange rate.

REFERENCES

Barro, R. 1978. "A Stochastic Equilibrium Model of an Open Economy under Flexible Exchange Rates." *Quarterly Journal of Economics* 92 (February): 149–64.

Bilson, J. 1978. "Rational Expectations and the Exchange rate." In *The Economics of Exchange Rates: Selected Studies*, edited by J. Frenkel and H. Johnson. Reading, Mass.: Addison-Wesley.

Calvo, G., and C. Rodriguez. 1977. "A Model of Exchange Rate Determination with Currency Substitution and Rational Expectations." *Journal of Political Economy* 85 (June): 617–25.

Dornbusch, R. 1980. *Open Economy Macroeconomics*. New York: Basic Books.

_____. 1976. "Expectations and Exchange Rate Dynamics." *Journal of Political Economy* 84 (December): 1161–76.

Dornbusch, R., and S. Fischer. 1980. "Exchange Rates and the Current Account." *American Economic Review* 70 (December): 960–71.

Frenkel, J. Forthcoming. "Flexible Exchange Rates in the 1970's." In *Economic Interdependence and Flexible Exchange Rates*, edited by J. Bhandari and B. Putnam. Cambridge, Mass.: MIT Press.

Frenkel, J., and K. Clements. 1980. "Exchange Rates in the 1920's: A Monetary Approach." In *Development in an Inflationary World*, edited by M. J. Flanders and A. Razin. New York: Academic Press.

Frenkel, J., and M. Mussa. 1980. "The Efficiency of Foreign Exchange Markets and Measures of Turbulence." *American Economic Review* 70 (December): 374–81.

Hodrick, R. 1978. "An Empirical Analysis of the Monetary Approach to the Determination of the Exchange Rate." In *The Economics of Exchange Rates: Selected Studies*, edited by J. Frenkel and H. Johnson. Mass.: Addison-Wesley.

Kouri, P. 1976. "The Exchange Rate and the Balance of Payments in the Short Run and in the Long Run." *Scandinavian Journal of Economics* 78: 280–304.

Mussa, M. 1980. "A Model of Exchange Rate Dynamics." Mimeographed, Chicago.

_____. 1979. "Empirical Regularities in the Behavior of Exchange Rates and Theories of the Foreign Exchange Market." In *Policies for Employment, Prices and Exchange Rates*, edited by K. Brunner and A. Meltzer, vol. 2. Carnegie-Rochester Conference Series. *Journal of Monetary Economics*, supp. pp. 9–57.

_____. 1978. "Sticky Prices and Disequilibrium Adjustment in a Rational Model of the Inflationary Process." CMBSE Report no. 7844. Chicago: University of Chicago, June.

_____. 1977. "Exchange Rate Uncertainty: Its Causes, Consequences, and Policy Implications." Paper presented at the Conference on International Financial Relations in a World of Uncertainty, sponsored by the Center for Monetary and Banking Studies of the Graduate Institute of International Studies, Geneva, Switzerland.

_____. 1976. "The Exchange Rate, the Balance of Payments and Monetary and Fiscal Policy under a Regime of Controlled Floating." *Scandinavian Journal of Economics* 78: 229–48.

_____. 1975. "Adaptive and Regressive Expectations in a Rational Model of the Inflationary Process." *Journal of Monetary Economics* 1 (October): 423–42.

Muth, J. 1960. "Optimal Properties of Exponentially Weighted Forecasts." *Journal of the American Statistical Association* (June):

Obstfeld, M. 1979. "Relative Prices, Employment and Exchange Rate Management in an Economy with Perfect Foresight." Mimeographed. New York: Columbia University, December.

Sargent, T., and N. Wallace. 1973. "Rational Expectations and the Dynamics of Hyper-inflation." *International Economic Review* 14 (June): 328–50.

Wilson, C. 1979. "Anticipated Shocks and Exchange Rate Dynamics." *Journal of Political Economy* 87 (June): 639–47.

13

A STOCHASTIC
GENERAL EQUILIBRIUM MODEL OF
THE OPEN ECONOMY UNDER
CONTROLLED FLOATING

INTRODUCTION

This chapter analyzes a rational expectations stochastic equilibrium model of the open economy under a regime of managed floating. The general equilibrium nature of the model results from the inclusion of explicit considerations of both the real and financial aspects of the economy. The focus of the analysis is on the optimal intervention policy or optimal degree of intervention in response to various external and domestic structural disturbances. We consider three kinds of structural shocks (domestic and foreign)—real expenditure shocks, real output supply shocks, and monetary disturbances. In each case we derive the optimal degree of intervention as a function of the structural parameters of the economy. An innovative feature of this framework is the attention given to the trade and capital accounts in the determination of the exchange rate (and the subsequent degree of intervention).

Previous stochastic models of the open economy have not, in general, considered the full general equilibrium interaction between the real and monetary aspects of the economy, nor have they analyzed the range of issues analyzed in this chapter. The papers by Barro (1978), Bilson (1978), and Mussa (1978), for example, ignore the real sector completely, as well as assume away interest-bearing capital assets. The latter assumption is also made by Saidi (1980). In addition, none of these papers consider managed floating but, instead, examine freely flexible exchange rates. Other recent contributions include Cox (1980), Turnovsky (in press), Bhandari (in press), and Driskill and McCafferty (1980).[1] Of these papers only Cox considers intervention policies, but then only in response to monetary disturbances. Further, the use of the instantaneous purchasing power parity relationship

241

removes any role for aggregate demand considerations in either the domestic or foreign economy.

This chapter may be viewed as an extension of the previous approaches to include a treatment of both the real and asset sectors of the economy, with a central role being assigned to the balance of payments in exchange rate determination. The results of our investigation indicate that the optimal domestic intervention policy (the optimum being defined by minimizing domestic price level variability) involves "leaning against the wind" if the predominant structural disturbances are foreign monetary in origin and "leaning with the wind" if they are due to foreign real expenditure shocks; the exact nature of the policy depends upon precise parameter magnitudes if the underlying disturbances result from stochastic shifts in foreign output supply. We also consider domestically occurring disturbance. In no case do we find that floating exchange rates are optimal, although a case for the optimality of pegged exchange rates does emerge if the principal source of variability is domestic monetary disturbances. In this way our analysis has implications for the "fixed versus flexible exchange rates" debate.

This chapter is organized as follows. The next section discusses the analytical framework, and the following section obtains the rational expectations solution to the model. The last section considers various structural disturbances, with the associated optimal intervention policies. In this section we also highlight the effects of these shocks on the trade balance.

THE MODEL

The analytical framework to be detailed below consists of two main building blocks. First, the structure of the large foreign economy is specified. This economy is large in the sense that it is not affected by economic events occurring in the domestic economy. In addition, it is assumed that the foreign economy is closed, the reason for the assumption being that we wish to avoid specifying a two-country model. Rather, we wish to concentrate on a moderately sized open domestic economy that is small enough to regard all foreign variables as being exogenously (although not independently) determined but large enough in export markets so that the domestic currency price of the exportable is endogenously determined.[2] The first stage of the analysis consists of obtaining the rational expectations solution to the foreign price level and interest rate in terms of the anticipated and unanticipated variables in that country. In the second stage these solutions are utilized in obtaining the ultimate rational expectations solution to the domestic (open) economy. The reason for this two-stage procedure is that movements in the foreign interest rate and price level are correlated in general (the nature of the correlation depending upon the precise stochastic shift involved). Consequently, it is not possible to assume that these variables are independently determined. Since it is the domestic economy that is under consideration, in the spirit of the one-country analysis it is assumed that it is only the domestic economy that engages in intervention operations with the foreign country making no attempt to defend specific exchange rates.

The Foreign Economy

The foreign economy is described by a standard discrete time stochastic IS-LM framework amended to include an aggregate supply relationship. Continuous equilibrium prevails in both the foreign commodity and money markets. Foreign aggregate demand is determined in the standard fashion by the level of real income, the level of the real interest rate, and an autonomous expenditure component in that country.[3] Aggregate supply is determined via a simple Lucas-type relationship—i.e., output supply is assumed to respond positively to unanticipated price increases. Thus, the foreign economy is described by the following log-linear relationships.[4] All parameters are defined positively:

$$Y_t^{*d} = G_t^* + \gamma_1^* Y_t^* - \gamma_2^* i_t^* + \gamma_3^*(E_t P_{t+1}^* - P_t^*), \tag{13.1}$$

$$Y_t^{*s} = \bar{S}^* + S_1^*(P_t^* - E_{t-1}, P_t^*) + \varepsilon_{3t}^*, \tag{13.2}$$

$$Y_t^{*d} = Y_t^{*s}, \tag{13.3}$$

$$M_t^* - P_t^* = \beta_0^* - \beta_1^* i_t^* + \beta_2^* Y_t^*, \tag{13.4}$$

$$M_t^* = \bar{M}^* + \varepsilon_{2t}^*, \tag{13.5}$$

$$G_t^* = \bar{G}^* + \varepsilon_{1t}^*, \tag{13.6}$$

$$\varepsilon_{it}^* \sim N(0, \sigma_{\varepsilon i}^2), \ i = 1, 2, 3.$$

Equation (13.1) describes foreign aggregate demand. G_t^* is an autonomous expenditure (fiscal) variable, Y_t^* is foreign real income, i_t^* is foreign nominal interest rate, and P_t^* is the foreign price level. The subscripts refer to the time period in question, while E_t is an expectations operator, the expectation being formed at time t for the next period. The real rate of interest is assumed to be defined in Fisherian fashion as the nominal rate minus the (next period) expected rate of inflation. The foreign supply curve is given by the Phillips curve (13.2), where $\bar{S}^*$ is the normal or trend component of supply, and S_1^* is the slope of the Phillips curve. Thus, cyclical output $(Y_t^{*s} - \bar{S}^*)$ responds positively to unanticipated inflation as measured by $(P_t^* - E_{t-1}, P_t^*)$. The stochastic component ε_{3t}^* is intended to characterize random supply (productivity) shifts occurring in the foreign economy. Considerable interest attaches to the transmission of supply (as well as other) disturbances from the foreign economy to the domestic country and to the nature of domestic intervention policy required to offset such shocks. The third equation is a statement of the commodity market equilibrium condition, while (13.4) asserts that continuous money market equilibrium prevails, the form of the money demand function being entirely conventional. Finally, (13.5) and (13.6) specify the stochastic processes governing nominal money supply and autonomous expenditure. Specifically, actual nominal money supply and autonomous expenditure are centered around their respective stationary or anticipated values $\bar{M}^*$ and $\bar{G}^*$. While other more complex stochastic processes could undoubtedly be hypothesized, we feel there is no advantage to be gained from a more complex stochastic structure for the issues under consideration. The random (unanticipated) terms are each assumed to be independently normally distributed with zero means and finite variances. The description of the foreign economy thus entails three anticipated or systematic variables ($\bar{S}^*$, $\bar{G}^*$, and $\bar{M}^*$) as well as three foreign innovations (i.e., ε_{it}, $i = 1, 2, 3$).

The Domestic Economy

In contrast to the foreign economy described above, the domestic economy is open. The openness of the economy results from trade in commodities and in riskless, interest-yielding one-period (government) securities. Domestic production is limited to a single final commodity, while domestic consumers have access to both domestic and foreign output. These goods are regarded by domestic agents as imperfectly substitutable. The domestic economy is small enough to regard the world supply of importables as well as the world supply of foreign currency-denominated securities to be infinitely elastic at the prevailing (exogenously determined) foreign currency price and yield, respectively. On the other hand, the domestic currency price of domestic output as well as the yield on domestic currency-denominated securities are endogenously determined.[5] Continuous monetary and commodity market equilibrium prevail in the domestic economy as well. However, domestic nominal money is not completely exogenous but is altered via an assignment rule-type intervention function to defend specific exchange rate targets—i.e., the domestic economy manages its exchange rate vis-à-vis the foreign currency. Clearly, either fixed or floating exchange rate regimes will be special cases of the managed float. A key feature of the specification of the domestic economy is the rehabilitation of the balance of payments in the determination of the currency exchange rate (and hence the extent of intervention).

Aggregate demand for domestic output is given by the sum of domestic absorption and the net real trade surplus. In the interest of computational simplicity it is assumed that domestic absorption is determined by the level of domestic real income alone, while the balance of trade is determined both by income (which determines imports) and by the terms of trade (which determine both exports and imports). In logarithmic form aggregate demand can be approximated by

$$Y_t^D = G_t + \theta_1 T_t + \theta_2 A_t, \quad \theta_1 > 0, \quad 0 < \theta_2 < 1, \tag{13.7}$$

where G_t is an autonomous component of expenditure, T_t is the real trade balance measured in natural units, and A_t is the logarithm of domestic private absorption.[6] Absorption is determined by income, i.e.,

$$A_t = \gamma_1 Y_t, \quad 0 < \gamma_1 < 1, \tag{13.8}$$

while the trade balance is assumed to be linear in the logarithm of the terms of trade and income:

$$T_t = \alpha_1 (E_t + P_t^* - P_t) - \alpha_2 Y_t. \tag{13.9}$$

In (13.9) the Marshall-Lerner condition is presumed satisfied. Combining equations (13.7) through (13.9) and assuming that the autonomous expenditure variable G_t is generated by a random process similar to (13.6), as well as imposing the commodity market equilibrium requirement, we have

$$Y_t(1 - \theta_2 \gamma_1 + \theta_1 \alpha_2) = \bar{G} + \theta_1 \alpha_1 (E_t + P_t^* - P_t) + \varepsilon_{1t}. \tag{13.10}$$

Since both θ_2 and α_1 are less than unity, it is clear that aggregate income from the demand side is positively related to the terms of trade $(E_t + P_t^* - P_t)$.

Aggregate supply in the domestic economy is described by a Lucas-type relationship resembling (13.2):

$$Y_t = \bar{S} + S_1 (P_t - E_{t-1}, Q_t) + \varepsilon_{3t}, \tag{13.11}$$

where Q_t is the domestic price index, and ε_{3t} is a domestic supply innovation. The difference between (13.11) and (13.3) results from the use of the index Q_t rather than the national price level in (13.11). This procedure appears more appropriate for an economy whose agents are concerned with both the national price level and the price of importables. A derivation of (13.11) based on domestic wage contracting behavior is provided in the Appendix to Chapter 13.

Domestic money market equilibrium is characterized by

$$M_t - Q_t = \beta_0 - \beta_1 i_t + \beta_2 Y_t + \varepsilon_{2t} \tag{13.12}$$

analogously to (13.4). Again, in view of the openness of the domestic economy, nominal money balances are deflated by the price index rather than the price level. The stochastic component ε_{2t} is to be interpreted as a domestic money demand disturbance.[7] The price index is assumed to be of simple log-additive variety, that is,

$$Q_t = \delta P_t + (1 - \delta)(E_t + P_t^*), \quad 0 < \delta < 1. \tag{13.13}$$

The next stage in the development of the model is the specification of total balance of payments. Assume that capital flows (measured in terms of domestic output) occur at a finite rate in proportion to the covered differential between yields on domestic currency and foreign currency-denominated securities. Thus,

$$c_t = c_1[i_t - i_t^* - (E_t E_{t+1} - E_t)],$$

where c_1 measures the rate of capital inflow in response to the covered differential in favor of the domestic economy.[8] The sum of the trade balance and the capital account equals the overall rate of reserve accumulation. Since the banking sector is suppressed and all money is assumed to be high-powered money, the balance of payments equation can be approximated by

$$\alpha_1(E_t + P_t^* - P_t) - \alpha_2 Y_t + c_1[i_t - i_t^* - (EE_{t+1} - E_t)]$$
$$= M_t - M_{t-1}.[9] \tag{13.14}$$

The final step in the model is the intervention function. Specifically, we assume that intervention occurs according to the derivative-control feedback rule hypothesized in (13.15):

$$M_t - M_{t-1} = -\mu(E_t - E^0), \tag{13.15}$$

where μ is the intervention parameter, and E^0 is the preannounced publicly known target exchange rate that the authorities attempt to defend. If $\mu < 0$, we subsequently refer to this policy as being of the "leaning against the wind" variety, while if $\mu > 0$, the authorities "lean with the wind." The random variables ε_{it}, $i = 1, 2, 3$ are assumed to be generated by independent "white noise" processes with zero means and finite variances. This along with the assumption that expectations are rational in the Muthian sense completes the specification of the domestic economy.

Thus, the specification of the home economy includes the predetermined and anticipated variables $\bar{G}$, E^0, $\bar{S}$, and M_{t-1} as well as three domestic innovations (i.e., unanticipated shocks) ε_{it}. Since, the foreign variables P_t^* and i_t^* occur in the specification of the domestic economy, prior to obtaining the rational expectations solution for this economy, it is first necessary to solve for these foreign variables in terms of the foreign anticipated variables and foreign innovations. The next section obtains the two-stage solution to the entire model.

THE RATIONAL EXPECTATIONS SOLUTION

The first stage in the solution consists of obtaining the rational expectations solution for the foreign economy described by equations (13.1) through (13.6). Specifically, we wish to obtain the solutions to the foreign price level P^* and interest rate i^* in terms of foreign anticipated variables and innovations. Given the log-linearity of the structure, it is clear that the ultimate solutions to P^* and i^* will be of the forms hypothesized in (13.16) and (13.17):

$$P_t^* = W_1 \varepsilon_{1t}^* + W_2 \varepsilon_{2t}^* + W_3 \varepsilon_{3t}^* + W_4 \bar{G}^* + W_5 \bar{M}^* + W_6 \bar{S}^* \quad (13.16)$$

and

$$i_t^* = U_1 \varepsilon_{1t}^* + U_2 \varepsilon_{2t}^* + U_3 \varepsilon_{3t}^* + U_4 \bar{G}^* + U_5 \bar{M}^* + U_6 \bar{S}^*, \quad (13.17)$$

where the W_i and U_j are as yet undetermined coefficients, which are to be obtained via an ex-post solution to the model itself. Solving for the foreign price level from the money market relation (13.4), we obtain

$$P_t^* = M_t^* - \beta_0^* + \beta_1^* i_t^* - \beta_2^* Y_t^*. \quad (13.18)$$

Note that

$$(P_t^* - E_{t-1}, P_t^*) = W_1 \varepsilon_{1t}^* + W_2 \varepsilon_{2t}^* + W_3 \varepsilon_{3t}^*$$

and

$$(E P_{t+1}^* - P_t^*) = -(W_1 \varepsilon_{1t}^* + W_2 \varepsilon_{2t}^* + W_3 \varepsilon_{3t}^*).$$

Substitute in (13.18) for M_t^* from (13.5), for i_t^* from (13.17), and for Y_t^* from the aggregate supply relation (13.2) after utilizing the above relations.

The result is

$$P_t^* = \bar{M}^* + \varepsilon_{2t}^* - \beta_0^* + \beta_1^*(U_1\varepsilon_{1t}^* + U_2\varepsilon_{2t}^* + U_3\varepsilon_{3t}^* + U_4\bar{G}^*$$
$$+ U_5\bar{M}^* + U_6\bar{S}^*) - \beta_2^*\bar{S}^* - \beta_2^*S_1^*(W_1\varepsilon_{1t}^*$$
$$+ W_2\varepsilon_{2t}^* + W_3\varepsilon_{3t}^*) - \beta_2^*\varepsilon_{3t}^*. \tag{13.19}$$

Equating (13.19) coefficient by coefficient to (13.16), we obtain the first set of simultaneous relations (13.20):

$$W_1 = \beta_1^*U_1 - \beta_2^*S_1^*W_1, \tag{13.20a}$$

$$W_2 = 1 + \beta_1^*U_2 - \beta_2^*S_1^*W_2, \tag{13.20b}$$

$$W_3 = \beta_1^*U_3 - \beta_2^*S_1^*W_3 - \beta_2^*, \tag{13.20c}$$

$$W_4 = \beta_1^*U_4, \tag{13.20d}$$

$$W_5 = 1 + \beta_1^*U_5, \tag{13.20e}$$

$$W_6 = \beta_1^*U_6 - \beta_2^*. \tag{13.20f}$$

Next, we obtain another set of relations involving the (W_i, U_j) by following the identical procedure as above except that the aggregate demand relation (13.1) is used to eliminate Y_t^*. The equation analogous to (13.19) is

$$P_t^* = \bar{M}^* + \varepsilon_{2t}^* - \beta_0^* + \beta_1^*(U_1\varepsilon_{1t}^* + U_2\varepsilon_{2t}^* + U_3\varepsilon_{3t}^* + U_4\bar{G}^*$$
$$+ U_5\bar{M}^* + U_6\bar{S}^*) - \frac{\beta_2^*}{1-\gamma_1^*}\bar{G}^* + \frac{\beta_2^*}{1-\gamma_1^*}\varepsilon_{1t}^* + \frac{\beta_2^*\gamma_2^*}{1-\gamma_1^*}$$
$$\times (U_1\varepsilon_{1t}^* + U_2\varepsilon_{2t}^* + U_3\varepsilon_{3t}^* + U_4\bar{G}^* + U_5\bar{M}^* + U_6\bar{S}^*)$$
$$+ \frac{\beta_2^*\gamma_2^*}{1-\gamma_1^*}(W_1\varepsilon_{1t}^* + W_2\varepsilon_{2t}^* + W_3\varepsilon_{3t}^*), \tag{13.21}$$

whence the relations:

$$W_1 = \beta_1^*U_1 - \frac{\beta_2^*}{1-\gamma_1^*} + \frac{\beta_2^*\gamma_2^*}{1-\gamma_1^*}U_1 + \frac{\beta_2^*\gamma_2^*}{1-\gamma_1^*}W_1, \tag{13.22a}$$

$$W_2 = 1 + \beta_1^*U_2 + \frac{\beta_2^*\gamma_2^*}{1-\gamma_1^*}U_2 + \frac{\beta_2^*\gamma_2^*}{1-\gamma_1^*}W_2, \tag{13.22b}$$

$$W_3 = \beta_1^*U_3 + \frac{\beta_2^*\gamma_2^*}{1-\gamma_1^*}U_3 + \frac{\beta_2^*\gamma_2^*}{1-\gamma_1^*}W_3, \tag{13.22c}$$

$$W_4 = \beta_1^* U_4 - \frac{\beta_2^*}{1 - \gamma_1^*} + \frac{\beta_2^* \gamma_2^*}{1 - \gamma_1^*} U_4, \qquad (13.22d)$$

$$W_5 = 1 + \beta_1^* U_5 + \frac{\beta_2^* \gamma_2^*}{1 - \gamma_1^*} U_5, \qquad (13.22e)$$

$$W_6 = \beta_1^* U_6 + \frac{\beta_2^* \gamma_2^*}{1 - \gamma_1^*} U_6. \qquad (13.22f)$$

The complete solutions to P_t^* and i_t^* are obtained by solving for the six duples (W_i, U_i), $i = 1, 2, \ldots, 6$ by utilizing each of the six pairs involved in (13.20) and (13.22). These are

$$P_t^* = \frac{\beta_1^*}{\Delta^*} \varepsilon_{1t}^* + \frac{\gamma_2^*}{\Delta^*} \varepsilon_{2t}^* - \frac{\beta_2^* [\beta_1^* (1 - \gamma_1^*) + \gamma_2^*]}{\Delta^*} \varepsilon_{3t}^*$$

$$+ \frac{\beta_1^*}{\gamma_2^*} \bar{G}^* + \bar{M}^* - \left[\frac{\beta_1^* (1 - \gamma_1^*)}{\gamma_2^*} + \beta_2^* \right] \bar{S}^* \qquad (13.23)$$

and

$$i_t^* = \frac{1 + \beta_2^* S_1^*}{\Delta^*} \varepsilon_{1t}^* - \frac{[\gamma_2^* + (1 - \gamma_1^*) S_1^*]}{\Delta^*} \varepsilon_{2t}^*$$

$$+ \frac{(1 - \gamma_1^*)[\beta_2^* S_1^* (1 - \beta_2^*) - \beta_2^*] + \beta_2^* \gamma_2^*}{\Delta^*} \varepsilon_{3t}^*$$

$$+ \frac{1}{\gamma_2^*} \bar{G}^* - \frac{(1 - \gamma_1^*)}{\gamma_2^*} \bar{S}^*, \qquad (13.24)$$

where

$$\Delta^* = \gamma_2^* (1 + \beta_2^* S_1^* + \beta_1^*) + \beta_1^* S_1^* (1 - \gamma_1^*) > 0.$$

Before proceeding with the second stage of the solution to the entire model, it is useful to review briefly the nature of the solutions (13.23) and (13.24) for the foreign economy. First, it can be seen that an anticipated (and permanent) increase in the foreign nominal money supply raises the foreign price level equiproportionately while not affecting the foreign interest rate: anticipated foreign money is completely neutral. On the other hand, an unanticipated foreign monetary expansion as represented by $\varepsilon_{2t}^* > 0$ raises the price level P^* but less than proportionately. The transitory price increase is accompanied by the usual decline in the interest rate. Turning next to the effects of expenditure expansion, it can be seen that an anticipated increase in the latter increases both the price level and interest rate. The same qualitative effects emerge for an unanticipated expenditure increase, although the coefficients on ε_{1t}^* and $\bar{G}^*$ in (13.23) make it clear that an anticipated expenditure increase is likely to affect the foreign price level proportionately more severely than the corresponding unanticipated disturbance. Finally, an anticipated supply (capacity) expansion lowers both the foreign price level and interest rate, while the analogous unanticipated shock also clearly reduces the price level, its effect upon the nominal interest rate being indeterminate without a priori restrictions. Thus, while both kinds of supply disturbances will unambiguously lower the price level (as expected), these effects upon the interest rate could be in opposite directions. It can be verified, however, that if β_2^* (the income elasticity of money demand) is in the neighborhood of unity, the interest effect following an unanticipated supply expansion is also negative.

We now turn to the second stage of the complete rational expectations solution, which involves the solution to (13.7) through (13.15), the solution being conditional upon the results derived above and stated in (13.23) and (13.24). Following the procedure utilized above, we hypothesize the following pure forward-looking linear solutions to the domestic price level and exchange rate. Given these solutions, it is possible to obtain the ultimate solution to all other variables of interest:

$$P_t = V_1 \varepsilon_{1t} + V_2 \varepsilon_{2t} + V_3 \varepsilon_{3t} + V_4 \varepsilon_{1t}^* + V_5 \varepsilon_{2t}^* + V_6 \varepsilon_{3t}^* + V_7 M_{t-1}$$
$$+ V_8 E^0 + V_9 \bar{G} + V_{10} \bar{S} + V_{11} \bar{S}^* + V_{12} \bar{M}^* + V_{13} \bar{G}^*$$

$$(13.25)$$

and

$$E_t = \pi_1 \varepsilon_{1t} + \pi_2 \varepsilon_{2t} + \pi_3 \varepsilon_{3t} + \pi_4 \varepsilon_{1t}^* + \pi_5 \varepsilon_{2t}^* + \pi_6 \varepsilon_{3t}^* + \pi_7 M_{t-1}$$
$$+ \pi_8 E^0 + \pi_9 \bar{G} + \pi_{10} \bar{S} + \pi_{11} \bar{S}^* + \pi_{12} \bar{M}^* + \pi_{13} \bar{G}^*, \quad (13.26)$$

where the V_i and π_i are again as yet undetermined coefficients. Equations (13.25) and (13.26) express the domestic price level and exchange rate in terms of their ultimate determinants—that is, the three domestic innovations (ε_{it}, $i = 1, 2, 3$), foreign innovations (ε_{it}^*, $i = 1, 2, 3$), and all the predetermined domestic and foreign variables. The technique of solution, as earlier, requires the derivation of two simultaneous sets of 13 relations, each involving one pair of ($V_i, \pi_i; i = 1, 2, \ldots, 13$). It should be noticed that an explicit dynamic process is implied by (13.25) and (13.26) because of the presence of the lagged term, i.e., M_{t-1}. It can be verified that the process is stable.

The first step consists of expressing (13.11) alternatively as

$$Y_t = \bar{S} + S_1(P_t - E_{t-1}, P_t) - S_1(1 - \delta)E_{t-1}(E_t + P_t^* + P_t) + \varepsilon_{3t}$$

$$(13.11')$$

and then transforming this equation to ultimate reduced form by using (13.25) and (13.26) to substitute into (13.11'). Next, use (13.10) to solve for the domestic price level as

$$P_t = E_t + P_t^* - \frac{1 - \theta_2\gamma_1 + \theta_1\alpha_2}{\theta_1\alpha_1} Y_t + \frac{\bar{G}}{\theta_1\alpha_1} + \frac{\varepsilon_{1t}}{\theta_1\alpha_1} \quad (13.27)$$

and substitute for E_t from (13.26), for P_t^* from (13.16), and for Y_t from the equations obtained by a transformation of (13.11'). The result is an ultimate reduced-form solution for P_t in terms of its fundamental determinants analogous to (13.19) or (13.21). To facilitate ready reference, we state this equation in the Appendix to Chapter 13—see (13.11A). Equating net coefficients identically to zero from (13.11A) yields the first set of relations as stated in (13.28):

$$V_1 = \pi_1 + \frac{1}{\theta_1\alpha_1} - \frac{S_1V_1(1 - \theta_2\gamma_1 + \theta_1\alpha_2)}{\theta_1\alpha_1}, \quad (13.28a)$$

$$V_2 = \pi_2 - \frac{S_1V_2(1 - \theta_2\gamma_1 + \theta_1\alpha_2)}{\theta_1\alpha_1}, \quad (13.28b)$$

$$V_3 = \pi_3 - \frac{S_1V_3(1 - \theta_2\gamma_1 + \theta_1\alpha_2)}{\theta_1\alpha_1} - \frac{1 - \theta_2\gamma_1 + \theta_1\alpha_2}{\theta_1\alpha_1}, \quad (13.28c)$$

$$V_4 = \pi_4 + W_1 - \frac{S_1V_4(1 - \theta_2\gamma_1 + \theta_1\alpha_2)}{\theta_1\alpha_1}, \quad (13.28d)$$

$$V_5 = \pi_5 + W_2 - \frac{S_1V_5(1 - \theta_2\gamma_1 + \theta_1\alpha_2)}{\theta_1\alpha_1}, \quad (13.28e)$$

$$V_6 = \pi_6 + W_3 - \frac{S_1V_6(1 - \theta_2\gamma_1 + \theta_1\alpha_2)}{\theta_1\alpha_1}, \quad (13.28f)$$

$$V_7 = \pi_7 + S_1(1 - \delta)(\pi_7 - V_7)\left(\frac{1 - \theta_2\gamma_1 + \theta_1\alpha_2}{\theta_1\alpha_1}\right), \quad (13.28g)$$

$$V_8 = \pi_8 + S_1(1 - \delta)(\pi_8 - V_8)\left(\frac{1 - \theta_2\gamma_1 + \theta_1\alpha_2}{\theta_1\alpha_1}\right), \quad (13.28h)$$

$$V_9 = \pi_9 + \frac{1}{\theta_1\alpha_1} + S_1(1 - \delta)(\pi_9 - V_9)\left(\frac{1 - \theta_2\gamma_1 + \theta_1\alpha_2}{\theta_1\alpha_1}\right),$$
$$(13.28i)$$

$$V_{10} = \pi_{10} - \frac{1 - \theta_2\gamma_1 + \theta_1\alpha_2}{\theta_1\alpha_1} + S_1(1 - \delta)(V_{10} - \pi_{10})$$

$$\times \left(\frac{1 - \theta_2\gamma_1 + \theta_1\alpha_2}{\theta_1\alpha_1}\right), \quad (13.28j)$$

$$V_{11} = \pi_{11} + W_6 + S_1(1 - \delta)W_6\left(\frac{1 - \theta_2\gamma_1 + \theta_1\alpha_2}{\theta_1\alpha_1}\right)$$

$$+ S_1(1 - \delta)(\pi_{11} - V_{11})\left(\frac{1 - \theta_2\gamma_1 + \theta_1\alpha_2}{\theta_1\alpha_1}\right), \quad (13.28k)$$

$$V_{12} = \pi_{12} + S_1(1 - \delta)W_5\left(\frac{1 - \theta_2\gamma_1 + \theta_1\alpha_2}{\theta_1\alpha_1}\right)$$

$$+ S_1(1 - \delta)(\pi_{12} - V_{12})\left(\frac{1 - \theta_2\gamma_1 + \theta_1\alpha_2}{\theta_1\alpha_1}\right) + W_5,$$
$$(13.28l)$$

$$V_{13} = \pi_{13} + W_4 + S_1(1 - \delta)W_4\left(\frac{1 - \theta_2\gamma_1 + \theta_1\alpha_2}{\theta_1\alpha_1}\right)$$

$$+ S_1(1 - \delta)(\pi_{13} - V_{13})\left(\frac{1 - \theta_2\gamma_1 + \theta_1\alpha_2}{\theta_1\alpha_1}\right). \quad (13.28m)$$

The second set of relations is obtained by utilizing the domestic money market relation (13.12) to solve for P_t after using (13.13) and (13.15) and eliminating the domestic interest rate via the balance of payments equation (13.14). Thus, the solution for P_t is obtained as

$$\delta P_t = M_{t-1} - \mu E_t + \mu E^0 - (1 - \delta)E_t - (1 - \delta)P_t^* - \beta_0$$

$$+ \beta_1 i_t^* + \beta_1(EE_{t+1} - E_t) - \left[\beta_2 + \frac{\beta_1(1 - \theta_2\gamma_1)}{c_1\theta_1} \right] Y_t$$

$$+ \frac{\beta_1}{c_1\theta_1} \bar{G} + \frac{\beta_1}{c_1\theta_1} \varepsilon_{1t} - \frac{\beta_1\mu}{c_1} E_t + \frac{\beta_1\mu}{c_1} E^0 - \varepsilon_{2t}. \quad (13.29)$$

Next, substitute for E_t from (13.26), again; for P_t^* and i_t^* from (13.16) and (13.17). The result is another ultimate reduced-form relationship for P_t from which the second set of relations stated in (13.30) can be obtained by equating net coefficients to zero. This equation is also stated fully in the Appendix to Chapter 13—see 13.12A.

$$\delta V_1 = - \left(\mu + 1 - \delta + \beta_1 + \frac{\beta_1\mu}{c_1} \right) \pi_1 + \frac{\beta_1}{c_1\theta_1}$$

$$- S_1 V_1 \left[\frac{\beta_2 c_1\theta_1 + \beta_1(1 - \theta_2\gamma_1)}{c_1\theta_1} \right], \quad (13.30a)$$

$$\delta V_2 = - \left(\mu + 1 - \delta + \beta_1 + \frac{\beta_1\mu}{c_1} \right) \pi_2 - 1 - S_1 V_2$$

$$\times \left[\frac{\beta_2 c_1\theta_1 + \beta_1(1 - \theta_2\gamma_1)}{c_1\theta_1} \right], \quad (13.30b)$$

$$\delta V_3 = - \left(\mu + 1 - \delta + \beta_1 + \frac{\beta_1\mu}{c_1} \right) \pi_3$$

$$- \left[\frac{\beta_2 c_1\theta_1 + \beta_1(1 - \theta_2\gamma_1)}{c_1\theta_1} \right]$$

$$- S_1 V_3 \left[\frac{\beta_2 c_1\theta_1 + \beta_1(1 - \theta_2\gamma_1)}{c_1\theta_1} \right], \quad (13.30c)$$

$$\delta V_4 = - \left(\mu + 1 - \delta + \beta_1 + \frac{\beta_1\mu}{c_1} \right) \pi_4 + \beta_1 U_1 - (1 - \delta)W_1$$

$$- S_1 V_4 \left[\frac{\beta_2 c_1\theta_1 + \beta_1(1 - \theta_2\gamma_1)}{c_1\theta_1} \right], \quad (13.30d)$$

$$\delta V_5 = -\left(\mu + 1 - \delta + \beta_1 + \frac{\beta_1 \mu}{c_1}\right)\pi_5 + \beta_1 U_2 - (1 - \delta)W_2$$

$$- S_1 V_5 \left[\frac{\beta_2 c_1 \theta_1 + \beta_1(1 - \theta_2 \gamma_1)}{c_1 \theta_1}\right], \tag{13.30e}$$

$$\delta V_6 = -\left(\mu + 1 - \delta + \beta_1 + \frac{\beta_1 \mu}{c_1}\right)\pi_6 + \beta_1 U_3 - (1 - \delta)W_3$$

$$- S_1 V_6 \left[\frac{\beta_2 c_1 \theta_1 + \beta_1(1 - \theta_2 \gamma_1)}{c_1 \theta_1}\right], \tag{13.30f}$$

$$\delta V_7 = 1 - \left(\mu + 1 - \delta + \frac{\beta_1 \mu}{c_1}\right)\pi_7 + S_1(1 - \delta)(\pi_7 - V_7)$$

$$\times \left[\frac{\beta_2 c_1 \theta_1 + \beta_1(1 - \theta_2 \gamma_1)}{c_1 \theta_1}\right], \tag{13.30g}$$

$$\delta V_8 = -\left(\mu + 1 - \delta + \frac{\beta_1 \mu}{c_1}\right)\pi_8 + \left(\mu + \frac{\beta_1 \mu}{c_1}\right)$$

$$+ S_1(1 - \delta)(\pi_8 - V_8)\left[\frac{\beta_2 c_1 \theta_1 + \beta_1(1 - \theta_2 \gamma_1)}{c_1 \theta_1}\right], \tag{13.30h}$$

$$\delta V_9 = -\left(\mu + 1 - \delta + \frac{\beta_1 \mu}{c_1}\right)\pi_9 + \frac{\beta_1}{c_1 \theta_1} + S_1(1 - \delta)$$

$$\times (\pi_9 - V_9)\left[\frac{\beta_2 c_1 \theta_1 + \beta_1(1 - \theta_2 \gamma_1)}{c_1 \theta_1}\right], \tag{13.30i}$$

$$\delta V_{10} = -\left(\mu + 1 - \delta + \frac{\beta_1 \mu}{c_1}\right)\pi_{10}$$

$$- \left[\frac{\beta_2 c_1 \theta_1 + \beta_1(1 - \theta_2 \gamma_1)}{c_1 \theta_1}\right] + S_1(1 - \delta)(\pi_{10} - V_{10})$$

$$\times \left[\frac{\beta_2 c_1 \theta_1 + \beta_1 (1 - \theta_2 \gamma_1)}{c_1 \theta_1} \right], \tag{13.30j}$$

$$\delta V_{11} = - \left(\mu + 1 - \delta + \frac{\beta_1 \mu}{c_1} \right) \pi_{11} + \beta_1 U_6 - (1 - \delta) W_6$$

$$+ S_1 (1 - \delta) W_6 \left[\frac{\beta_2 c_1 \theta_1 + \beta_1 (1 - \theta_2 \gamma_1)}{c_1 \theta_1} \right]$$

$$+ S_1 (1 - \delta)(\pi_{11} - V_{11}) \left[\frac{\beta_2 c_1 \theta_1 + \beta_1 (1 - \theta_2 \gamma_1)}{c_1 \theta_1} \right], \tag{13.30k}$$

$$\delta V_{12} = - \left(\mu + 1 - \delta + \frac{\beta_1 \mu}{c_1} \right) \pi_{12} + \beta_1 U_5 - (1 - \delta) W_5$$

$$+ S_1 (1 - \delta) W_5 \left[\frac{\beta_2 c_1 \theta_1 + \beta_1 (1 - \theta_2 \gamma_1)}{c_1 \theta_1} \right]$$

$$+ S_1 (1 - \delta)(\pi_{12} - V_{12}) \left[\frac{\beta_2 c_1 \theta_1 + \beta_1 (1 - \theta_2 \gamma_1)}{c_1 \theta_1} \right], \tag{13.30l}$$

$$\delta V_{13} = - \left(\mu + 1 - \delta + \frac{\beta_1 \mu}{c_1} \right) \pi_{13} + \beta_1 U_4 - (1 - \delta) W_4$$

$$+ S_1 (1 - \delta) W_4 \left[\frac{\beta_2 c_1 \theta_1 + \beta_1 (1 - \theta_2 \gamma_1)}{c_1 \theta_1} \right]$$

$$+ S_1 (1 - \delta)(\pi_{13} - V_{13}) \left[\frac{\beta_2 c_1 \theta_1 + \beta_1 (1 - \theta_2 \gamma_1)}{c_1 \theta_1} \right]. \tag{13.30m}$$

The complete rational expectations solution to the domestic economy is now obtained by solving (13.28) and (13.30) simultaneously for each of $(V_i, \pi_i; i = 1, 2, \ldots, 13)$ after substituting for the known foreign economy coefficients $(U_j, W_j; j = 1, 2, \ldots, 6)$. The next section discusses the nature of the solution and of the optimal intervention policy in each of several specific cases.

THE NATURE OF THE SOLUTION AND OPTIMAL INTERVENTION POLICY

As indicated above, the solution to the model is obtained by solution of each of the 13 pairs of simultaneous equations involved in (13.28) and (13.30). Once the coefficients V_i and π_i are obtained, the solution to other domestic variables follows easily. For the purposes of this chapter, however, we shall be concerned primarily with the domestic price solution for the reason that we wish to consider the optimal degree of intervention in the exchange market, and the optimality criterion we adopt involves the minimization of domestic price level variability. Given the simple form of the aggregate supply function, this criterion coincides with the minimization of domestic output (income) variance (except in the case of domestic aggregate supply disturbances). While other optimality criteria can doubtless be considered, we feel the one adopted here useful enough in view of the authorities' concern with stabilization.[10] Further, in what follows below we consider each type of disturbance and the associated degree of optimal intervention separately. The merit of this approach is to disentangle the effects of anticipated from unanticipated disturbances and of foreign from domestic shocks.

Anticipated Disturbances

Consider first the effects of foreign anticipated shocks. A foreign anticipated and correctly perceived (by both domestic and foreign residents) monetary expansion as characterized by an increase in the foreign money supply component $\bar{M}^*$ will affect the domestic price level and exchange rate in the proportions V_{12} and π_{12}, respectively. These are (from (13.28l) and (13.30l):

$$V_{12} = \frac{\mu\left(1 + \dfrac{\beta_1}{c_1}\right)}{\mu\left(1 + \dfrac{\beta_1}{c_1}\right) + 1} < 1$$

and

$$\pi_{12} = -\cfrac{1}{\mu\left(1 + \cfrac{\beta_1}{c_1}\right) + 1} > -1.$$

Consequently, the foreign anticipated monetary disturbance is positively transmitted to the home economy in the form of a less-than-proportionate price level increase and a less-than-proportionate spot appreciation. At the same time, as seen from (13.23) above, the foreign price level increases equiproportionately. The lack of neutrality in the domestic economy or the failure of insulation from the external disturbance can be seen to be completely the result of attempting to manage the exchange rate. As the above expression makes clear, if the domestic authorities allow the exchange rate to float freely (i.e., $\mu = 0$), the domestic price level becomes independent of the foreign disturbance ($V_{12} = 0$) with the implication that the spot exchange rate now undergoes equiproportionate appreciation.

It can also be verified that the response of the domestic price level is decreasing in c_1 (the degree of capital market integration) and increasing in β_1 (the interest sensitivity of domestic money demand). The former property has some bearing on the issue of whether a relatively open economy is more vulnerable to external disturbances than one that is less open. The derivative $\partial V_{12}/\partial c_1 < 0$ implies that if openness is to be measured in terms of degree of financial market integration between the domestic economy and the rest of the world, openness contributes to increased insulation and not to increased susceptability to foreign influences. As a related point note that even though increased capital market integration provides better insulation in the sense of lowering V_{12}—the domestic price level increase—there is clearly a finite lower bound, and even if $c_1 \to \infty$ (perfect capital mobility), the domestic price level still increases, albeit in the (reduced) proportion ($\mu/\mu + 1$). The qualitative result, therefore, that only a policy of nonintervention will eliminate the variability of the domestic price level (and hence domestic output) in the face of anticipated external monetary disturbances, is unchanged.

It is also instructive to review briefly the effects of such a disturbance on the domestic trade balance. The change in the domestic trade balance following an increase in $\bar{M}^*$ can be written as

$$\Delta T_t = \alpha_1 \Delta P_t^* + \alpha_1 \Delta(E_t - P_t) - \alpha_2 \Delta Y_t,$$

which upon substituting for the relevant expressions becomes

$$\Delta T_t = [\alpha_1 + \alpha_2 S_1(1 - \delta)](1 + \pi_{12} - V_{12}) = 0. \tag{13.31}$$

Thus, the domestic trade balance is completely unaffected by the anticipated external monetary shock. Moreover, this result is independent of the exchange rate regime. The movement in the capital account must consequently mirror the net change in reserves via intervention. If the exchange rate is fully flexible, the capital account must also necessarily remain unchanged. On the other hand, if the authorities attempt to defend a specific exchange rate E^0, the change in the domestic money supply (indicating the extent of intervention) can be seen to be

$$\Delta M_t = -\mu \Delta E_t = \frac{\mu}{\mu \left(1 + \dfrac{\beta_1}{c_1}\right)} > 0.$$

Consider next the effects of an anticipated external expenditure expansion as characterized by an increase in $\bar{G}^*$. Such a disturbance could result from a publicly known and anticipated fiscal operation conducted in the foreign country and is seen to be transmitted to the domestic economy as given by the following coefficients (obtained via solution to [13.28m] and [13.30m]):

$$V_{13} = \frac{\beta_1^* \left(\mu + \dfrac{\beta_1 \mu}{c_1}\right) + \beta_1}{\gamma_2^* \left(\mu + 1 + \dfrac{\beta_1 \mu}{c_1}\right)} > 0$$

and

$$\pi_{13} = \frac{\beta_1 - \beta_1^*}{\gamma_2^* \left(\mu + 1 + \dfrac{\beta_1 \mu}{c_1}\right)} \gtrless 0.$$

Hence, the domestic price level is seen to increase following such an external disturbance, while its effect upon the spot exchange rate is dictated by the difference between the interest sensitivities of the domestic and foreign money demand functions. It can also be verified that increased capital mobility increases the absolute exchange rate response, while its effect upon the price change is unclear and depends again upon intercountry differences in money demand parameters. Moreover, a regime of freely floating exchange rates does not afford full insulation from this disturbance, for it can be seen that

$$V_{13} \bigg/ {}_{\mu = 0} = \frac{\beta_1}{\gamma_2^*} > 0$$

and

$$\pi_{13} \bigg/ {}_{\mu = 0} = \frac{\beta_1 - \beta_1^*}{\gamma_2^*}. \tag{13.32}$$

Comparison of (13.32) with the foreign price solution (13.23) indicates a point of some interest. To the extent that money demand functions do not exhibit intercountry variation (i.e., $\beta_1 = \beta_1^*$) it can be seen that the domestic exchange rate remains unaltered (i.e., fixed de facto) despite the floating exchange rate regime, while the domestic and foreign price levels are affected to an identical equiproportionate extent ($\Delta P = \Delta P^*$). Hence, the foreign anticipated expenditure shock is fully passed on to the domestic economy, notwithstanding the flexibility of the exchange rate. This result is the exact analogue of the earlier result that under fixed exchange rate regime, an anticipated external monetary disturbance affects both price levels equiproportionately while the exchange rate remains unaltered de jure. Thus, there is a complete correspondence between the effects of anticipated external monetary shocks under fixed exchange rates and those of anticipated foreign real expenditure disturbances under floating exchange rates.

The trade balance implications of this disturbance are qualitively identical to those in the earlier case. Specifically, the change in the balance of trade can be written as

$$\Delta T_t = [\alpha_1 + \alpha_2 S_1 (1 - \delta)](W_4 + \pi_{13} - V_{13}),$$

which can again be shown to be zero, independently of the nature of the exchange rate regime. Meanwhile, the capital account balance under managed floating is given by the extent of intervention and is seen to be

$$\Delta M_t = -\mu \Delta E_t = \frac{-\mu(\beta_1 - \beta_1^*)}{\gamma_2^* \left(\mu + \dfrac{\beta_1 \mu}{c_1} + 1 \right)},$$

that is, the capital account can be in deficit or surplus depending upon the relation between the two money market parameters.

Consider finally the nature of the intervention policy required to insulate the domestic price level (and output) from this foreign disturbance. From the expression for V_{13} given earlier it is clear that V_{13} will be zero if the degree of intervention is given by

$$
\mu^* = \frac{-\beta_1}{\beta_1^* \left(1 + \frac{\beta_1}{c_1} \right)} < 0, \tag{13.33}
$$

that is, to offset the effects of external anticipated expenditure disturbances, domestic intervention policy must be of the "leaning with the wind" variety. An important consideration, however, for the success of the policy indicated by (13.33) is that $\beta_1 \neq \beta_1^*$. It is easy to verify that if this were not the case, the coefficient V_{13} "blows up" for $\mu = \mu^*$.

As a final exercise for anticipated disturbances consider the implications of an announced and anticipated devaluation of the target exchange rate E^0.[11] Following the revision in the target, both the domestic price level and exchange rate increase by an identical percentage extent, although the increase falls short of the extent of the devaluation in the target:

$$
V_8 = \pi_8 = \frac{\mu \left(1 + \frac{\beta_1}{c_1} \right)}{\mu \left(1 + \frac{\beta_1}{c_1} \right) + \mu} < 1.
$$

Hence, the domestic terms of trade remain unaltered as does the level of domestic output, implying in turn that the domestic trade balance is unaffected. We now turn to an examination of unanticipated external and domestic shocks.

Unanticipated Disturbances

We first examine the consequences of a random unanticipated foreign money supply expansion as characterized by the unsystematic component of foreign money supply taking on a positive value, i.e., $\varepsilon_{2t}^* > 0$. The effect of this disturbance on the domestic price level is given by the coefficient V_5, which (from [13.28c] and [13.30c]) is seen to be

$$
V_5 = \frac{W_2 \left[\beta_1 + \mu \left(1 + \frac{\beta_1}{c_1} \right) \right] + \beta_1 U_2}{\Omega} \tag{13.34}
$$

where

$$\Omega = \alpha_1 c_1 \theta_1 \delta + \alpha_1 S_1 \beta_1 (1 - \theta_2 \gamma_1) + \alpha_1 S_1 c_1 \theta_1 \beta_2 + c_1$$

$$\frac{\times \left(\beta_1 + \mu + 1 - \delta + \dfrac{\beta_1 \mu}{c_1} \right) [\theta_1 \alpha_1 + S_1 (1 - \theta_2 \gamma_1 + \theta_1 \alpha_2)]}{c_1 \theta_1 \alpha_1}$$

$$> 0.$$

The coefficients W_2 and U_2 measure the movements in the foreign price level and interest rate, respectively, and were stated earlier. The first point of interest is that, unlike the case of an anticipated foreign money supply disturbance, flexible exchange rates fail to provide insulation of the domestic price level. As can be seen from (13.34),

$$V_5 \Big/ {}_{\mu\,=\,0} = \frac{\beta_1 (W_2 + U_2)}{\Omega}. \tag{13.35}$$

More interesting, upon substitution of the already derived coefficients W_2 and U_2, (13.35) can be shown to be negative. Thus, while the unsystematic foreign monetary shock raises the foreign price and output level, it is negatively transmitted to the domestic economy if the latter maintains a policy of floating exchange rates and price level and output level movements in the two countries are negatively correlated. The result of negative transmission of externally occurring monetary disturbances is in stark contrast to the implications of existing one-country stochastic models such as those of Saidi (1980), Turnovsky (in press), and Barro (1978). In these papers, it will be recalled, the foreign monetary disturbance can only be characterized by an exogenous change in the world price level holding fixed the foreign interest rate. The underlying source of the shift in the world price level is not considered, and neither is the concomitant adjustment in the interest rate. This procedure amounts to treating $W_2 > 0$ and $U_2 = 0$ in equation (13.35), in which case it follows that the domestic price level is positively affected. It may then be concluded that the results from single-country models may be potentially quite misleading; to adequately consider the issue of international propagation of economic disturbances, account must first be taken of the nature of the underlying stochastic shift and its full ramifications upon the economy in which it occurs.

To eliminate the induced variability of the domestic price level (and output)—and hence to insulate the domestic economy—requires a degree of intervention such that $V_5 = 0$. That is,

$$\mu^* = - \frac{\beta_1 \left(\dfrac{U_2}{W_2} + 1 \right)}{\left(1 + \dfrac{\beta_1}{c_1} \right)}, \tag{13.36}$$

since

$$\left(\frac{U_2}{W_2} + 1 \right) = - \frac{[\gamma_2^* + (1 - \gamma_1^*)S_1^*]}{\gamma_2^*} > |1|.$$

It follows that the policy indicated by (13.36) is of the "leaning against the wind" variety (i.e., $\mu^* > 0$) and is given more precisely by

$$\mu^* = \frac{\beta_1 [\gamma_2^* + (1 - \gamma_1^*)S_1^*]}{\gamma_2^* \left(1 + \dfrac{\beta_1}{c_1} \right)} > 0. \tag{13.36'}$$

The only domestic structural parameters that (13.36') depends upon are again β_1 and C_1 and can be shown to be increasing in both.[12] A related point of interest is that although V_5 is increasing in both α_1 and $\delta(\alpha_1$ measures the degree of commodity market integration and δ is another measure of the extent of openness), the optimal policy itself is independent of these parameters.

The effect of the disturbance upon the domestic trade balance can be shown to be

$$\Delta T_t = V_5 \left[\frac{S_1(1 - \theta_2\gamma_1)}{\theta_1} \right], \text{ sign } (\Delta T_t) = \text{sign } (V_5). \tag{13.37}$$

Consequently, a policy of floating exchange rates, which implies that $V_5 < 0$ as seen above, will result in a domestic trade balance deficit that is mirrored by a capital surplus. On the other hand, the pursuit of the intervention policy indicated by (13.36') results in insulation of the trade balance as well, that is, $\Delta T_t/_{\mu^*} = 0$. Finally, it can be seen that the extent of the exchange rate movement permitted under (13.36') must be precisely of such an extent that it offsets the movement in the foreign price level induced by the foreign monetary expansion:

$$\Delta E_t \Big/_{\mu^*} = - W_2 = - \frac{\gamma_2^*}{\Delta} < |1| .[13] \tag{13.38}$$

On comparing (13.38) with the exchange rate response in the absence of intervention, it is clear that the later case is associated with a larger (absolute) exchange rate movement, which is given by

$$\Delta E_t \Big/_{\mu = 0} = - W_2 + \left[\frac{\theta_1 \alpha_1 + S_1 (1 - \theta_2 \gamma_1 + \theta_1 \alpha_2)}{\theta_1 \alpha_1} \right]$$

$$\times \left[\frac{\beta_1 (W_2 + U_2)}{\Omega} \right]. \tag{13.39}$$

The reduced exchange rate volatility under the optimal policy is, of course, the result of "leaning against the wind."

Next, consider the effects of a foreign unanticipated expenditure disturbance, that is, $\varepsilon^*_{f_t} > 0$. As seen earlier, this has the consequence of increasing both the foreign price level and interest rate. Its effect on the domestic price level is given by the coefficient V_4, which can be computed to be

$$V_4 = \frac{\left[\beta_1 + \mu \left(1 + \frac{\beta_1}{c_1} \right) \right] W_1 + \beta_1 U_1}{\Omega} > 0 \text{ for } \mu > 0. \tag{13.40}$$

From (13.40) it can be seen that this disturbance is transmitted positively to the domestic economy for all "leaning against the wind" policies, including under freely floating exchange rates, in which case the effect is

$$V_4 \Big/_{\mu = 0} = \frac{\beta_1 (W_1 + U_1)}{\Omega} > 0. \tag{13.41}$$

Equation (13.41) indicates again that the domestic price response is proportional to the sum of the foreign price level and interest rate responses and also underscores the fact that results from a one-country model, which would effectively set $U_1 = 0$, would understate the degree of transmission. However, since both W_1 and $U_1 > 0$, the direction of domestic price movement predicted by a small-country model is indeed correct (unlike the previous case), although its magnitude is not.

In view of the fact that the domestic price level is positively affected by the external disturbance for all $\mu \geq 0$, the optimal intervention policy (one that leaves the domestic price level unaffected following the shock) must be one of "leaning with the wind." In terms of structural parameters the optimal degree of intervention is given by

$$u^* = - \frac{\beta_1 \left(\frac{1 + u_1}{W_1} \right)}{1 + \frac{\beta_1}{c_1}} < 0 \tag{13.42}$$

While the effect on the trade balance is

$$\Delta T_t \bigg/_{\mu = 0} = V_4 \left[\frac{S_1(1 - \theta_2 \gamma_1)}{\theta_1} \right], \tag{13.43}$$

that is, the trade balance moves into surplus and remains in surplus for all degrees of intervention $\mu > \mu^*$, while $\Delta T_t/_{\mu=\mu^*} = 0$ again.[14] It is also intuitively clear and easy to verify that the extent of exchange rate appreciation called forth by the optimal policy given by (13.42) is proportionately greater than that which would have occurred as a natural consequence of a floating exchange rate regime (i.e., $| \Delta E_t | /_{\mu=\mu^*} > | \Delta E_t | /_{\mu=0}$). The exaggerated extent of exchange rate volatility that must be tolerated as the price of stabilizing the domestic price and output level in the present case is somewhat in contrast to the earlier case for foreign monetary disturbances where it was seen that the pursuit of the optimal policy (given by [13.36']) not only stabilized the price level but also reduced exchange rate volatility.

The next type of externally occurring disturbance we consider is a random output expansion in the foreign country as characterized by $\varepsilon_{3t}^* > 0$. Following this disturbance, the foreign price level declines, as seen above, while its effect on the domestic price level is given by

$$V_6 = \frac{\left[\beta_1 + \mu \left(1 + \frac{\beta_1}{c_1} \right) \right] W_3 + \beta_1 U_3}{\Omega}. \tag{13.44}$$

Under freely floating exchange rates the domestic price would have been affected to the extent of

$$V_6 \bigg/ \mu = 0 = \frac{\beta_1(W_3 + U_3)}{\Omega} =$$

$$- \frac{\beta_1(1 - \gamma_1^*)\beta_2^*[1 + \beta_1^* - S_1^*(1 - \beta_2^*)]}{\Omega}$$

$$\gtrless 0. \tag{13.45}$$

Once again, the effect on the domestic price level is linearly related to the sum of the foreign price level and interest rate responses. Owing to the ambiguity, it is now not clear whether a small-country analysis that ignores U_3 would overstate or understate the extent of transmission to the domestic economy. One point is clear, however: such a small country would inevitably produce the result of negative transmission, while this result is not necessarily ensured in the present framework.[15] Given the ambiguity in (13.45), it is not surprising that the precise nature of the optimal intervention policy is indeterminate without further a priori restrictions. If, for example, $\beta_2^* = 1$, the optimal policy calls for "leaning against the wind" as in the case of external monetary disturbances:

$$\mu^* = - \frac{\beta_1(W_3 + U_3)}{\left(1 + \dfrac{\beta_1}{c_1}\right) W_3} . \tag{13.46}$$

The trade balance implications of the supply shock are qualitatively similar to those for $\varepsilon_{2t}^* > 0$, provided that $\beta_2^* = 1$, and similar to those for an external expenditure shock if $S_1^* > (1 + \beta_1^*)/(1 - \beta_1^*)$ for $\beta_1^* \neq 1$.

We now turn to an investigation of domestically generated disturbances, that is, ε_{1t}, ε_{2t}, and ε_{3t}. Consider first the case of domestic monetary shocks as represented by $\varepsilon_{2t} > 0$. From equations (13.28b) and (13.30b) the effect on the domestic price level can be computed to be simply

$$V_2 = -\frac{1}{\Omega} < |1| . \tag{13.47}$$

Thus, a positive money demand shock is deflationary, as expected, and affects the trade balance negatively as seen from

$$\Delta T_t = V_2 \left[\frac{S_1(1 - \theta_2\gamma_1)}{\theta_1} \right] < 0.$$

To ensure price stability (or output or trade balance stability), the required policy is clearly one of fixed exchange rates ($\mu \to \infty$). Therefore, if the predominant source of randomness in the economy is the domestic money market, it can be said that a regime of pegged exchange rates is superior to any managed float (or to floating exchange rates).

A domestically generated random expenditure disturbance affects the domestic price level in the proportion given by the coefficient V_1, which is obtained from (13.28a) and (13.30a) as

$$V_1 = \frac{c_1 \left[\mu \left(1 + \dfrac{\beta_1}{c_1} \right) + 1 - \delta + \beta_1 \right] + \alpha_1 \beta_1}{\theta_1 \alpha_1 c_1 \Omega} > 0,$$

$$(13.48)$$

while under freely floating exchange rates the domestic price level is moderated and is given instead by

$$V_1 \Big/_{\mu\, =\, 0} = \frac{c_1(1 - \delta + \beta_1) + \alpha_1 \beta_1}{\theta_1 \alpha_1 c_1 \Omega} > 0 \qquad (13.49)$$

Consequently, an intervention policy that stabilizes the price level in the face of this disturbance must necessarily involve "leaning with the wind," the precise degree of intervention being

$$\mu^* = - \frac{[c_1(1 - \delta + \beta_1) + \alpha_1 \beta_1]}{c_1 + \beta_1} < 0. \qquad (13.50)$$

Several aspects of (13.50) should be noted. First, it is clear from (13.11') that domestic price stabilization will again ensure domestic output stabilization but not insulation of the trade balance (see [13.10]). Consequently, the price stabilization policy will diverge from the trade balance stabilization policy in this case. Second, the optimal policy required by (13.50) depends not only on the parameters c_1 and β_1, as did the earlier policies, but also on δ (degree of openness) and α_1 (degree of commodity market integration). It can be verified that while μ^* in (13.50) is increasing in α_1 and decreasing in δ, the effects of c_1 and β_1 upon the optimal degree of intervention are (unlike in previous instances) ambiguous. The case of perfect capital mobility ($c_1 \to \infty$) is of no special interest, although for $\alpha_1 \to \infty$ (i.e., the case of purchasing power parity—see [13.27]) the optimal policy is clearly one of pegged exchange rates. Finally, as may be expected, the domestic price stability must necessarily be achieved at the expense of enhanced exchange rate variability. The proportionate exchange rate appreciation that results from the pursuit of (13.50) can be calculated from (13.10) to be

$$\Delta E_t \Big/_{\mu\, =\, \mu^*} = - \frac{1}{\theta_1 \alpha_1}$$

and is inversely related to the degree of commodity market integration (α_1).
Coming now to the trade balance implications of the domestic

expenditure disturbance, the change in the trade balance attendant upon such a shock is given by

$$\Delta T_t = \left[\frac{V_1 S_1 (1 - \theta_2 \gamma_1) - 1}{\theta_1} \right].^{16} \tag{13.51}$$

It is immediately clear from (13.51) that the optimal policy given by (13.50), which sets $V_1 = 0$, will not insulate the trade balance but will, in fact, leave the latter in deficit. A deficit would also have emerged with a floating exchange rate in view of the fact that the terms of trade $(E_t + P_t^* - P_t)$ decline and real income increases following the disturbance.

It is possible to compute the intervention policy that is optimal from the point of view of stabilizing the trade balance rather than the price (and output) level. Using (13.51), the trade balance-stabilizing degree of intervention, $\hat{\mu}$, can be obtained via a solution to

$$V_1(\hat{\mu}, \dots) = \frac{1}{S_1(1 - \theta_2 \gamma_1)} > 0. \tag{13.52}$$

It can be shown that $\hat{\mu}$ derived from (13.52) involves "leaning against the wind" $(\hat{\mu} > 0)$ in direct contrast to the price stabilization policy given by (13.50), which requires "leaning with the wind." Hence, there may be a fundamental conflict between price stabilization and trade balance stabilization (or internal balance and external balance) when the underlying structural disturbances in the economy concern domestic real expenditure. It will be recalled that such a conflict was not observed for the disturbances considered earlier. Further, if the trade balance is to be stabilized, a domestic price level increase must be tolerated—since $V_1(\hat{\mu}, \dots) > 0$ (see [13.52])—corresponding to which exchange depreciation is called for. The extent of exchange depreciation necessitated by the requirement of trade balance stability is given by

$$\Delta E_t \bigg/ \mu = \hat{\mu} = \frac{\alpha_1 + \alpha_2 S_1}{\alpha_1 S_1 (1 - \theta_2 \gamma_1)} > 0. \tag{13.53}$$

While under floating exchange rates the domestic expenditure expansion leads to spot appreciation and the extent of the spot appreciation required by a policy of price stabilization exceeds that which would have occurred anyway in the absence of intervention, an intervention policy designed to ensure trade balance stability necessitates spot depreciation.

Finally, consider a random unanticipated supply increase in the domestic economy, that is, $\varepsilon_{3t} > 0$. Following such a disturbance, the domestic price level responds to the extent V_3, while the proportionate change in domestic income (output) is given by $(S_1 V_3 + 1)$. From equation (13.28c) and (13.30c) it can be shown that

$$V_3 = -\frac{-c_1\left[\beta_1 + \mu\left(1 + \dfrac{\beta_1}{c_1}\right) + 1 - \delta\right](1 - \theta_2\gamma_1 + \theta_1\alpha_2)}{c_1\theta_1\alpha_1\delta} - \frac{\alpha_1[c_1\theta_1\beta_2 + \beta_1(1 - \theta_2\gamma_1)]}{c_1\theta_1\alpha_1\delta}$$

$$< 0 \tag{13.54}$$

Given V_3, it can be demonstrated that $(S_1 V_3 + 1) > 0$. Consequently, the random supply (productivity) expansion has the predictable consequence of lowering the domestic price level and increasing the domestic output level. These conclusions are qualitatively unaltered if the regime being considered is one of floating exchange rates rather than the managed float. A policy of intervention that stabilizes the domestic price level must involve "leaning with the wind," the precise degree of intervention being given by

$$\mu^* = -\frac{\alpha_1[c_1\theta_1\beta_2 + \beta_1(1 - \theta_2\gamma_1)]}{(c_1 + \beta_1)(1 - \theta_2\gamma_1 + \theta_1\alpha_2)} - \frac{c_1(1 - \delta + \beta_1)}{(c_1 + \beta_1)} < 0. \tag{13.55}$$

It is possible to assess the contribution of each parameter to μ^*, but this will be left to the interested reader. One special case is of interest, however. It can be seen that if commodity markets are perfectly integrated (purchasing power parity holds), the optimal price stabilization policy is of pegged exchange rates. A similar conclusion was found to be true above for domestic expenditure disturbances. A difference between the two kinds of real domestic disturbances arises to the extent, however, that in the present case price stabilization is neither equivalent to output stabilization nor to trade balance stabilization. Further, while the pursuit of the optimal price stabilization policy in the case of expenditure shocks necessitates an exaggerated extent of spot appreciation, this is not the case in the present circumstances. In fact, if the dgree of intervention is given by (13.55) (i.e., the domestic price level is stabilized), exchange rate depreciation is called for, the extent of which is given by (using [13.10])

$$\Delta E_t\Big/_{\mu\,=\,\mu^*} = \frac{1 - \theta_2\gamma_1 + \theta_1\alpha_2}{\theta_1\alpha_1} > 0. \tag{13.56}$$

A related point of interest is that while the price level can indeed be stabilized by using (13.55), the price that must be paid for this results not only from the required exchange depreciation that must be tolerated but also from increased income instability. As indicated above, in the absence of intervention the increase in income following the supply shock is $(S_1 V_3 + 1)$, which in view of $V_3 < 0$ is less than proportionate. However, if the degree of intervention is given by (13.55), then $V_3 = 0$, so that the income increase is now exactly equiproportionate. Hence, there is a sense in which there is a potential conflict between price and output stability if the primary source of disturbances in the economy is domestic output supply.

The effect of the random supply disturbance upon the trade balance can be computed by the procedure discussed earlier to be proportional to the change in domestic output and is

$$\Delta T_t = \frac{1 - \theta_2 \gamma_1}{\theta_1} (S_1 V_3 + 1) > 0, \tag{13.57}$$

i.e., the trade balance moves into surplus following the supply shock. Moreover, if the domestic price level is stabilized, a greater trade surplus is generated in view of the exaggerated income movement that results. Finally, if the domestic authorities' objective is output and trade balance stabilization, it can be verified that the intervention policy dictated by this choice may involve "leaning against the wind" and requires price deflation.

CONCLUSION

This chapter has constructed and analyzed a stochastic equilibrium model of the open economy that manages its exchange rate. The focus of the analysis is on the implications of various anticipated and unanticipated externally and domestically generated disturbances. A key feature of the model developed in this chapter is the rehabilitation of the balance of payments as a determinant of the exchange rate. Another distinguishing aspect of this framework is that it is able to consider foreign disturbances in a more complete manner than existing small-country models. This is done by first obtaining the rational expectations solution to the world (foreign) economy and then utilizing these results in solving the model for the domestic economy. Once this is done, it is seen that the results emerging from this model are quite different from those of conventional models. For example, the latter inevitably produce the result that an unanticipated foreign price level increase under floating exchange rates is positively transmitted to the domestic economy via a less-than-proportionate increase in the domestic price level. Our investigation shows that an unanticipated external disturbance is not positively but negatively transmitted. The reason for the difference in results is that the external monetary expansion not only raises the foreign price level but also reduces the foreign interest rate. A small-country analysis, being unable to consider the source of the foreign price level increase, ignores the interest rate fall that is attendant upon the increase in the foreign price level following an unexpected foreign monetary expansion and, consequently, presents a potentially misleading picture. Similar conclusions hold for other externally occurring disturbances.

The main results of this chapter can be summarized as follows. The optimal (from the point of view of either domestic price or output stability) exchange rate policy for anticipated foreign monetary disturbances is one of freely floating exchange rates. If the external anticipated disturbance results from a foreign expenditure shock, the optimum policy calls for "leaning with the wind." The success of this policy is contingent upon variation inter-country money demand parameters. There is a close correspondence between the effects of anticipated external monetary disturbances under pegged exchange rates and those of anticipated foreign expenditure shocks under floating exchange rates. In each case the domestic price response is exactly equal in proportionate terms to the foreign price movement. In no case do external anticipated disturbances affect the domestic trade balance. This result is independent of the nature of the exchange rate regime.

A random unexpected foreign monetary expansion is negatively transmitted to the domestic economy and induces a domestic trade deficit if no activist intervention policy is pursued. This result is in sharp contrast to results emerging from small-country models. A policy of price stabilization will also ensure income stability and trade balance stability and is of the "leaning against the wind" variety. This policy also reduces exchange rate volatility in comparison with the floating exchange rate regime. An unanticipated external expenditure expansion increases the price level in both countries if the authorities do not intervene in the exchange market. As in the earlier case, the domestic price level response is proportional to the sum of the external price and interest rate percentage movements, and a small-country analysis would tend to underestimate the extent of the transmission. If there is no intervention, the trade balance moves into surplus. The optimal price stabilization policy requires "leaning with the wind" and also stabilizes the output level and the trade balance. However, an exaggerated extent of exchange rate appreciation must be tolerated as a consequence of this policy. If the foreign disturbance is a random supply increase, the effect on the domestic economy is contingent upon precise parameter magnitudes. Consequently, it is not clear if domestic intervention policy should "lean with the wind" or "against the wind," although a persuasive case for the latter can be made based on plausible parameter values.

If the predominant source of stochastic shifts in the economy is in the domestic money market, a policy of pegged exchange rates is superior to any managed float regime from the point of view of domestic price or output level stability. Randomly generated domestic expenditure increases affect the domestic price level positively if there is no intervention. Domestic price and output stabilization can be ensured by "leaning against the wind," although unlike the earlier cases this policy will not achieve trade balance stability and will, in fact, leave the domestic balance of trade in deficit. Thus, there may be an inherent conflict between the internal and external objectives of the authorities. A conflict is also present if an unanticipated domestic supply expansion is considered, although the conflict is now not only between internal and external objectives but also between two internal objectives, that is between price and output stability. The supply disturbance lowers the domestic price level under floating exchange rates. Consequently, an intervention policy that sought to stabilize the price level would need to be one of "leaning with the wind." Such a policy, however, would generate enhanced output and trade balance variability.

APPENDIX TO CHAPTER 13

A derivation of (13.7) proceeds as follows. Denote by a caret the level of a variable measured in natural units, except the trade balance T_t, which is already expressed in nonlogarithmic form. Then, by definition

$$\hat{Y}_t = \hat{A}_t + T_t + \hat{G}'_t, \tag{13.1A}$$

where $\hat{A}_t$ is domestic private absorption, and $\hat{G}_t$ is domestic autonomous expenditure. Taking logarithms of (13.1A), obtain

$$\log \hat{Y}_t \equiv Y_t = \log(\hat{A}_t + T_t + \hat{G}'_t) = \log(\exp \log \hat{A}_t + T_t + \exp \log \hat{G}'_t).$$

Expanding by a first-order Taylor series,

$$Y_t = B^0 + \frac{1}{B^0}(T_t - T^0) + \frac{\hat{A}^0}{B^0}(A_t - A^0) + \frac{\hat{G}'^0}{B^0}(G'_t - G^{0\prime}), \tag{13.2A}$$

where $B^0 \equiv (\exp^{\log \hat{A}^0} - T^0 + \exp^{\log \hat{G}'^0})$ is determined by the initial linearization point. Collecting coefficients,

$$Y_t = k^0 + \theta_1 T_t + \theta_2 A_t + \frac{\hat{G}'^0}{B^0} G'_t, \tag{13.3A}$$

where $\theta_1 \equiv 1/B^0 > 0$ and $\theta_2 \equiv (\hat{A}^0/B^0) < 1$.

For convenience and without loss of generality, define $G_t \equiv (\hat{G}^{\prime 0}/B^0)G_t'$. Suppressing the constant term, rewrite (13.3A) as

$$Y_t = G_t + \theta_1 T_t + \theta_2 A_t, \tag{13.4A}$$

which is the same as (13.7). The autonomous term G_t is linearly proportional to the logarithm of government (autonomous) expenditure and, consequently, can be used to represent domestic fiscal policy.

A derivation of the supply function is based on the following considerations. Assume that laborers negotiate to achieve a fixed-target wage rate in terms of the previous period price index, that is,

$$x = W_t - E_{t-1}, Q_t, \tag{13.5A}$$

where x is the fixed-target real wage. Labor supply is perfectly elastic at this wage rate. Assuming that the only variable input into the production process is labor, the production function can be assumed to be given by

$$Y_t = \varepsilon N_t, \tag{13.6A}$$

where N_t is the logarithm of the employment level and $0 < \varepsilon < 1$. Employment is determined by the marginal productivity condition

$$\varepsilon = \frac{\partial \log \hat{Y}}{\partial \log \hat{N}} = \frac{\partial \hat{Y}}{\partial \hat{N}} \frac{\hat{N}}{\hat{Y}} = \left(\frac{\hat{W}}{\hat{P}} \frac{\hat{N}}{\hat{Y}} \right), \tag{13.7A}$$

whence

$$\log \varepsilon = (W_t - P_t) + (N_t - Y_t). \tag{13.8A}$$

Substituting from (13.6A),

$$W_t = P_t + \ln \varepsilon + (\varepsilon - 1)N_t,$$

while from (13.5A)

$$W_t = x + E_{t-1}, Q_t.$$

Thus,

$$P_t + \ln \varepsilon + (\varepsilon - 1)N_t = x + E_{t-1}, Q_t,$$

or

$$N = -\frac{x}{1-\varepsilon} + \frac{\ln \varepsilon}{1-\varepsilon} + \frac{1}{1-\varepsilon}(P_t - E_{t-1}, Q_t). \quad (13.9A)$$

Substitute from (13.9A) into (13.6A) to obtain

$$Y_t = \frac{\varepsilon \ln \varepsilon - \varepsilon x}{1-\varepsilon} + \frac{\varepsilon}{1-\varepsilon}(P_t - E_{t-1}, Q_t). \quad (13.10A)$$

Equation (13.10A) is clearly of the form of (13.11) used in the text. The complete form of (13.11A) mentioned in the text is

$$
\begin{aligned}
P_t = {}& \pi_1\varepsilon_{1t} + \pi_2\varepsilon_{2t} + \pi_3\varepsilon_{3t} + \pi_4\varepsilon_{1t}^* + \pi_5\varepsilon_{2t}^* + \pi_6\varepsilon_{3t}^* + \pi_7 M_{t-1} \\
& + \pi_8 E^0 + \pi_9\bar{G} + \pi_{10}\bar{S} + \pi_{11}\bar{S}^* + \pi_{12}\bar{M}^* + \pi_{13}\bar{G}^* \\
& + W_1\varepsilon_{1t}^* + W_2\varepsilon_{2t}^* + W_3\varepsilon_{3t}^* + W_4\bar{G}^* + W_5\bar{M}^* + W_6\bar{S}^* \\
& + \frac{\bar{G}}{\theta_1\alpha_1} + \frac{\varepsilon_{1t}}{\theta_1\alpha_1} - \left(\frac{1 - \theta_2\gamma_1 + \theta_1\alpha_2}{\theta_1\alpha_1}\right) \\
& \times \{\bar{S} + S_1(V_1\varepsilon_{1t} + V_2\varepsilon_{2t} + V_3\varepsilon_{3t} + V_4\varepsilon_{1t}^* + V_5\varepsilon_{2t}^* + V_6\varepsilon_{3t}^*) \\
& - s_1(1-\delta)(W_4\bar{G}^* + W_5\bar{M}^* + W_6\bar{S}^*) - s_1(1-\delta) \\
& \times [(\pi_7 - V_7)M_{t-1} + (\pi_8 - V_8)E^0 + (\pi_9 - V_9)\bar{G}] \\
& + (\pi_{10} - V_{10})\bar{S} + (\pi_{11} - V_{11})\bar{S}^* + (\pi_{12} - V_{12})\bar{M}^* \\
& + (\pi_{13} - V_{13})\bar{G}^* + \varepsilon_{3t}\}, \quad (13.11A)
\end{aligned}
$$

while (13.11A) is explicitly given by

$$
\begin{aligned}
\delta P_t = {}& M_{t-1} - \left(\mu + 1 - \delta + \frac{\beta_1\mu}{c_1}\right)(\pi_1\varepsilon_{1t} + \pi_2\varepsilon_{2t} - \pi_3\varepsilon_{3t} \\
& + \pi_4\varepsilon_{1t}^* + \pi_5\varepsilon_{2t}^* + \pi_6\varepsilon_{3t}^* + \pi_7 M_{t-1} + \pi_8 E^0 \\
& + \pi_9\bar{G} + \pi_{10}\bar{S} + \pi_{11}\bar{S}^* + \pi_{12}\bar{M}^* + \pi_{13}\bar{G}^*) \\
& + \left(\mu + \frac{\beta_1\mu}{c_1}\right)E^0 - \beta_0 + \beta_1(U_1\varepsilon_{1t}^* + U_2\varepsilon_{2t}^* \\
& + U_3\varepsilon_{3t}^* + U_4\bar{G}^* + U_5\bar{M}^* + U_6\bar{S}^*) - (1-\delta)(W_1\varepsilon_{1t}^* \\
& + W_2\varepsilon_{2t}^* + W_3\varepsilon_{3t}^* + W_4\bar{G}^* + W_5\bar{M}^* + W_6\bar{S}^*) \\
& - \beta_1(\pi_1\varepsilon_{1t} + \pi_2\varepsilon_{2t} + \pi_3\varepsilon_{3t} + \pi_4\varepsilon_{1t}^* + \pi_5\varepsilon_{2t}^* + \pi_6\varepsilon_{3t}^*)
\end{aligned}
$$

$$+ \frac{\beta_1}{c_1\theta_1} \bar{G} + \frac{\beta_1}{c_1\theta_1} \varepsilon_{1t} - \varepsilon_{2t} - \left[\frac{\beta_2 c_1 \theta_1 + \beta_1(1 - \theta_2\gamma_1)}{c_1\theta_1} \right]$$

$$\times [\bar{S} + S_1(V_1\varepsilon_{1t} + V_2\varepsilon_{2t} + V_3\varepsilon_{3t} + V_4\varepsilon_{1t}^* + V_5\varepsilon_{2t}^* + V_6\varepsilon_{3t}^*)$$

$$- S_1(1 - \delta)(W_4\bar{G}^* + W_5\bar{M}^* + W_6\bar{s}^*) - S_1(1 - \delta)$$

$$\times \{(\pi_7 - V_7)M_{t-1} + (\pi_8 - V_8)E^0 + (\pi_9 - V_9)\bar{G}$$

$$+ (\pi_{10} - V_{10})\bar{S} + (\pi_{11} - V_{11})\bar{S}^* + (\pi_{12} - V_{12})\bar{M}^*$$

$$+ (\pi_{13} - V_{13})\bar{G}^*\} + \varepsilon_{3t}].$$

NOTES

1. It should be noted that all of these papers assume perfect mobility and, consequently, assign no importance at all to the balance of payments in exchange rate determination.

2. This asymmetric assumption—that is, "smallness" in import markets but not in export markets—is entirely standard in recent open macromodels.

3. The inclusion of the real rate of interest in the aggregate demand function does not enrich the results significantly. It will be seen below that when describing the domestic economy we exclude the real rate from the aggregate demand function in the interest of analytical simplicity.

4. All variables in the foreign and domestic economies except nominal interest rates are to be understood to be in logarithmic form.

5. At this juncture it should be pointed out that the assumption of the foreign economy being closed is not to be interpreted completely literally. For we have assumed that domestic consumption is not limited to domestic output alone—the openness of the domestic economy depends upon this. Strictly speaking, therefore, foreign production cannot equal foreign consumption, the discrepancy being accounted for by foreign exports (and imports). However, the essential point is that the foreign economy is very large in comparison with the domestic economy. Consequently, foreign exports (domestic imports) are only a negligible part of total foreign output. In this way equation (13.3) can be assumed to hold as a close approximation. As a related point, note that the assumed log-linearity of the model is itself an approximation to some presumably unknown "true" structure.

6. The derivation (13.7) is sketched in the Appendix to Chapter 13.

7. It will be recalled that in describing the foreign economy we interpreted ε_{2t}^* as a foreign money supply innovation. This was appropriate because of the exogeneity of foreign money supply. However, domestic money supply is not exogenous and, consequently, we characterize domestic monetary disturbances by a money demand innovation ε_{2t}. The asymmetry between the assumed source of monetary disturbances in the two countries is entirely inconsequential.

8. We are aware of the fact that a stock formulation of the capital market might be preferable to the flow formulation that is utilized here. The reason for our choice is that the latter simplifies an already complex set of calculations tremendously without compromising the nature of our results. The stock formulation would introduce infinite lags in solutions for all the endogenous variables. However, the current period results, which are all that this chapter is concerned with, are expected to be insensitive to whether the stock or flow formulation is used. This statement is based on the results from Driskill and McCafferty (1980) and Bhandari and

Turnovsky (1981). These papers utilize a stock formulation, but the conclusions are not seen to be sensitive to this specification, and a flow formulation would have yielded similar results. For recent use of the flow specification in a nonstochastic context, see Frenkel and Rodriguez (1980) and Dornbusch (1980). This list is not exhaustive.

9. It can be verified that provided that small disturbances are considered and equilibrium real balances can be normalized via an appropriate choice of nominal money units to unity, then (13.14) is indeed a close approximation.

10. Another possible candidate for the authorities' objective function could be one that not only considers domestic output or price stabilization but one that involves a weighted average of price and exchange rate variance. Such a criterion could presumably be justified on the grounds of internal and external balance. It should be clear, however, that in the present framework internal and external balance cannot be simultaneously obtained via a single policy instrument, except in certain special cases.

11. To economize on space we have not presented the results for an anticipated (planned) increase in the trend component of foreign output supply $\bar{S}^*$. As seen earlier, this leads to a decline in both the foreign price level and interest rate. The domestic price level can also be shown to decline following this shock, so that "leaning against the wind" is called for to restore the price level to its former level, that is, to ensure insulation. Once again, the domestic trade balance remains unaltered regardless of the exchange rate regime.

12. The fact that $\partial \mu^* / \partial c_1 > 0$ results from the fact that $\partial V_5 / \partial c_1 > 0$, which implies that an increased extent of financial market integration renders the domestic price level more vulnerable to random external monetary shocks. This result is in contrast to the earlier result for systematic external monetary disturbances where it was seen that $\partial V_{12} / \partial c_1 < 0$, indicating again that the conventional view associating increased openness (in some sense) with increased vulnerability of the domestic economy is to be accepted with caution. Note also that $\partial V_5 / \partial \alpha_1$ and $\partial V_5 / \partial \delta > 0$, while $\partial V_{12} / \partial \alpha_1$ and $\partial V_{12} / \partial \delta = 0$.

13. Recall that under $\mu = \mu^*$, the domestic price level and output are unaffected (insulated). From the aggregate demand equation (13.10) this is only consistent with $\Delta E_t = -\Delta P_t^*$.

14. For $\mu = \mu^*$ no trade balance effects emerge. The reason for this is intuitively clear. Since $\mu = \mu^*$ sets $V_4 = 0$, no price or output effects emerge. Further, from the aggregate demand relation (13.10) it follows that an unchanged domestic output level necessarily implies that the domestic terms of trade $(E_t + P_t^* - P_t)$ must be unaltered. Since the trade balance depends upon the terms of trade and income and these are unchanged, it follows that $\mu = \mu^*$ insulates the trade balance as well. This simple correspondence between insulation of the domestic price level and that of the trade balance will not be found to be true of domestically occurring shocks, as seen below.

15. For plausible parameter magnitudes such as $\beta_2^* = 1$, negative transmission also occurs in the current context.

16. The change in the trade balance can be computed by noting that $\Delta T_t = \alpha_1 \Delta P_t^* + \alpha_1 (\Delta E_t - \Delta P_t) - \alpha_2 \Delta Y_t$, which is $\Delta T_t = \alpha_1 (\pi_1 - V_1) - \alpha_2 S_1 V_1$. Next, substitute the known relation

$$(\pi_1 - V_1) = \frac{S_1 V_1 (1 - \theta_2 \gamma_1 + \theta_1 \alpha_2)}{\theta_1 \alpha_1} - \frac{1}{\theta_1 \alpha_1}$$

to obtain (13.51).

REFERENCES

Barro, R. J. 1978. "A Stochastic Equilibrium Model of an Open Economy under Flexible Exchange Rates." *Quarterly Journal of Economics* 92 (February): 149–64.

Bhandari, J. In press. "A Stochasti Macroequilibrium Approach to a Floating Exchange Rate Economy with Interest-Bearing Assets." *Weltwirtschaftliches Archiv.*

Bhandari, J., and S. Turnovsky. 1981. "Capital Mobility, Floating Exchange Rates and the Balance of Payments: A Stochastic Macroequilibrium Approach." Mimeographed, Carbondale.

Bilson, J. F. O. 1978. "Rational Expectations and the Exchange Rate." In *The Economics of Exchange Rates*, edited by J. A. Frenkel and H. G. Johnson, pp. 47–65. Reading, Addison-Wesley.

Cox, W. M. 1980. "Unanticipated Money, Output and Prices in the Small Economy." *Journal of Monetary Economics* 6 (June): 359–84.

Dornbusch, R. 1980. "Monetary Stabilization, Intervention and Real Appreciation." In *Open Economy Macroeconomics.* New York: Basic Books.

Driskill, R., and S. M. McCafferty. 1980. "Exchange Rate Variability, Real and Monetary Shocks, and the Degree of Capital Mobility under Rational Expectations." *Quarterly Journal of Economics*, 95 (November): 577–86.

Frenkel, J., and C. Rodriguez. 1980. "The Anatomy of the Exchange Rate Overshooting Hypothesis." Mimeographed, Chicago.

Mussa, M. 1978. "The Exchange Rate, the Balance of Payments and Monetary and Fiscal Policy under a Regime of Controlled Floating." In *The Economics of Exchange Rates*, edited by J. A. Frenkel and H. G. Johnson, pp. 47–65. Reading, Pa.: Addison-Wesley.

Saidi, N. H. 1980. "Fluctuating Exchange Rates and the International Transmission of Economic Disturbances." *Journal of Money, Credit and Banking* 4 (November) 575–91.

Turnovsky, S. J. In press. "Monetary Policy and Foreign Price Disturbances under Flexible Exchange Rates: A Stochastic Approach." *Journal of Money, Credit and Banking.*

ABOUT THE AUTHOR

Jagdeep S. Bhandari is Assistant Professor of Economics at Southern Illinois University, Georgetown University, and George Mason University. His professional papers have appeared in most major journals including *International Economics (final) Review, Quarterly Journal of Economics, European Economic Review, Journal of Money, Credit, and Banking, Southern Economic Journal, The Manchester School, Weltwirtschaftliches Archiv* and *The Journal of Macroeconomics.* He has recently edited a book entitled *Economic Interdependence and Flexible Exchange Rates* published by MIT Press.